Portfolio of
Ready-to-Use
Model Sales Scripts

PORTFOLIO OF READY-TO-USE MODEL SALES SCRIPTS

Howard S. Bishop

PRENTICE HALL
Englewood Cliffs, New Jersey 07632

Prentice-Hall International (UK) Limited, *London*
Prentice-Hall of Australia Pty. Limited, *Sydney*
Prentice-Hall Canada, Inc., *Toronto*
Prentice-Hall Hispanoamericana, S.A., *Mexico*
Prentice-Hall of India Private Limited, *New Delhi*
Prentice-Hall of Japan, Inc., *Tokyo*
Simon & Schuster Asia Pte. Ltd., *Singapore*
Editora Prentice-Hall do Brasil, Ltda., *Rio de Janeiro*

10 9 8 7 6 5 4 3

Library of Congress Cataloging-in-Publication Data

Bishop, Howard S.
    Portfolio of ready-to-use model sales scripts / Howard S. Bishop.
      p.   cm.

    ISBN 0-13-686031-1
    1. Selling.   2. Sales letters. I. Title.
  HF5438.25.B54 1988   88-23492
  658.8′2--dc19   CIP

ISBN 0-13-686031-1

PRENTICE HALL
BUSINESS & PROFESSIONAL DIVISION
A division of Simon & Schuster
Englewood Cliffs, New Jersey 07632

Printed in the United States of America

How This Book Will Help You

WHO SHOULD READ THIS BOOK?

This book is for the in-the-trenches sales and marketing representative who is sometimes stumped about what to say in a customer or prospect situation.

You could be an entry level salesperson looking for answers or a veteran salesperson looking for *new* answers who realizes, thanks to Ben Franklin, that "we need to be reminded four times as often as we need to be taught." In either case, this book has the answers for you.

You realize that you don't have time to develop all of the tools you need to do your job better and could use a lot of help with the "what to say" basics.

WHY SHOULD YOU READ THIS BOOK?

Every salesperson on this planet gets tongue-tied from time to time and needs help with that "right" line or phrase that will turn a prospect's expressed or implied "no" into a "yes," or deal effectively with an objection or a put-off. This book provides, in the form of specific scripts, proven sales techniques, communication strategies, and implementation tactics that will make your sales calls more effective and enable you to close more sales.

For example, when your prospect says, "Your price is too high," this book will teach you to say something like "That could be true. You see, we try to be 10 percent better, not 5 percent cheaper." You'll find over 400 other ways to deal with prospect objections, customer complaints, and all those other things that get in the way of your doubling sales.

We will provide you with model scripts and letters that have worked for me, have worked for my clients, and will work for you. They will save you time and let you do the creative job you are capable of doing for your company or organization. They are based on a lot of lessons I've learned in finding out the right way to do things. This is the kind of advice that is based on on-the-job experience. It will put you on the right track right away.

THE THREE-PRONGED APPROACH

Paraphrasing Arthur H. ''Red'' Motley, nothing happens until a customer is created. Sometimes, however, we forget that selling is a three-edged sword. Some salespeople are good at personal calls, but hate the telephone and think of writing letters like they think of having root canal work done. Other salespeople are good on the telephone but seem to have agoraphobia and hesitate to leave their offices even for a cup of coffee. Still others write well but use their letters as a protective shield when a personal touch is necessary.

If you rely solely on personal calls, you are using time ineffectively. You could call as many people in an hour as you see in a day. With help (from a secretarial assistant or a computer) you could contact by mail as many customers or prospects in an hour as you could call on the telephone in a day.

In this book, I'll show you exactly how to combine all three communication tools (telephone, mail, and personal calls) in a way that will increase the effectiveness of your selling effort exponentially. Rather than just discussing the tools, I'll provide specific telephone and personal call scripts and suggested letters you can use with your prospects.

HOW TO USE THIS BOOK

The chapters are organized in a logical sequence. Pick out from the Table of Contents the problem you have to solve right now—the kinds of things you've had sales-closing obstacles with in the past. *But*, try to deal with the book in a chapter-by-chapter way as it is organized.

List some of the most common objections you get from prospects and customers. Then find the suggested answers in this book. Mark those that you are particularly comfortable with and add some of your own, using this book as a guide. Through this exercise, you'll find yourself coming up with the right responses far more frequently.

As a sales manager you can use this book in your sales training programs as an outline or curriculum guide. Use your group or individual sessions to improve the scripts and adapt them to your own selling situation.

In the process of preparing this book, I did just that with a client. The salespeople were given some suggested scripts to study before the training session. They adapted and improved the scripts. By the end of the session we had the beginnings of a custom-made sales script book for the client's special situations.

FINAL NOTE

While I've tried to use the term ''salesperson'' throughout the book (unless an anecdote referred to a specific lady or gentleman), continually using ''he or she'' or avoiding gender in every instance would get awkward and slow down the reading. I recognize that salespeople, customers, and prospects are not always men and hope that the salespeople who happen to be women will understand and accept the use of the pronoun ''he.''

Howard S. Bishop

Table of Contents

Chapter 9: Using Customer Complaints as an Opportunity 149

APPENDIX

Quick Scripts for Any and Every Occasion

Portfolio of
Ready-to-Use
Model Sales Scripts

1

Breaking Through the Initial Appointment Barrier

INTRODUCTION

For most salespeople, the initial appointment (usually involving some form of ''cold'' call) is the most difficult chore in selling and the one most often shunted aside. I remember holding a seminar at which over 50 salespeople were present. Only three answered ''yes'' to the question, ''Do you like making cold calls?'' One person who answered ''yes'' said that she didn't mind cold calls since she had her people make them.

But, it doesn't have to be that way. Getting the initial appointment can be an exciting challenge if you look upon it as a game. Change your perception of rejection and you'll change the reality of cold call selling. Unless you are doing something very wrong, you should get at least one appointment if you make 20 calls. (You may even get five or more.)

So, decide to make those 20 calls even if you get an appointment with the first one. If you don't get an appointment in the first 20, tell yourself that the law of averages dictates that you'll get two appointments in the next 20 so they will be even more fun.

When you get the appointments, congratulate yourself on these successful calls and forget about those people who didn't want to see you just now. Analyze what you may have done differently on the successful calls so you can repeat the process. Also, don't give up on any prospect in your file until you have a very good indication that there is clearly a lack of interest. (Hanging up when you mention your name is a pretty good indication of the prospect's lack of interest.)

Now let's look at some specific scripts that will help you fill your appointment book:

SCRIPT 1.1. THE INITIAL COLD, *COLD* CALL—GETTING PAST THE RECEPTIONIST

OBJECTIVE: Tackle the most difficult situation first. You don't have a trade show lead, bingo card, or referral—just an idea that this is a good prospect for you. You *have* done your homework and *know* that your prospect can use your company's product or service, but the prospect doesn't know you and you don't know your prospect. You may have gotten the name from a trade directory or from reading local business magazines and have found that the prospect is doing some things (like a new manufacturing operation) that will make your product or service useful to the prospect.

Let's assume that you are in the business of selling turnkey computer hardware/software systems. ("Turnkey," in this case, means that you will handle the whole installation and take responsibility for its effectiveness.) Your prospect is in the tooling business so there is a possibility of selling a CAD/CAM (Computer-Aided Design/Computer-Aided Manufacturing) system in addition to the usual business system including payroll, billing, accounts receivable, accounts payable, check-writing, and general ledger accounting.

In doing your homework, you have found from a local business listing service that your prospect has 35 employees, does about $5 million a year in gross revenues, and has, in addition to the normal machine shop equipment, a deep-hole trepanning machine or lathe. You can guess that, without a computer (you got this particular piece of information from a computer installation listing service) that his manual systems for accounting and billing, never mind production scheduling, are grossly inadequate. Let's follow a typical (or perhaps atypical) scenario for this prospect:

SALESPERSON: Good morning. This is Stuart Davidson from Cardinal Business Services. May I speak with Mr. Harkins, please?
RECEPTIONIST: I'll see if I can put you through.

SCRIPT 1.1A. MAKING THE PROSPECT'S SECRETARY YOUR ALLY

SECRETARY: Mr. Harkins office. May I help you?
SALESPERSON: Yes, this is Stuart Davidson from Cardinal Business Services. May I speak with Mr. Harkins, please?
SECRETARY: May I ask what this is about? (You see, of course, that Mr. Harkins gets a lot of calls and she is being very protective. He is, after all, the president of the company.)

TIP: At this point, most sales books would tell you not to talk with the secretary if you can't get through to the president. Nonsense! Presidents usually have very competent administrative assistants who will be asked to advise them on important decisions. Make this person your friend! He or she is probably used to being passed over and will welcome the opportunity to be brought into your confidence about the important message you want conveyed to the president. Other books provide suggestions on how to trick the secretary into putting you through. Dangerous! You need this person as an ally.

SALESPERSON: Our company has just recently developed a complete, integrated computer system for companies in the machining business and I know Mr. Harkins would be interested in knowing what we have done *for companies like yours*.

TIP: Don't overlook the importance of the phrase in italics. You are not just a peddler of computer systems. *You* are offering to share the benefit of your experience with a company that may have the same kind of problems that you have solved in the past for similar companies.

SECRETARY: Well, Mr. Harkins isn't in right now and he has a lot of companies calling him to sell him a computer.

SCRIPT 1.1B. TREATING THE SECRETARY LIKE A PERSON

SALESPERSON: I'm sorry. I missed your name (she didn't give it) when you answered the phone. May I ask your name, please?

TIP: You stopped that negative dead end *cold*. Since a person's name is one of his most cherished possessions, you are ready to get back to *your* script in a positive way. You will stand out among Mr. Harkins' calls by being attentive in this way.

SECRETARY: Oh, my name is Mrs. Ryan, Kylie Ryan.
SALESPERSON: Well, Mrs. Ryan, I assume that since you are answering Mr. Harkins' phone that you are very much involved in the executive management activities of the company.

TIP: How can she say no? By saying "yes," however modestly, she has invited further discussion with you about your product.

SECRETARY: Well, I do help Mr. Harkins make some of the decisions—he's just so busy.
SALESPERSON: The system we have has worked very well in *companies like yours*—machine shops that do about $5 million in sales and have 30 to 40 employees. I really think that you and Mr. Harkins would like to see the kinds of time-saving and efficiency advantages it could produce.

TIP: Again, contrary to conventional wisdom, you have made the secretary (administrative assistant?) a partner in your quest to see Mr. Harkins. How can she not be on your side at this point?

SECRETARY: Well, Mr. Harkins is very busy with our new trepanning machine . . .

SCRIPT 1.1C. CLOSING THE SECRETARY ON THE APPOINTMENT

SALESPERSON: I can understand that. What I am suggesting is a way that you can all be a little less busy in the future handling details that neither you nor Mr. Harkins have time for. Do you handle a lot of the administrative routine?

> TIP: This is an open-ended question designed to elicit a response that will lead to the next appointment-closing question. It also happens to appeal to the sense of importance of a person who usually gets walked by (or on) by most of Mr. Harkins' callers.

SECRETARY: Well, yes, I do. I handle the payroll because it's confidential and I handle the job cost control summaries which are out of control and I handle the general ledger.

> TIP: Now she's warming up to you. How many callers do you suppose express an interest in her important activities as opposed to those who treat her like a clerk?

SCRIPT 1.1D. SETTING UP THE APPOINTMENT

SALESPERSON: The systems my company has developed for *companies like yours* are designed to bring those things that may be out of control back into control. Would next Wednesday or Thursday be better for you and Mr. Harkins?

> TIP: Besides the usual "give them a choice of two yeses instead of a yes and no" approach, we involved Mrs. Ryan in the presentation appointment. This is *exactly* the opposite approach from the "don't talk with anyone but the boss" nonsense you hear from the conventional sales gurus.

SECRETARY: Let me put you down for 11:00 on Thursday. I'll tell Mr. Harkins that it's important that he talk with you.

Done deal! Nicely done. If you had been able to reach Mr. Harkins, your job might have been a bit easier. Here's how that conversation would go, picking up from the point that Mrs. Ryan answered the phone and decided to put you through after you explained the *benefit* you were offering.

SCRIPT 1.2. GETTING THE FIRST APPOINTMENT WITH THE "BUSY" PROSPECT

> OBJECTIVE: The objective is the same as in Script 1.1. We want an appointment with our prospect to result from this phone call.

(We are picking up from the point in Script 1.1 where Mrs. Ryan decides to put you through to Mr. Harkins.)

SALESPERSON: Our company, Cardinal Business Services, has just recently developed a complete, integrated computer system for companies in the machining business. I'd like to share with you what we've learned about how to apply this system *to companies like yours*.

> TIP: If your prospect were relatively unsophisticated, you might not want to use the scary term, "computer." You could, with this and other products, use terms like

"money-saving system" or "time-saving product." Again, notice that key phrase, "companies like yours."

MR. HARKINS: With the problems I have, the last thing in the world I need is a computer system to worry about.

SCRIPT 1.2A. GETTING THE PROSPECT TALKING

SALESPERSON: I can understand exactly how you feel. Our other clients *in businesses like yours* have felt the same way. What do you feel is your biggest problem right now?

> TIP: We asked another open-ended question. There is little point in trying to sell a prospect something before we understand why he is or may not be buying. Besides tossing the ball to Mr. Harkins, we may get a little insight into how to develop a benefits pitch that is specifically Mr. Harkins-oriented.

MR. HARKINS: My biggest problem right now is that I don't have time to talk to you. I don't know what my crazy machinists are doing in the shop right now.

SCRIPT 1.2B. KEEPING THE PROSPECT TALKING

SALESPERSON: I can understand that, especially in such a high-pressure business as yours. MY goal is to *eliminate* those problems—not add to them. Mr. Leewen at Christian Machine Tools felt exactly the same way. He wouldn't see me until 7:00 p.m. because he had the same pressures you have. When I explained what we could do, he kept me there until after 10:00.

> TIP: You had to provide a "grabber" before you lost Mr. Harkins to the shop. Mentioning a name he is likely to know will at least stop him in his tracks. Third-party referrals are particularly effective, especially if the person you are calling is likely to know the third party, even as a competitor.
>
> Obviously, you don't give away any confidential information, but name-dropping doesn't hurt in this kind of situation. (You will, of course, have cleared the use of Mr. Leewen's name and business situation with Mr. Leewen before you drop the name.)

MR. HARKINS: Chris Leewen bought your system? That guy is still back in the dark ages!
SALESPERSON: Mr. Leewen is discussing our system for his company. You understand, Mr. Harkins, why I can't go into any detail on this.

> TIP: Now you've whetted Mr. Harkins' appetite. If his competitor is interested in your system, he *has* to pay attention. Remember that you can *always* find a third-party referral person whose name will ring a bell with the person you are talking with. I know a salesperson who always makes it a point to talk with a competitor of the person she is making a call on just so she can say "Well, I was talking with . . ." She didn't say she got anywhere with the prospect—only that she was talking with the person or the company.

MR. HARKINS: Well, it sounds like you just might have something I'd be interested in looking at—not buying, mind you—just looking at.
SALESPERSON: Mr. Harkins, would Wednesday or Thursday be better for you? I could be

there at 5:00 P.M. either day so you don't cut into your plans with the shop.
MR. HARKINS: Make it Thursday, but 4:00 P.M. would be fine. I don't want to keep you out too late.

Another done deal! Do you see how easy it was, recognizing the obstacles and principles spelled out in the beginning of this chapter? Let's review what we did and look at how easy and simple it was to do.

CRACKING THE "BUSY" PROSPECT SUMMARY POINTS

1. We *proacted*. We picked up the phone and called a likely prospect for our product months or even years before he recognized he needed us. We didn't wait from a referral from Mr. Leewen if, indeed, we would have ever sold him *or* gotten a referral. We didn't wait for a bingo card to come in from a trade magazine or for a lead from another source. We *proacted* instead of *reacting*. A good start.

2. We didn't even think about rejection. We did our homework and *knew* that this prospect *needed* our system. All we had to do was to convince Mr. Harkins (or Mrs. Ryan) that we had a real *benefit* to offer.

3. We knew our package would work for the prospect. (We haven't yet sold Christian Machine Tools, but we have done enough work with this similar operation to feel confident that we have a deal for Mr. Harkins that will be to his benefit.)

4. We didn't fall into the trap that most sales "experts" lay for us by telling us that "you don't talk to secretaries." We made Mrs. Ryan an ally. By giving her the credit she is undoubtedly due, we got at least part way to a sale.

5. We created the environment where, if the prospect didn't ask for the appointment, Mrs. Ryan or Mr. Harkins were at least very receptive to our suggesting that it should happen. We paved the way for a future successful, appointment-resulting call. (Actually, we could have written the script so Mrs. Ryan or Mr. Harkins would have asked for the appointment before we suggested it and it would have been only a little less believable.)

6. We talked *benefits*—valued added components of our system *to the company we were talking to*. We didn't talk about computer power, megabytes, or anything else that our prospect couldn't relate to. We tried to get him where he lives.

7. The third-party referral bit we used is, admittedly, a bit of a shortcut. There is *no way* that Mr. Harkins is not going to be interested in anything that Mr. Leewen may be interested in. This situation exists in every industry and is a legitimate way to arouse interest.

8. We consistently used the phrase "businesses like yours." This is another form of the third-party referral, but makes it clear that we are not just salespeople shooting in the dark. *We have a real benefit to offer to our prospect based on work we have done already—with companies like his.*

9. Most important, we didn't count on the old features-benefits approach to get us the appointment. *We asked questions* that let the prospect sell himself on the appointment. To have a successful sales call, in person or over the phone, the salesperson should, in most cases, be *listening* about 60% of the time. When a salesperson is talking he isn't getting any useful information and has no idea whether or not the prospect is paying attention. When the prospect is talking you know you have his attention.

SCRIPT 1.3. SELLING THE SECRETARY WITH A THIRD-PARTY REFERRAL

OBJECTIVE: To obtain an appointment to discuss our system. (We'll use the same CAD/CAM system example as in Scripts 1.2 and 1.3.) *This* time, however, we have a built-in advantage. Mr. Weber from Stuart Aircraft Company, a client of ours and a customer of Mr. Harkins, has, with a little help and guidance from us, suggested that we talk with Mr. Harkins.

Since we already know the value of talking with the secretary or administrative assistant (see Script 1.1), we will assume that we get put right through to Mr. Harkins.

SALESPERSON: Good morning. This is Stuart Davidson from Cardinal Business Services. May I speak with Mr. Harkins, please?

RECEPTIONIST: I'll see if I can put you through.

SECRETARY: Mr. Harkins' office, May I help you?

SALESPERSON: Yes, this is Stuart Davidson from Cardinal Business Services. May I speak with Mr. Harkins, please?

SECRETARY: I don't recognize your name. Does Mr. Harkins know you?

SALESPERSON: Don Weber from Kyle Aircraft Company asked me to call Mr. Harkins.

SCRIPT 1.3A. GETTING THE SECRETARY ON YOUR SIDE

SECRETARY: Well, Mr. Harkins isn't in right now. May *I* help you?

TIP: At this point you could find out when Mr. Harkins will be back, leave your name (and phone number—you just might get lucky with a call back), and thank Mrs. Ryan. Rather than do that, let's let Mrs. Ryan in on what we're doing. Besides developing a future ally, we're letting Mr. Harkins know why we're calling. Since we've been referred by his customer, Mr. Weber, Mr. Harkins *is* going to talk with us. Knowing what we will be calling about will give him a chance to think about our product—positively or negatively. If the thoughts are positive, we're one step closer to a sale. If they are negative, we'll get them out in the open on our next call and will ask questions to turn the negatives into positives.

SALESPERSON: Our company, Cardinal Business Services, has done some work for Mr. Weber in streamlining his engineering design and manufacturing operations. Mr. Weber thought that Mr. Harkins could use some similar help and wanted me to talk with him.

TIP: You are calling because Mr. Harkins' customer *wanted* you to. You imply that both you and Mr. Harkins have to go along with the customer's request. Also, we didn't talk about any of the other aspects of our system—accounts receivable, cost accounting, etc. There will be time for that when we get in the door. Or, we can talk to Mrs. Ryan about it in the same way we did in Script 1.1 if Mr. Harkins isn't in the next time we call. For now, we'll give Mrs. Ryan only one "grabber"—streamlining engineering and manufacturing operations.

SECRETARY: We could certainly use some streamlining. I'll tell Mr. Harkins you called.

SALESPERSON: Thank you. Please be sure to mention that I'm calling at Mr. Weber's request. What is the best time to reach Mr. Harkins?

SECRETARY: He's usually in his office after 4:00, when most of the shop people have left.

SALESPERSON: Thank you for your help, Mrs. Ryan. I'll look forward to talking with you tomorrow after 4:00.

> TIP: A small touch. We could have just said a quick "thank you." Instead, we used the secretary's name and paved the way to her recognizing us the next time we call and made it a point to express appreciation—two more steps toward developing a relationship and two more steps closer to a sale.

We're off to a good start, having created a favorable, businesslike impression but thanks mostly to the use of Mr. Weber's name. You can see how much easier your job will be if you have these kinds of names to use. This should suggest that your referral-obtaining efforts get a bit more priority than they may have in the past. Let's now go to a conversation with the prospect.

SCRIPT 1.4. USING THIRD-PARTY REFERRALS WITH PROSPECTS

SALESPERSON: Good afternoon, Mrs. Ryan, this is Stuart Davidson from Cardinal Business Services. How are you today?

SECRETARY: Oh, hello, Mr. Davidson. I told Mr. Harkins about your call. He's still in the shop. Let me see if I can page him for you.

> TIP: She *did* remember us thanks to taking an extra few seconds to make an impression. Further, she followed through with Mr. Harkins.

SALESPERSON: Fine, thank you. I'll hold on.

SECRETARY: (after a minute) Mr. Harkins is on his way back to his office. He'll be with you in a minute.

SCRIPT 1.4A. MAKING THE SECRETARY YOUR SALES PARTNER

SALESPERSON: Mrs. Ryan, may I ask you a question while we're waiting? Do you handle a lot of the administrative routine for Sheraton Machining (Mr. Harkins' and Mrs. Ryan's company)?

SECRETARY: Well, I handle the payroll and supervise the accounts receivable and credit collection among other things.

SALESPERSON: At some point we might discuss how Cardinal Business Services (keep mentioning the name) systems might be able to save you some time and hassle in these areas.

SECRETARY: Well, we could certainly use it. Oh here's Mr. Harkins.

> TIP: You use the waiting time effectively. No big pitch—just planting a seed. If you have to wait for Mr. Harkins when you meet for your appointment, you just might have a chance to chat about Mrs. Ryan's problems and concerns in the accounting and administrative areas. She may even bring it up. Teasers can sometimes be more effective than outright pitches.

SCRIPT 1.4B. GETTING THROUGH TO THE PROSPECT

MR. HARKINS: Hello.

SALESPERSON: Hello, Mr. Harkins. This is Stu Davidson from Cardinal Business Services. I think Mrs. Ryan told you that Dave Weber from Kyle Aircraft suggested that I call you.

> TIP: Your name and your company's name is mentioned again. Also, whether you are on a first-name basis with Mr. Weber or not, the use of the first name implies that you are, indeed, close.

MR. HARKINS: Yes. How do you know Dave?

SALESPERSON: Cardinal Business Services just recently installed a system that we expect will save Kyle Aircraft about $50,000 per year.

> TIP: You don't know Mr. Harkins' level of sophistication, nor his feeling about computers, so you stayed away from the term, "computer." You don't yet know his "hot buttons," so you don't give any specific information until you've had a chance to ask questions. You did, however, provide a grabber that has to provoke interest.

MR. HARKINS: How did you manage to do that?

SCRIPT 1.4C. GETTING THROUGH BY GETTING INFORMATION

SALESPERSON: Good question. We helped him make some changes in his engineering and manufacturing operations. May I ask *you* a question, Mr. Harkins?

> TIP: We don't want to talk specifics until we know how they relate to Mr. Harkins' operations and what will turn him on. At the same time, we can't brush the question aside. By providing an answer, however vague, we've bought some time and the right to ask a question that will get things back on the track *we* want them running on.

SALESPERSON: What do you feel is *your* biggest problem in your engineering and manufacturing departments?

> TIP: We took the ball back by asking an open-ended question. Let's see if Mr. Harkins bites.

MR. HARKINS: I'd like to know a little more about what you did for Dave Weber.

> TIP: Oops. He's been through the control-through-questions bit before. We'll have to try harder. We have, of course, discussed with Mr. Weber the amount of information we can discuss with Mr. Harkins or other prospects.

SALESPERSON: We installed a system that cuts drawing and drafting time in half for most projects. Is this the kind of thing that would interest *you*?

> TIP: We fed out a little more information, being careful to avoid being specific and not mention the term, "computer." We also tried to get the ball back with another hard-to-avoid question.

MR. HARKINS: Who wouldn't be interested? How much does this system cost and what is it?

SCRIPT 1.4D. SELLING THROUGH INFORMATION GATHERING

SALESPERSON: Those are two good questions at once. Before I can answer, I need a bit of information. How many people do you have in your engineering and manufacturing departments?

> TIP: Again, you are trying to get back in control and get information you will need later. Also, by keeping Mr. Harkins on the phone and interested in talking, you will have increased his *time investment* in you, making it that much easier to get the next appointment. No one wants to admit that time was wasted, so the more time you can get a prospect to spend, the more time you are likely to get in the future—as long as you keep doing things right.

MR. HARKINS: I have four people in the engineering department and two manufacturing engineers.
SALESPERSON: And what kind of support people do you have in these two departments?
MR. HARKINS: There are two secretaries, one for each department, and two draftsmen. I guess I should say "draftspersons" since one is a woman.

> TIP: Now you're getting the kind of information you'll need to approach the size of the opportunity—pre-proposal information. We've also kept Mr. Harkins talking—like *boiling a frog*. To boil a frog, you don't throw him into hot water. He'll just jump out. You put him in tepid water and gradually turn up the heat. Before he knows it, he's cooked. It's the same with prospects.

SALESPERSON: Well, from what I know about your company so far it sounds like you might be able to get the same benefits from our system that Dave Weber did.

> TIP: Don't push, the hook isn't set yet. Pause and let Mr. Harkins' curiosity prompt him to make the move and *invite* you for an appointment.

MR. HARKINS: Well, how do I find out more about this system and whether or not it makes sense for me?

> TIP: Perfect. Now *Mr. Harkins* is asking appointment-closing questions.

SCRIPT 1.4E. CLOSING FOR THE APPOINTMENT

SALESPERSON: I'm sure you're very busy with your operation. What is the best time for us to meet?

> TIP: You headed off the "too busy" stall. You didn't yet ask for the appointment— you're leading up to that with another "boil a frog" question.

MR. HARKINS: Well, I usually get free of the shop around 4:00 and clean up the stuff in my office.
SALESPERSON: Why don't we plan on getting together around 5:00? Would Tuesday or Wednesday next week be better for you?

TIP: We gave him the usual choice of two "yeses" instead of a "yes" or a "no," but we also implied that our time is valuable or that we are booked this week by suggesting "next week."

MR. HARKINS: Make it Wednesday. Anytime between 4:30 and 5:00 is fine. And, make sure you bring some information on what this would cost.
SALESPERSON: Fine, I'll look forward to seeing you then.

Great! Another done deal. And you kept Mr. Harkins on the phone long enough for him to feel he has put a time investment in your project. We didn't discuss any of the other aspects of our system. There will be time enough for that with Mrs. Ryan. We avoid the mistake a lot of salespeople make—confusing the prospect by giving him more than one central issue to focus on.

SCRIPT 1.5. DEVELOPING PROSPECTS WITH TRADE SHOW LEADS

It's said that it takes an average of five calls to close the typical industrial sale, but an average of only two calls to close the typical trade show lead. It may be that the people saying this are those who sponsor trade shows, but the point has a good deal of validity. Let's look at setting up the initial appointment that we got from a trade show or that was forwarded to us. We'll stick with the Cardinal Business Services example and pick up from the point where we've gotten through to the prospect. (See page 2 for a description of the product and pages 3-8 for scripts on dealing with the secretary.)

OBJECTIVE: We want an appointment with the prospect. To maximize our time, first we want to *qualify* the prospect. Was she just a looker at the trade show or did she see something that fits an immediate need? All we have is a name, "Sherie Wendell," and a title, "MIS (Management Information Systems) Director." In checking our local business directory, we found that her company, ABC Moving & Storage, employs 35 people and does about $4 million in annual sales volume.

SALESPERSON: Good morning Ms. Wendell. This is Stuart Davidson from Cardinal Business Systems.

TIP: "Ms." is usually a safe bet until you find out whether it is "Miss", "Ms.", or "Mrs." Pause after mentioning the name of your company to see if it rings a bell from the show. If nothing else, you should act as though it should so Ms. Wendell will think it should.

MS. WENDELL: Do I know you?
SALESPERSON: You don't know *me*, but you do know our company. Apparently you stopped by our booth at the Arizona Computer Exposition and asked one of our people to have someone follow through with more information.

TIP: Pause again instead of rushing into a pitch. You just might get some information that will be helpful in leading the conversation.

MS. WENDELL: Oh yes, now I remember. You were demonstrating a system that would let us track orders from estimate to billing and give us some control over our drivers' and contractors' activities.

TIP: By pausing and waiting, you have a direction to go in with your questions.

SCRIPT 1.5A. QUALIFYING THE TRADE SHOW LEAD PROSPECT

SALESPERSON: Yes, that's been one of our most successful systems. We've installed about a dozen *in companies like yours*. Do you presently have a computer system in your company?

MS. WENDELL: We have a terminal on line to our central agency office and they handle payroll for us, but our billing is still done manually. You say you've done work for moving and storage companies before?

TIP: Now she's taking control by asking questions. Get it back, remembering that you can't just brush the question aside.

SALESPERSON: Yes, as a matter of fact I was working last week on integrating a billing system into a total traffic management system. About how many invoices a month do you send out?

TIP: By using the term "traffic management system" you've shown familiarity with her industry. The question should make her think and get her off trying to control *your* call.

MS. WENDELL: I'd have to get the exact numbers from our billing department, but it's enough for us to be concerned about doing it more efficiently.

SALESPERSON: What do you feel is your biggest problem with billing right now?

TIP: The hook is in her mouth since she expressed a problem and a need. Following right up with another question keeps *her* talking and *you* in control. You should also get the information you need to set the hook.

MS. WENDELL: Getting invoices out fast enough. We don't get paid until our clients get their bills.

SCRIPT 1.5B. GETTING THE PROSPECT IN FOR A DEMONSTRATION

SALESPERSON: Yes, that's the same problem CSS Moving & Storage had. We were able to cut the time required to process invoices in half. Would you like to learn more about how we were able to do this?

MS. WENDELL: Well, sure. Could you come in and talk with me about it?

TIP: Well, it looks like we have a good prospect. Let's push for a bigger commitment of her time and a better chance to move the sales process a few steps ahead.

SALESPERSON: I'd be happy to. (A good idea just occurred to you.) In order to save you time and give you a good idea of what our system could do for you, why don't I reserve some time in our demonstration room and *show* you rather than just telling you about the benefits of the system?

TIP: This is the "boil a frog" theory again. By getting her in *your* office, you have more control over the interview and make her commit more of her time than she would have given you in her office. You've also made her feel important and enhanced your own status as a professional organization by "reserving time in the demonstration room."

MS. WENDELL: Well . . .

SCRIPT 1.5C. CLOSING FOR THE APPOINTMENT

SALESPERSON: We're located right on Camelback Road, about 15 minutes from your office. We could schedule a demo for early morning, late afternoon, or around lunchtime. What would be best for you?

TIP: Again, the choice of two or more "yeses."

MS. WENDELL: I guess I have to almost pass by your place on my way to work, so morning should be better.
SALESPERSON: Good. Let me just check the demo room appointment book. We could fit you in at 8:30 next Tuesday or at 9:30 on Thursday. Which could be better for you?
MS. WENDELL: Thursday would work better.

TIP: Some people like to be taken out for lunch, some people like an excuse to leave the office early, and some even like to have an excuse to sleep later. Your original choices of times gave Ms. Wendell all three options.

SALESPERSON: Fine. I'll talk with one of our tech reps to make sure we have the system you'd like to see up and running. Look forward to seeing you Thursday.

Done deal. There is an obvious need for your product that could be developed into a sale. When you get together next Thursday, you'll further qualify Ms. Wendell by finding out just how much authority she has to authorize purchases, who else will be involved, and whether they have the money to buy your system. You might consider calling on Wednesday to confirm the appointment and asking if Ms. Wendell would like to invite anyone else from her company to come along.

Had the person not qualified—presently has an effective computer system, too small a company, home office handles all computer purchases, etc.—you would have kept the card in your "C" file (as in "A," important; "B," less important; and "C," even less important) for follow up in six months or so and perhaps added the person to your mailing list.

LETTER 1.1. CONFIRMING AND RESELLING THE APPOINTMENT

OBJECTIVE: We want to make sure the prospect keeps the appointment and avoids the post-cognitive dissonance syndrome—that feeling that sets in after a decision is made that suggests that the decision wasn't such a good one. We also want the prospect to show up in our office with a sense of positive expectancy. Finally, we want to close the gap between the making of the appointment and the demonstration with some additional prospect-oriented reasons for buying from us.

Dear (Prospect)   [Phone number]

Enjoyed talking with you on the phone last Thursday and having the opportunity to discuss how we can help solve your billing problems.

I'm looking forward to seeing you on Tuesday the ninth at 8:00 a.m. Our technical service manager has already set up a demonstration that will show you quickly how our system can deal with *your* particular situation.

As you can tell from the address, we're on City Line Avenue, exactly 1 mile from the expressway, on the right-hand side, right after the Lord & Taylor store.

I've enclosed a recommendation letter from Dennis Moving and Storage that may give you some idea of what we'll be able to do for you. Of course, *your* system would be custom-tailored for *your* operation.

Call in the meantime if you have any questions. See you on the ninth at 8:00 a.m.

TIP: Let's review what we did with this brief letter:

- We wrote it the way we would talk with the prospect in person—no stilted language.
- We included a phone number to save time later. How many times have you reviewed correspondence and then had to start digging through your notes or prospect cards to find the number?
- We restated the problem discussed. This letter is addressed specifically to the prospect. It's not a cookie-cutter form letter.
- We indicated that we had made an investment in time and effort to set up the demonstration. This won't completely insure against a no-show, but it should reinforce the prospect's sense of commitment to the appointment.
- We provided specific directions. We don't want the prospect coming in late and frazzled because she couldn't find our office. (In some cases it may be worthwhile to pick up the prospect so you have a captive and can spend time in the car doing some soft selling.)
- We included a recommendation letter from a company in the same business. *You* could tell your prospect how great you are, but it's a lot more effective coming from a third party.
- The "I/you" count is right. This is a final check for any customer or prospect letter. Count the number of times "I," "we," and "ours" are mentioned compared to the number of "you," "your," and "yours" that are included. There should always be more of the latter. In this case, there are 10 "yous" to seven "Is" so we're right on track.
- (Not mentioned) We included a capabilities brochure to provide some additional selling material to whet our prospect's appetite, and our business card.

Personal calls and demonstrations are *expensive* so it makes good time management sense to use the phone and direct mail for another contact with the prospect as often as you can. Letters, leave-behind literature, brochures, and newsletters keep your name in front of the prospect, head off PCD (post-cognitive dissonance), and contribute importantly to the sale. The prospect has to deal with you and your message one more time even if it's only to circular-file your material.

With the price of computers and word-processing equipment so low, a form letter that doesn't look like a form letter should be sent after almost every contact with a prospect and sometimes in between contacts. This applies as well to a one-person office as to a 100-person salesforce.

SCRIPT 1.6. SELLING BY DEMONSTRATING

Specific scripts for the first call or demonstration will vary considerably from product to product, company to company, and prospect to prospect. By now, you've gotten the idea of scripts—they are guides, not highly structured, canned pitches that leave no room for inter-action between you and the prospect. They include a lot of questions so you are *listening* most of the time. You are now ready to write your own script and agenda for your prospect's visit. We'll use Cardinal Business Services again and you can adapt this outline to your prod-uct or service. (See page 2 for a description of the product.) Here is a guide to help you.

OBJECTIVE: We want to close the prospect. This probably won't happen on the first call, but let's keep our sense of positive expectancy alive. (If you shoot for the moon, you may miss and fall back to earth. If you shoot for the sun and miss, you still have a chance at the moon.)

The minimum we want from this call is to get most of the informa-tion we need for a specific proposal. We want the prospect to leave with the feeling that our system is a must and all that needs to be done before installation is to clear away a few obstacles and set a date.

DEMONSTRATION CHECKLIST

1. Prepare an agenda for the meeting even if it includes only four or five items:
   Welcome and introductions .... SD
   Brief meeting with president .... NG
   Outline of needs .... SW

   TIP: This is the prospect's turn to talk. She will tell your people what is important to her and give them a lead on how she is to be sold. *You get control over a sales situation by giving up control.*

   Basic product demonstration .... TR
   Fitting the product to the needs .... SD
   Client discussion .... All

   TIP: At this point the "prospect" has become a "client." If you and your people think this way, you will get her thinking this way.

   Proposal and follow up .... SW/SD

2. Send out the agenda with a brief note so it arrives a day or two before the meeting. It's another reminder of the meeting, further proof that you've made a time-and-effort investment, an indication that the prospect (client) is expected to participate actively in the meeting and a way to enhance the feeling of positive expectancy on the part of the prospect.

3. Have a changeable letter sign board in your lobby:

> WELCOME
>
> SHERIE WENDELL
> MANAGEMENT INFORMATION SYSTEMS DIRECTOR
> ABC MOVING AND STORAGE COMPANY

This obviously makes the prospect feel important. It also communicates the message to other visitors that something is going on (perphaps they would like to see their names on a sign) and helps out with step 4 below.

    If you don't already have one of these sign boards (they start at less than $100), get one. You can get them from most stationery stores or contact one of the factories directly. Among the manufacturers who make these are:

    Weber Costello, 183 Edwards Drive, Jackson, TN, 38302-2687 (901-442-4440).

    Stempel Mfg. Co., P.O. Box 391, Coleman, TX, 76384 (915-625-3530).

4. Make sure everyone in your office knows that you have a V.I.P. (Very Important Prospect) coming in. The receptionist should be alerted, and, when the first woman shows up near the appointment time, she should ask, "Ms. Wendell?" If it's not Ms. Wendell you haven't lost anything. If it is, she has to be flattered by being recognized.

5. Have coffee, soft drinks, and possibly doughnuts or finger sandwiches (depending on the time of day) available. Alternatively, have someone immediately come in to the conference area, *address your prospect by name*, mention what drinks and other goodies are available, and ask what she would like.

6. It may sound obvious, but pay attention to your office housekeeping. That box of computer paper may have been in the corner so long that you no longer see it. Count on it to detract from your presentation in your prospect's mind.

7. Have (clean) ashtrays available so the prospect may smoke if she wishes (unless your building has a clearcut no-smoking policy). If she doesn't smoke, nobody else does—and make sure nobody smokes in the conference room before your meeting.

8. No alcohol before or during the meeting. Don't count on getting an order signed by getting the prospect tipsy. It could be cancelled the next day just as easily and her hangover will erase positive feelings about her visit. If the meeting is scheduled for late afternoon, you might want to consider having wine available for *after* the meeting, but stay away from the hard stuff. You could be legally liable if your prospect gets in a traffic accident because you plied her with booze.

    With this guide you should be ready to prepare your agenda and script. This "script" will probably be an *outline* of the points you want to cover since you want plenty of room and opportunity for prospect participation. Remember, in sales interviews or demonstrations as in any other relationship, *you get control by giving it up.*

SCRIPT 1.7. DEMONSTRATING IN THE PROSPECT'S OFFICE

It should be obvious from Script 1.6 that your best bet is to have the first call take place in *your* office. There should always be a demonstration of some kind on the first call even if you are selling pencils or paper clips. Your office is the best place for this. You can control the interruptions, impress the prospect with your professionalism, and make the prospect truly feel like a V.I.P. (Very Important Prospect) on the way to making her a C.C. (Closed Client).

If you really have no control over this, even after offering to send a limo to pick up your prospect (sometimes not a bad idea for really I.P.'s), here is a guide to the first call in the prospect's office.

> OBJECTIVE: The same as in Script 1.6—close the prospect, or, if this doesn't happen, get the information you need for a complete proposal and leave the prospect with the impression that the system is a must for her. We have one other objective—get the prospect into our office so we can put Script 1.6 on the stage.

SALESPERSON: Good morning, I'm Stuart Davidson from Cardinal Business Systems. (Hand receptionist your business card.) Ms. Wendell is expecting me. Is it "Miss" or "Mrs." Wendell?
RECEPTIONIST: It is *definitely* "Ms." I'll see if she's in her office.

> TIP: Good information. This tells us to be even more careful to make sure we act as though we were talking to a management information systems director, not a woman—no flirting, no cutesy remarks, and no "What's a nice girl like you doing in a place like this?" In fact, strike the word "girl" from your vocabulary unless you're talking about someone under 10. Older than 10 they are young ladies, ladies, or women.

SCRIPT 1.7A. MAKING AN ALLY OF THE RECEPTIONIST

RECEPTIONIST: Ms. Wendell says she will be with you in 5 minutes or less. That's a cute bird on your card.
SALESPERSON: Thanks. It helps people remember us. (Reaching into briefcase) Since you like the bird, here's a noteholder for you with the cardinal on it.
RECEPTIONIST: (Looking at noteholder) "Our Systems Sing for You." A bit corny isn't it?
SALESPERSON: Maybe, but so is "How do you spell relief." The cardinal *is* a songbird— and, corny or not, the slogan helps people remember us. And, our systems really do sing.

> TIP: The receptionist is obviously not busy typing invoices or stuffing envelopes and wants to talk, so it does no harm to develop a new friend and possible future ally. Rebuffing her friendliness could mean her announcing you next time as "that clown from the bird company" as opposed to "that nice Mr. Davidson from Cardinal Business Services." Also, other people will see the noteholder with the distinctive red logo.

RECEPTIONIST: Excuse me. That might be Ms. Wendell now. (Pause) Yes, Ms. Wendell says to go right in. It's the second door on the right.

SCRIPT 1.7B. PRE-DEMONSTRATION QUESTIONS TO ASK

You say, "Thank you," enter Ms. Wendell's office, and exchange pleasantries. You have a portable computer with you with a demonstration disk on your billing system. For now, you tuck it unobtrusively in a corner. Before running the demonstration, you need:

- to get more information on the problem areas,
- to get more of an idea of what Ms. Wendell's hot buttons are, and
- to take control of the interview by asking questions.

Rather than explore all the possible dialogue that could take place, let's suggest some questions that you might want to ask.

SCRIPT 1.7C.

SALESPERSON: Ms. Wendell, you mentioned the billing area as a critical problem for you. Could you tell me what the three biggest problems in this area are?

TIP: By specifying "three," you're controlling the interview. Ms. Wendell can't get off the hook by saying something vague like "Everything." She also has to think logically about the problems, so she can't think about controlling. Yet, *she* is doing the talking. *You get control by giving it up.*

SCRIPT 1.7D.

SALESPERSON: How do you feel about computerized systems in general? Have you had a good deal of prior experience with computerized systems?

TIP: It's important that you know whether or not you're dealing with a computerphobe (a person who *hates* computers) or with someone looking for an excuse to have one installed. You have to know her level of awareness so you don't talk down to her or over her head.

SCRIPT 1.7E.

SALESPERSON: If you were convinced today that this were the absolute solution to all your billing problems, what would the next step be before we trained your people and installed the system?

TIP: You ask this before the demo since you want to find out whether Ms. Wendell has the authority to approve the purchase or if there is another buying influence actively involved. If there is someone else who has to approve the purchase, you might want to have Ms. Wendell invite this person to see the demonstration— after you have gotten her confidence and after assuring her (without saying it) that you don't want to step on her toes or go over her head.

SCRIPT 1.7F.

SALESPERSON: If you were convinced that this system would cut your billing time in half with no extra cost, how much time would it take to get the purchase of the equipment approved?

TIP: Part of your discussion now and your final proposal will center on the cost-effectiveness of your product. Obviously, the software and hardware is going to cost money. Put the focus on labor savings and payback period.

SCRIPT 1.7G.

SALESPERSON: Let's make a specific list of your expectations of the "perfect" system for you. What would the list include?

SCRIPT 1.7H.

SALESPERSON: Now that you've seen what we have done for *companies like yours* and what we can do for you, do you have any reservations about placing an order?

SCRIPT 1.7I.

SALESPERSON: Would you like me to make arrangements for you to see the system we installed at Dennis Moving and Storage Company?

TIP: Obviously, you have Dennis's approval to do this and Dennis and ABC Moving & Storage are not competitors of your prospect.

IN CLOSING

We discussed the obstacles that get in the way of making new appointments, getting new prospects, and turning them into customers. We pointed out ways to resolve these problems and turn them into opportunities.

Then we took the most difficult appointment-setting situation of all—the cold, unknown prospect—and provided a specific, step-by-step script to close the deal; in this case, an appointment.

We worked it two ways—where you are dealing with the secretary or administrative assistant, who is usually an obstacle, or with the principal. We used the *"businesses like yours"* phrase to take full and complete advantage of the third-party referral syndrome and demonstrate how easy it can be to get that first appointment.

Great so far. Unfortunately, first appointments seldom result in sales unless you're into aluminum siding or driveway repaving. In the next chapter, we'll talk about how to close the sale on the second, third, fourth, or fifth sales call.

2

Closing on the Second, Third, Fourth, or Fifth Appointments

INTRODUCTION

You made the first sales call or held the first demonstration and broke the ice with your prospect. The prospect now knows who you are and what your company can do. You didn't make the sale, but because you are not in a one-call-close business, you didn't really expect to. You developed interest that now has to be translated into action steps.

There is an old selling cliché that holds that most industrial sales closes are made on the fifth sales call. Most salespeople, according to a continuation of the cliché, give up on the third or fourth sales call. Both elements of this cliché are supported by a wealth of market research evidence. Perhaps this is why wisdom like this is called a "cliché." If there weren't a great deal of truth in "wisdom" like this, the statements probably would be called hyperboles or untruths. Maybe they are called clichés just because there really is a great deal of truth in them that we should heed.

In the last chapter we dealt with how to get the first appointment. It doesn't end there, however. Unless your salespeople have a unique product, they will encounter the "Well, we're happy with our present supplier but will keep you in mind" syndrome, or the prospect may want to shop around for competitive products and/or pricing. Persistence is one of the few things that will crack this kind of account. But, what do you do? What do you say after you've given your best pitch? What do you say after you've said "Hello"? This chapter will suggest some ideas, letters, and specific scripts for the second, third, and fourth sales call so your salespeople can hit the magic fifth.

LETTER 2.1. FOLLOWING UP ON THE INITIAL CALL OR DEMO

A lot of the work we will suggest in closing accounts will be between-appointments activities. While there is no substitute for face-to-face contact with a prospect, it's just too expensive to rely on personal calls as the only means of communication. The exact number will vary according to the circumstances, but you should plan on something like three letters and five phone calls to every personal call you make in order to utilize your time in the best way. If your prospect is in the same office building you are, you might scale these numbers back. If your prospect is in Waubansee, Kansas and you are headquartered in West Olive, Massachusetts, you might rely on the mail and the phone a bit more.

If you don't yet have a personal computer or have access to one, get one soon. Even with minimal typing skills you'll find that you can put stuff on the screen (monitor or CRT—Cathode Ray Tube) almost as fast as you can dictate. *And*, you can store the letters you write to prospects, call them up, copy them into another file, and write a personalized letter to another prospect with just a few key strokes. You'll also make small modifications in your basic "form" letters that will continue to hone your approach and make your efforts even more successful.

Now, let's look at a suggested first follow-up letter to Mr. Harkins, the machine shop owner from Script 1.1. The letter should be written and mailed within three days after your appointment:

> OBJECTIVE: Recall in your prospect's mind the positive elements of your call, keep him interested, and pave the way for the next (hopefully closing) appointment.

Dear Mr. Harkins,

Thanks very much for taking time away from your hectic activities to spend some time discussing how *Cardinal Business Services* can help your business to grow, be more profitable, and be more organized.

> TIP: All machine shop owners (and, probably, most other entrepreneurs) like to think that they are the only ones who have hectic activities. Also, we didn't mention our product or its *features*—we talked *benefits* to our prospect.

You recall that we spent a fair amount of time talking about your frustration over the fact that it takes months for your accountant to come up with a financial statement. This is certainly understandable. No businessman can wait until June to find out whether or not he made money in January.

> TIP: This is the grabber, hook, or hot button that you identified and remember from your notes, and it provides the segue from your appointment to this letter to keep the effort on a smooth continuum.

I've asked our financial statement specialist to develop some information on how our package would work in your specific situation to give you the financial facts you need.

> TIP: Can't you just picture Mr. Harkins appreciating the *personal* attention to his needs and waiting for your "financial statement specialist" to come up with *his* answer?

You will hear from me when I have an answer to your problem from our specialist. If you have any questions in the meantime, please call me at 617-822-6471.

> TIP: Short, sweet, and non-pushy. You came across as being interested in solving Mr. Harkins' problem, not selling your system. This mention of a "financial statement specialist" is another version of the third-party referral technique we talked about in Chapter 1.
>
> You also did something that few salespeople do—you stopped before you peaked. You didn't try to close because you realized you couldn't. You turned the heat up (as in boiling a frog, page 10). It wouldn't be the least bit surprising if Mr. Harkins called *you* in a few days, especially since you provided the invitation with your phone number, to see what your specialist has come up with for *him*.

KEEPING TRACK OF PROSPECT PROGRESS—ACCOUNT PROFILE AND CALL SHEETS

It's important to keep careful notes of your progress so you can review where you are and where you've been at any time without trusting to your memory. Figures 2.1 and 2.2 suggest a very convenient way to do this without having to worry about filling out complicated forms. You just use them to jot down what happened so you'll know what the next step should be.

You can keep these sheets in a conventional three-ring binder arranged by importance, timeliness, city, zip code, or any other system that will help you follow through on the good start you've made. (Copies of the sheets on which there has been activity during the week or month sent to the sales manager could make a good substitute for the conventional call report forms.)

> OBJECTIVE: Provide an easy-to-use recordkeeping system that will provide immediate and complete information on what has happened with all prospects, including prospects' individual "hot buttons" and special interests.

SCRIPT 2.1. GETTING THE IMPORTANT SECOND APPOINTMENT

It's very possible that you may have done such a good selling job that Mr. Harkins will call you before you have a chance to call him, but not likely. The reality is that you have to make the call. It should happen within seven to ten days after your appointment which means less than a week after Mr. Harkins has received (not necessarily read) your letter. Here's how it might go:

ACCOUNT PROFILE AND CALL SHEET

COMPANY
NAME _____ CONTACT _____
ADDRESS _____ ALTERNATE _____
CITY _____ STATE _____ ZIP _____ PHONE _____
HOT BUTTONS _____
COMMENTS _____
_____
_____

Date   Activity
_____
_____
_____
_____
_____
_____
_____
_____
_____
_____
_____
_____
_____
_____
_____
_____
_____

Figure 2.1

OBJECTIVE: Continue to reinforce the positive first impression you made, keep your name in the front of Mr. Harkins mind, and set up what hopefully will turn out to be a sale-closing appointment.

SALESPERSON: Good morning, Mr. Harkins. How is that aircraft part that had to be done in titanium going?

TIP: You got this from your notes (Account Profile and Call Sheet, Figure 2.1, above) so you could demonstrate that you really are interested in Mr. Harkins' business.

MR. HARKINS: We're going to be late on it. That crazy machinist I had working on it had the drill set all wrong. I had to straighten it out.

SCRIPT 2.1A. PROVIDING PROSPECT-ORIENTED BENEFITS

SALESPERSON: I guess it would make your job a lot easier if you had all the specs immediately available so you or your machinists could do things right from the beginning of a job.

ACCOUNT CALL SHEET

Date   *Activity*

_____
_____
_____
_____
_____
_____
_____
_____
_____
_____
_____
_____
_____
_____
_____
_____
_____
_____
_____
_____
_____
_____
_____
_____

Figure 2.2

TIP: Maybe financial statements isn't the right grabber so switch your thinking to what the prospect's current hot button is.

MR. HARKINS: Sure it would, but there are so many variables in this business. You have to be there to see what is going on.

SALESPERSON: (Switching topics) You know, one of our other clients had a similar problem and we were able to solve most of it with our job-estimating application package—a neat thing that takes a lot of information out of your head and gets it down on paper for your estimators to follow.

SCRIPT 2.1B. CLOSING FOR THE APPOINTMENT

SALESPERSON: (Quickly—Mr. Harkins still has his pride.) Of course, nothing will substitute for the kind of experience *you* have, but I think it would be to your advantage to take a look at this and tell me how it might work for a *company like yours*.

TIP: Mr. Harkins *has* to be the expert, so let him *be* the expert. You can let him teach you while he is selling himself on your system.

MR. HARKINS: Well, I don't have much time, but I might be willing to take a look at what you have.

TIP: Great. You've whetted his appetite enough so he's suggesting an appointment. Might as well go for it now and forget, for now, your financial statement specialist and that report.

SALESPERSON: Wednesday at 4:00 p.m. was good for you the last time we met. Is that still a good time?
MR. HARKINS: Make it 4:30. We're just so busy.
SALESPERSON: Fine, I'll look forward to seeing you Wednesday at 4:30.

Now you have that critical second appointment set up. You are going in to discuss the job estimating or even job scheduling aspects of your system, but you bring along the report from your "financial statement specialist" hoping for an opening to introduce it. With luck, you might even get a commitment to the system on this second call.

Because we are still anticipating that it might take five calls to close this prospect, we want to be sure that we leave something in our back pockets as a reason for a third call. We want to assume, of course, that we can sell the prospect on any of these calls and want to have this positive mental attitude going in. We still, however, keep something in reserve for the next call just in case we have to make it before the final sale.

DEALING WITH THE "THIRD" PARTY IN A SALE

You had your second appointment with Mr. Harkins and it went fairly well, despite the interruptions from his head journeyman machinist. He was skeptical about the ability of your job scheduling system to keep track of what he (probably inadequately) keeps in his head, but promised to show it to his daughter Wendy who is a senior in college looking forward to her Mechanical Engineering Degree before she joins her father's business. He's interested, but is copping out by bringing in that third party who just may or may not be reachable for awhile. You can use this to your advantage.

Now you've learned that there might be a third-party influence—a far more common phenomenon than most salespeople recognize. Often, the third call is not on the primary buying influence, but on a third party. Dad is nondegreed old school, but may be willing to listen to his daughter. Obviously, you will make arrangements to get together with the daughter to discuss your ideas and, not so incidentally, your system.

This is a bit touchy since Mr. Harkins knows it all and can't believe that Wendy can provide that much help. You handle this by suggesting that it will be a good part of her education to see what real world problems are all about. He's skeptical at first because you foiled his cop-out plans by offering to get together with Wendy. You smooth this over by telling him that *you* would be interested in finding out what "they" are teaching kids at college these days. (Expressing a self-interest is a good way to gain credibility for your motives.) He agrees and gives you her phone number at Bucknell.

From here, it's fairly simple. If that third call *is* to a third party, the mere mention that your prospect suggested that you get in touch with the third party and arrange an appointment is usually enough to guarantee that you will get to see the person. If you were selling a benefit plan, the third party might be your prospect's accountant or attorney. If you were selling original art, the third party might be your prospect's designer. They *will* see you because of *their* interest in the prospect. Let's look at how we'll set up this appointment:

SCRIPT 2.2. SELLING THE THIRD PARTY ON AN APPOINTMENT

OBJECTIVE: You want to set up an appointment to explain what you are presenting to Mr. Harkins and get his daughter's agreement that the system makes sense for Mr. Harkins' company.

SALESPERSON: Good morning Wendy. ("Ms. Harkins" would make you sound too much like a salesperson and a stranger.) This is Stu Davidson from Cardinal Business Services. Gerhardt, your father, asked me to call you.

TIP: Pause to see what kind of reaction you get. For all you know, Mr. Harkins may be divorced and estranged from his daughter who can't stand him and you're being set up.

WENDY: Oh yes. What's dear vater ("father" in German) up to now?
SALESPERSON: He's considering installing one of our computer systems . . .
WENDY: Well, it's about time.

SCRIPT 2.2A. FINDING OUT WHERE THE THIRD PARTY IS COMING FROM

SALESPERSON: Oh good. I'm glad you feel that way. I understand that you're a mechanical engineering senior and that you'll be joining the company when you graduate later this year.

TIP: Get to know Wendy a little before you push for an appointment. Get her to feel comfortable talking with you.

WENDY: Yes. Full time that is. I've worked at the company every summer for the past five years. I'll graduate in June and then spend a month with some relatives in Würzburg taking side trips around Europe.

TIP: Jot this bit of information down on your Account Profile and Call Sheet for future reference.

SALESPERSON: That sounds great. After what you must have gone through during the past four years you *deserve* some time off. Have you had much experience with computer systems?
WENDY: Some. My minor is in Computer Science.

SCRIPT 2.2B. CLOSING THE APPOINTMENT WITH THE THIRD PARTY

SALESPERSON: That's great. I'll look forward to talking with you and explaining what we're proposing for your company.

TIP: This is a jump ahead, but by assuming that the appointment is a given, you just might get Wendy to do that too.

WENDY: Me?
SALESPERSON: Yes. Your father asked me to get together with you to explain what we're proposing and get your thoughts and, hopefully, approval of the direction we're going in.
WENDY: He wants *my* approval?
SALESPERSON: He'd like you to see what we plan to do and provide some advice from

your viewpoint on the value of the system to the company. Do you get a break in classes during the day or would it be better to see you after classes?

> TIP: We might as well get the commitment for an appointment while Wendy is still in shock. Notice that we're leading up to the appointment with a nonthreatening question and the choice of two "yeses" bit.

WENDY: Well, on Tuesdays and Thursdays I have a three-hour break from eleven to two.
SALESPERSON: Fine. Let's get together for lunch either on or off campus. Would next Tuesday or Thursday be better for you?
WENDY: Well, I have an exam on Friday, so let's make it Tuesday. Why don't you meet me outside the Student Union at 11:30?

> TIP: You'd prefer off-campus, but the lady doesn't know you so go along with the meeting site. When you get there you'll have an opportunity to suggest a different place for lunch.

SALESPERSON: Fine. I'll be driving a blue Merkur with "CARDCO" on the license plate. Look forward to seeing you next Tuesday at 11:30.

Another done deal. You know that you'll be dealing with a pretty sophisticated young lady, so you'll want to come prepared. You want to make an ally of Wendy, so you might want to bring along some material from your office that she'll find helpful in her Computer Science courses. These extra little touches with prospects, third parties, secretaries, and receptionists will accumulate and pay off in better relationships, a happier workday, and more closed sales.

LETTER 2.2. GETTING A THIRD-PARTY RECOMMENDATION LETTER

Let's assume that you have made the appointment with the third party (Wendy, Mr. Harkins' daughter in this case) and have explained the benefits of your system. Wendy is sold on the system and its benefits for the Harkins' company (the third party doesn't have to pay for it, so this is fairly easy in most cases). Now, the ball is back in your court. Here's what to do:

1. Get the third party to write a letter to your prospect "so there is no misunderstanding" about what was discussed and agreed upon.

2. Get a definite commitment that the third party *will* call your prospect with observations and recommendations *before* a certain time. Tell the third party that you will be calling your prospect in the next two days and that you will count on the prospect having been contacted before you call.

3. Try to get the letter written before you leave the third party's office. You might even have a copy of the last third-party recommendation letter you got written with you to make it easier. In Wendy's case you might offer to draft a letter for her and send it to her for signature or revision. Here's what the recommendation letter might look like (Wendy's would, of course, be a little less formal in tone).

SAMPLE THIRD-PARTY RECOMMENDATION LETTER

Dear (Your Prospect):

I met recently with Stuart Davidson of Cardinal Business Services to discuss their computerized general ledger accounting system and its application for your company.

Based on the demonstration I saw, the system looks good. It has all the elements you should be looking for in an accounting package and seems relatively easy to use without a lot of training.

I was also impressed with Cardinal's customer base. In checking with some of their clients, I found that they seem to enjoy an excellent reputation for installation, training, and follow-through service. Their people are highly regarded by their clients.

Based on what I've seen so far, I would recommend that you pursue this to the final proposal stage. I'd be happy to meet with you and/or Mr. Davidson to discuss the proposal and its application.

> TIP: The writer is, of course, looking for more billable hours. Why not? That's what he does for a living. By starting off right with this third party and keeping him informed, you should be able to keep him from being an eleventh hour deal killer. You also might get referrals to some of his other clients.

LETTER 2.3. KEEPING THE SALE GOING WITH THE THIRD-PARTY "THANK YOU" LETTER

This letter is just as important as a follow-up letter to a prospect. You certainly want to thank the third party for his courtesy even if he *was* being paid to spend the time with you. You want to stress some of the more important points that you agreed upon during your meeting in terms of how your system would be beneficial to your prospect. You also have the opportunity to develop a relationship with this person for other third-party referrals. (See Chapter 1, Script 1.4, page 8.)

SAMPLE THIRD-PARTY "THANK YOU" LETTER

Dear (Third Party):

Thanks very much for taking the time to review the computerized general ledger accounting we are proposing for Harkins Machining.

Your kind words and your recommendation are very much appreciated. We're very proud of our product and our reputation and it's gratifying to have a professional such as you endorse our efforts.

Your points on how easily an effective cost accounting system could be integrated into the total system were right on the mark. We feel that this is one of the main advantages of the system to a company like Harkins.

I'd be happy to meet with you and any of your clients whom you think could use a similar system on a no-cost, no-obligation, and no-pressure basis.

Thanks again for your help. Look forward to working with you again soon.

> TIP: Short, sweet, and to the point. Remember the "I/you" count from Chapter 1, page 14? In this case we scored nine to four, "you's" over "I's", so the letter passes this test with flying colors. Send a copy to your prospect—for more than just common courtesy reasons.

SCRIPT 2.3. WRAPPING UP THE PRE-CLOSE DETAILS

With our third-party appointment and follow-up letter complete, you're ready to go back to work on Mr. Harkins. You want to call him the day after you talk with the third party and tell him that you had a good meeting, explored some interesting ideas, and that you feel even more confident that there is a match between your company's capabilities and your prospect's needs. You have, however, a couple of points that you want one of your systems specialists to investigate in more detail before you get back to your prospect. (This adds to the importance of the meeting and to the stature of the prospect in your eyes—remember how you boil a frog.)

Next, review your notes (Account Profile and Call Sheet) to plan your strategy for the fourth call on your prospect. Here is a suggested script you can use.

SCRIPT 2.3A. GETTING THE PRE-CLOSE APPOINTMENT

OBJECTIVE: Get the next appointment which could be a sale-closing one.

SALESPERSON: Good morning, Mr. Harkins. This is Stuart Davidson from Cardinal Business Services. I had a very interesting meeting with your daughter Wendy last week, as we discussed.

MR. HARKINS: Oh, good. She told me she learned something from you. Amazing. I haven't been able to teach her anything in 23 years.

SALESPERSON: Well, she did raise a couple of interesting points that I've had our system specialist check out and I think we're ready for a final proposal that will answer all the needs that you and she raised.

> TIP: Might as well go for the beginning of a "trial close" now, but pause and see if you can get the prospect to suggest the interview. It may not happen, but it's worth a shot. If he doesn't make the suggestion, you can always do it yourself in a minute or two.

MR. HARKINS: Well, when would you like to come in and discuss it?

> TIP: This is the best situation—your prospect has suggested the next appointment. If he hadn't, you would have said something like, "Would late afternoon Tuesday or Wednesday, be better for you to discuss the proposal?"

SALESPERSON: Wendy told me that she doesn't have classes on Wednesday afternoon, so why don't we make it at 3:00 p.m. next Wednesday and ask Wendy to join us?.

TIP: *You* want Wendy to be there so Mr. Harkins doesn't put off any decision until he has "had a chance to discuss it with his daughter." His daughter probably won't make any difference at all in the decision, but you have eliminated at least this reason for your prospect to put off making a buying decision on your next call.

Eliminating Final Objections

MR. HARKINS: Well, I don't know that Wendy has to be here. She's pretty busy with school.

TIP: Don't buy this. He's still reaching for a reason to put off making a decision.

SALESPERSON: Mr. Harkins, you asked me to see Wendy (that famous "third person") to discuss my proposal for a very good reason. Actually, she had some very good ideas and an excellent understanding of what we are trying to do, so I think she should be there.

TIP: Push hard for this so you eliminate the next excuse Mr. Harkins will have.

MR. HARKINS: Well, okay, if you really think that makes sense. We'll see you at 3:00 p.m. next Wednesday. I'll call Wendy and tell her.

TIP: Don't buy this either. Mr. Harkins probably won't call and could very well find a reason to put off the decision because he "wants to discuss it with Wendy."

SALESPERSON: I need to talk to Wendy to clarify a couple of points she raised, so why don't I just tell her about our meeting. I'll give you a call if there is any problem with her schedule.

TIP: Cut him off at the pass on this attempt to delay making a decision.

MR. HARKINS: (Knowing he's been outsmarted—something he really appreciates, believe it or not, in a salesperson.) Okay, Okay. See you and Wendy on Wednesday.

Done deal! After recording our notes on the Harkins' page in the Account Profile and Call Sheet and calling Wendy, we're ready to start preparing for the appointment.

Well, at least it *was* done. The next day Mr. Harkins called back with the news that Wendy had exams for the next two weeks (probably true) and the request that we make the appointment for two weeks from Wednesday. We know from our discussion with Wendy that it is, indeed, exam time, so this isn't just a stall. And, Mr. Harkins suggested a date without our having to push for it so we're still very much in the ball game. Let's look at some ways to turn this delay to our advantage.

Keeping the Sale Going Between Appointments

We're doing pretty well so far and don't want to lose what we've gained. We have to keep Mr. Harkins' interest alive and our name in front of him in a positive way since we just might close on the next call.

This is where the "boil a frog" theory comes in handy. You remember from our previous discussion that you don't boil a frog by dumping him into hot water—he'll just jump out. You boil a frog by putting him in tepid water where he's comfortable and gradually turn the heat up. Before he knows it, he's cooked.

Closing a sale involves the same process. By asking the prospect questions that he has to say yes to, you turn the heat up gradually.

SCRIPT 2.4.

SALESPERSON: You really want a more efficient operation don't you, Mr. Harkins?

By using trial closes you turn the heat up more.

SCRIPT 2.5.

SALESPERSON: Do you see how this system would give you monthly reports on a timely basis?

SCRIPT 2.6.

SALESPERSON: Do you think you would prefer to lease the equipment or buy it outright? (Up even more.)

Let's look at a checklist of things we can do before the next appointment so we can boil our frog.

PRE-CLOSE CHECKLIST

1. You took careful notes during your discussions with Mr. Harkins and Ms. Harkins, focusing on what their company's needs are, the kinds of *benefits* your product can provide and where their hot buttons are.

2. Review these notes, looking for all of the "hooks" and "grabbers." For example, Mr. Harkins mentioned his frustration at finding that jobs that looked profitable when they came into the shop turned out to have more problems than were anticipated. This is your clue to point out how your system can accommodate a really neat estimating package that will help keep the same mistakes from happening over and over.

3. Mr. Harkins talked about his dismay at not finding out until June that he didn't make any money in January and February. This is your clue to push the general ledger accounting package that is part of your system and point out in the proposal that it will generate reports by the tenth of the following month.

4. Find some "new" piece of information about a benefit that, based on your notes of the first and subsequent appointments, will be of interest to your prospect.

5. Call Mr. Harkins with just enough information about this "new" idea to whet his appetite and make him look forward to your next appointment.

6. Stay on the lookout for magazine articles, newspaper items, or other information that might be of interest to Mr. Harkins whether or not they tie directly to the system you are trying to sell him or not. Keep a file of these "send withs" so you always have a reason to keep your name in front of a live, hot prospect.

CLOSING THE SALE

At this point your prospect, Mr. Harkins, has the idea that you're pretty serious about making this sale. He's going to be alert for any attempt to close and will take it as a matter of pride that he resisted strongly until he bought. We're going to surprise Mr. Harkins. We'll tell him and Wendy right up front what we intend to do so we get that out of the way. Then we'll go on to our final presentation steps (which are really and have always been trial closings).

Mr. Harkins has had your proposal for three weeks now, and you called after one week to make sure he received it and would go over it at least twice before your meeting. He agreed. You answered some questions on your follow-up call a week later. You sent a copy to Wendy. She had some questions which you answered over the phone. She also assured you that she has told her father that the system makes sense for the company and has promised her support at the meeting.

SCRIPT 2.7. PREPARING FOR THE CLOSE

SALESPERSON: Hello, Ger't. Hello Wendy. How did you make out on your exams, Wendy?

WENDY: Well, I don't know yet, but I think I did pretty well on most of them.

SALESPERSON: Good. I know you're both very busy, so let me suggest an agenda for our meeting today. We'll discuss any final questions you may have on the system, the software, or the hardware. Then we'll discuss the people who will be involved in the system and set a date for installation and a training schedule for your people.

> TIP: There. No tricky trial closes, no backing in to a close, and no devious games that will divert attention from what we want to accomplish. (Actually, we were closing from the first call and at every presentation since then.) We made it clear up front that we expect to close today so that's out of the way. Also note the term "final questions," further indicating that we are going to close today.

MR. HARKINS: Wait a minute. I haven't said that I'm going to buy your computer yet.

SCRIPT 2.8. USING THE THIRD PARTY IN CLOSING

WENDY: Oh, Vatti. We've gone over this before. The system is right, the company is right, and, while the price may be a bit higher than we expected or might get from someone else, we're losing money every day we postpone putting this in.

> TIP: Smart lady. Obviously the work we did with her is paying off. Also, from the way she's talking, she will play an even more important role in the company than we had thought. Do your work right and the third party is an ally. Don't and the third party is a deal killer, especially if the third party is an attorney, an accountant, or anyone else who feels his turf threatened. However, the old man can still kill the sale himself, so we can't make the mistake of just talking with Wendy.

SCRIPT 2.9. THE TRIAL CLOSE

MR. HARKINS: (enjoying seeing his daughter take charge) Well, maybe, but there's no point in Stu knowing that just yet. Let him work for it.

SALESPERSON: Mr. Harkins, I think you would agree that I *have* worked for it. This is one of the best proposals and best systems designs I've seen our people do—and they've done a lot of good ones.

SALESPERSON: (pulling out a pre-typed order form) Why don't we talk about an installation date so I can schedule our people? We can have all of the hardware in our shop burnt in and tested with your system by the fifteenth of next month. How about installation on the twentieth? Then we could spend a half day on Wednesday, Friday, and the following Tuesday training your people.

> TIP: Did you see a close here? We pulled out an order form and started to fill in information *assuming* that the deal was closed. If we act this way, maybe Mr. Harkins and Wendy will. Contrary to conventional wisdom, people *do* like to buy—they just don't like making decisions. Because you've done your homework and between-appointments work so well, you've found out what you need to know to make the decision for them. So make it for them and then ask them to agree with you.

SCRIPT 2.10. HANDLING FINAL QUESTIONS

MR. HARKINS: I have a couple of questions. Do we really need all those computers and terminals?

SALESPERSON: No, not right away. That's why we've suggested starting with one central computer and only four PCs (personal computers). We'll set up the LAN (Local Area Network—a bunch of wires that ties together all the computers, terminals, and printers) to accommodate up to ten PC work stations, but the initial installation and order form you'll sign today will just be for the first four.

> TIP: ". . . sign today." Act like getting the order is a given and it just might be.

MR. HARKINS: Do we have to go through this all over again when we want to add work stations?

SALESPERSON: No. Page 17 of the proposal shows the cost of adding each additional station, including hookup to the Local Area Network. We can do this in an hour or two. The ability to expand this easily is one of the beauties of this system. (Pause to see if Mr. Harkins has any other questions.) Wendy, do *you* have any other questions?

WENDY: Yes. There's something I meant to ask you the last time we talked. Can we add word processing to the system like the spreadsheet package?

SCRIPT 2.11. CLOSING THE SALE

SALESPERSON: Yes. We have a word processing package that sells for less than $100. It will take us about 20 minutes to install it and about a half a day to train you people to use it. (Pause—wait for someone else to break the silence.) Well, Mr. Harkins, what would you like me to do now?

TIP: How's that for a slick close? Poor Mr. Harkins has been rehearsing his objections and close-resisting strategies for two days. Now, *he* has the ball and only one way to run with it.

MR. HARKINS: Wendy?
WENDY: Dad?
MR. HARKINS: What day is the twentieth?

TIP: *That* is a clear-cut buying signal. The only way you can blow it at this point is to open your mouth. You have a question on the table, so sit there with your mouth shut until it's answered.

WENDY: That's a Tuesday, Vatti, our slowest day.

TIP: In doing your own preparation and rehearsal you consulted your Account Profile and Call sheet and found that you had noted that Tuesday is, indeed, the slowest day. That's why you suggested the twentieth.

MR. HARKINS: You know, liebe Tochter, that *you* are going to have to make this work.
WENDY: I'm counting on it, Vatti, just as soon as I get back from Europe. I'm sure Mr. Davidson (she called you ''Stu'' when her father wasn't there) will help me if I get in any trouble.

TIP: There's an obvious attraction between Stu and Wendy. (Stu isn't married.) Stu has wisely kept everything on a friendly but businesslike level. It may be a different story when the order is signed and Wendy gets back from Europe.

MR. HARKINS: What do you want me to sign?

Done deal. You didn't get the order because of a smooth, countdown close or any of the other tactics conventional sales gurus urge. You got it because you did a thorough, professional job with every step. You started closing from the first contact with Mr. Harkins. Selling may be a numbers game, but it is the *quality* of effort that makes the numbers work.

SCRIPT 2.12. MAKING SURE THE SALE STAYS CLOSED

Your fifth appointment with Mr. Harkins will be a PCD preventative. (Post-Cognitive Dissonance, see page 37. See also Letter 2.4, The Post-Cognitive Dissonance Letter, page 37.) You might arrange to be there on the twentieth to introduce the tech reps working on the job and at the first training session to introduce your training people. Then, you'll want to follow up two to three weeks later to make sure the installation is working well and see if you can pick up a couple of referrals. Just incidentally, Wendy will be back from Europe.

SCRIPT 2.13. DEALING WITH A NON-CLOSE

Let's look at a different fifth call—Sherie Wendell of ABC Moving & Storage. We'll assume that we've gone through all of the steps we went through with Harkins Machining and have completed our fourth appointment. On this last call, however, we get put off because ABC's central office has decided that they want to be involved with all computer purchases. ABC's president, for political reasons, has no choice but to go along so we can't close yet.

Naturally, you found out who in the Chicago central office is responsible (another third party), called her on the phone, sent her the proposal and all other material about Cardinal Business Services, and offered to fly out to Chicago to meet with her and discuss the proposal. So far, she has declined to meet with us. Fifth call:

SALESPERSON: How much do you know about the system?

SHERIE: Not a lot, but I went to an orientation session in Chicago last week. It looks pretty good.

SALESPERSON: How much choice do you have over whether to go with this system or look at something else?

SHERIE: None. I'm sorry, but central is going to take over our billing based on what we send them daily from our terminal here. Then, we're going on line with all the other terminals so we can route and schedule.

> TIP: Sherie does look distressed—she didn't know about this until recently, so didn't mislead you. You're shut out, so act like a gentleman for possible future business. Let her off the hook.

SALESPERSON: Well, I'm disappointed that we won't be working together on a system, but it sounds like you're going in the right direction. At this point, the only thing I guess I can do is wish you luck with your new system.

SHERIE: Yes. I'm sorry it turned out this way for you. I know you and your people put in a lot of work for us and it's appreciated.

SALESPERSON: Well, we don't get *every* sale we work on. It's possible that before or after your system is installed you'll need some local training or installation help. You've seen that we're capable of doing a good job in this area, so I hope we'll be the first people you'll call.

SHERIE: Certainly. I'm sorry about the system, but maybe we *will* be able to work together when the system is installed here. The software house is in Cupertino.

SALESPERSON: Fine. I'll check back with you in a month or two to see how things are going and what we might be able to do to help.

No deal—at least not for now. Well, we didn't say that we would win them all, no matter how well we did our work. This time that "third party" did us in. It's time now to put ABC in the "B" category of our Account Profile and Call Sheet file or notebook and follow up in two months. Circumstances could change, and we just might get some installation, modification, and training business even if they do go with the central traffic management system.

Don't worry about the loss. The late, great Vince Lombardi has been misquoted by a lot of people as having said something like, "Winning isn't everything—it's the only thing." Recent research indicates that what he really said was something like "Winning isn't everything—the *desire* to win *is*." We don't want to lose so often that we learn how to become "good losers," but we're going to forget this loss and go on to the next prospect with a desire to win.

LETTER 2.4. KEEPING THE SALE SOLD

If you've spent any time at all in sales, you've had the experience of selling a prospect only to find the order cancelled a few days later. Or, you find out some weeks later that while your prospect has accepted delivery, he's unhappy, making it unlikely that he will give you a recommendation letter or a referral. This is PCD or post-cognitive dissonance—"post" meaning after, "cognitive" meaning perceiving or being aware of, and "dissonance" meaning discord or lack of agreement. You may be familiar with its cousin, buyer's remorse—that feeling that sets in after a decision is made and the buyer begins to question the wisdom of his decision. Should he have shopped more? Should he have done more checking of competitors' products?

The way to head this off is to recognize that you have one more call to make and one more letter to write *after* you thought you had the order sewed up. The call (telephone and/or personal) can simply reinforce the reasons the buyer bought, assure him that he made the right decision, and make sure that there are no problems. Here's what the letter, signed by the president of the company or your boss, might look like.

Dear (Former Prospect, Now Customer):

Congratulations on your purchase of the Cardinal general ledger accounting system. We appreciate your order.

As I'm sure Stu Davidson told you, we have literally hundreds of successful installations of this system and thousands of happy users.

While Stu will be your main contact, our entire organization will be at your service to ensure a successful installation and complete future satisfaction, training, and support.

If you ever even *think* about being unhappy with our system, I hope you'll call me right away so we can solve any problem. Our job is to make sure that your system continues to run smoothly.

Thanks again for your order.

I can remember being very impressed when the appliance dealer from whom I bought a refrigerator called two weeks later. My first thought was "What now? Is he trying to sell me something else?" No. He just called to make sure that it was working satisfactorily. Wow. No one had ever done that before. Guess where I went to buy my next appliance? That quick two minutes did more to ensure a future sale than hundreds of dollars worth of advertising would have. Whatever your product or service, *you* can use the same effective technique to avoid *PCD*.

IN CLOSING

In the last two chapters we've talked about how to get the first appointment and how to turn this first appointment into a closed sale and the prospect into a customer. We learned that there is a lot more to selling than slick techniques pulled off in face-to-face interviews with a prospect. There is homework, preparation, between-appointments phone calls, and follow-through letters. There are receptionists, secretaries, and third parties who can be a helpful part of the selling process if dealt with properly.

We did learn a few tested and proven techniques that you shouldn't hesitate to use as long as the prospect needs, can afford, and will get cost savings or other benefits from your product or service. The most important of these techniques is in concentrating on getting a full understanding of your prospect's needs and problems. As William James said, "A problem well-defined is half solved." If you properly identify these needs and relate your product to them as you go through the selling process, you'll find that you can make the decision for your prospect, get his agreement, and the close will be almost automatic.

3

Giving Sales a Boost—Ten Ways to Get Your Customers to Order Now

INTRODUCTION

We're all looking for an instant fix. We know that substantial sales results, like all other results, happen over a period of time, sometimes a long period of time. When we look for help, however, we forget about the long term and focus on tomorrow if not today. This isn't completely unfair, given the day-to-day world most of us salespeople find ourselves working in.

Long-term results mean long-term efforts and there are few shortcuts that have any longevity. However, there *should* be some ways to hype sales short-term and have these efforts be compatible and consistent with our long-term objectives. In this chapter, we'll suggest how to do just this.

We'll continue to use the computer hardware/software turnkey system from Cardinal Business Services as an example for most of the letters and scripts since it is a complicated sell that involves all the elements of a tangible product, intangibles, service, and other benefits.

LETTER 3.1. BOOSTING SALES WITH THE SPECIAL, LIMITED-TIME DISCOUNT OFFER

OBJECTIVE: Get the customer/prospect interested in placing at least a trial order based on the reputation of the company, the work you have done so far, *and* the special offer.

Dear (Prospect):

WOULD YOU LIKE TO ADD *TEN PERCENT* TO YOUR PROFIT MARGIN???

That's exactly what you have the opportunity to do right now if you agree to install our XK 246 system. From now until October 31st you can purchase the complete system at a 10% discount.

Further, we'll deduct the same discount from any peripheral equipment you purchase at the same time. You see, our factory is fairly slow at this time of the year and our manufacturing people want business. To get it, we'll pass our savings on to you.

Actually, this won't automatically add 10% to your bottom line. The cost savings benefits of the system and this 10% discount will probably be much greater.

You remember that the XK 246 system is *guaranteed* to handle *all* your bookkeeping problems, *all* your job cost control problems, *and* to deliver to you weekly reports that will let you run your business on a timely and effective basis.

I'll call you next week to discuss how you can take advantage of this offer and start saving money right away. If you can't wait until I call, please return the enclosed reply card and we'll put your request at the top of the list.

TIP: Let's look at some of the things we did in this fairly innocuous letter:

1. We offered an immediate benefit—the 10% discount. At the same time, we tied this to our prospect's *profit* margin. Who isn't interested in their profit margin?

2. We put a time limit on the offer to provide a sense of urgency and immediacy.

3. We offered a self-serving business interest to make the offer credible.

4. We resold the benefits of the system. (In some cases, a word-processing system that would tailor the letter to the last contact with the prospect would be appropriate.)

5. We promised to call the prospect so the follow-up won't be a surprise.

6. We provided a reply card to give us one more contact and chance for feedback.

SCRIPT 3.1. BOOSTING SALES WITH THE SPECIAL LIMITED-TIME DISCOUNT TELEPHONE CALL

OBJECTIVE: Follow up the letter and close an order over the phone. Failing this, close another appointment over the phone.

SALESPERSON: Good morning, Mr. Wendig, this is Glen Ryan from Morra Office Systems. How are you this bright and sunny morning?

MR. WENDIG: Good morning. It's snowing outside and half my people were late. How should I be?

SALESPERSON: Probably a little upset about what this will do to your productivity and efficiency. Speaking about productivity, did you get our mailing on the special 10% discount offer?

> TIP: This isn't exactly a subtle segue, but you did get Mr. Wendig on the subject without ignoring his concerns. It might be a good idea to think, ahead of time, about what the answers to your questions might be so you can jump in with a rejoinder that will bring your prospect back to *your* subject quickly.

MR. WENDIG: I saw something from your company, but don't remember what.

SALESPERSON: Well, you remember the system we talked about on the 16th of last month? That was the day your office manager had an emergency appointment with the dentist.

> TIP: This is where your Account Profile and Call Sheet (Figure 2.1, page 24) comes in handy. You have not only pinpointed Mr. Wendig's memory, but have shown some interest in his problems.

MR. WENDIG: Yes, I remember that you were in that day and even helped answer the phones.

SALESPERSON: Right. As I remember, one of the calls was from a customer who wanted to know where his quotation was. It took you over ten minutes to find it. Do you remember that?

MR. WENDIG: Well, I know that it wasn't at the tip of my fingers. I have a lot of orders in the works.

SCRIPT 3.1A. AROUSING INTEREST IN THE LETTER OFFER

SALESPERSON: This is what our letter was about. The system we discussed would give you the information you needed then in seconds. *And*, right now, you could save a lot of money by placing your order for the system you need. Wouldn't you like to be able to answer customers' questions in seconds instead of minutes?

MR. WENDIG: Sure, but we have so many orders . . .

SALESPERSON: Of course. But, you remember that I showed you how our system would let you call up *any* order and give you the complete status in less than 30 seconds. Why don't we set up a time for us to install it before you get another customer call?

MR. WENDIG: Well, I still have a couple more questions about how it would work for *us*. I'm not sure we're ready for it right now.

SALESPERSON: Why don't I bring it over and we'll give it a try for a day or so? That way you'll know for sure that it's the right system for you and you'll be able to see what it will do on a test basis.

MR. WENDIG: No, I'm not sure I can spare the time to work with you.

SCRIPT 3.2. GETTING THE DEMONSTRATION APPOINTMENT WITH A KEY EMPLOYEE

SALESPERSON: No problem. I'll work with Kylie who knows what has to be done and set it up with her. You can review the results at the end of the day.

TIP: Obviously, you *know* that Kylie, Mr. Wendig's assistant *wants* this system because you were smart enough to treat her as an important member of the company's management to sell *her* on the system as we suggested in Chapter 1. Get your system in for a trial and, perhaps, Kylie will take it from there.

MR. WENDIG: Well, I'm not sure Kylie has the time either, but if you can set up a meeting with her, go ahead and do it.

TIP: Mr. Wendig, as is often the case, has underestimated his assistant. *You*, however, were smart enough to see who would be one of the *real* buying influences in this situation. Kylie *will* find the time that is needed to work with you on the project and, not so incidentally, will bug the heck out of Mr. Wendig until he agrees to buy your system.

SPECIAL NOTE: We've talked before about that famous or infamous "third party." In this case, Kylie is obviously a good third-party candidate. Don't overlook the influence this third party can bring nor the existence of a "third party" in almost every selling situation.

SALESPERSON: Thank you, Mr. Wendig. I'll call Kylie and tell her that you suggested that we set up this trial when she has time.

TIP: This may not seem like a big win . . . yet. After all, you *didn't* close the order over the phone. All you did was get your prospect's agreement that you could talk with a key employee about your system—and on agreement to have it installed. What do you think the chances are that Mr. Wendell will ask you to pick up the hardware and take it back to your office?

USING CASE HISTORIES EFFECTIVELY

It's a marketing truth that publicity releases that show up as editorial copy in magazines are usually more effective than advertising in the same publications. Similarly, true case histories are usually more effective than selling letters, especially when accompanied by a recommendation letter from the case history subject.

Since you're dealing with basic facts, you also get to make claims for benefits that might be less credible in another type of sales letter or advertisement. As Dizzy Dean said, "If ya' done it, it ain't braggin' "

LETTER 3.2. GETTING THE APPOINTMENT WITH THE CASE HISTORY LETTER

OBJECTIVE: Describe a success story experienced by a customer that would be of interest to a prospect in order to get an appointment for a personal visit and demonstration.

Dear (Prospect):

WOULD YOU LIKE AN EXTRA THREE HOURS A WEEK?

Who wouldn't? Most of us don't have nearly enough time to get done what we would like to.

Well, more time is exactly what Glen Kristofferson, president of KGM Machining, got when he installed our job tracking system as a part of our cost estimating package. He can get details of a customer job in seconds instead of minutes. Mr. Kristofferson estimates savings of almost an hour a day just in getting information on jobs.

And, this is only the beginning of the benefits *you* could enjoy. By controlling the status of jobs through the Daily Activity Report the system provides, late deliveries at KGM have been almost eliminated and overtime has been cut by one-third.

I'll call you in a few days to set a time for us to discuss how *you* can enjoy similar benefits. If your need is more urgent than that, fill out and mail the enclosed card or call me at (406)-822-6471.

> TIP: Let's review what we did in this letter:
>
> 1. We provided a grabber by asking a question that almost has to be answered "yes."
> 2. Rather than our suggesting that this time savings benefit could happen for our prospect, we went the more credible route of describing a specific instance. (Of course, we have Mr. Kristofferson's letter on file.)
> 3. We then went on to describe additional benefits of our system that should be of interest to our prospect.
> 4. We included action steps.

SCRIPT 3.3. USING CASE HISTORIES TO GET APPOINTMENTS

> OBJECTIVE: Describe a customer success story in a limited amount of time in order to get an appointment for a personal visit and demonstration.

SALESPERSON: Good morning, Mrs. Coren. This is Stuart Davidson from Cardinal Business Services. You recall that we talked on the phone about a month ago. How are you this rainy day?

MRS. COREN: Up to my ears in paper work with no time to even get a cup of coffee.

SALESPERSON: Good.

MRS. COREN: *Good*?

SALESPERSON: Yes, *Good*. The reason I'm calling is to tell you how a client of mine in a *company like yours* cut down on his paper work and squeezed an extra three or four hours out of every week. (Pause and see if Mrs. Coren takes the bait.)

> TIP: In this case, getting the prospect to ask questions that you'd love to provide the answers to is a good strategy. You're still in control. Remember, your objective is to have *her* invite you to come in for an appointment rather than your having to push for it.

MRS. COREN: (no longer shuffling papers while talking with you) What did he do, lose a lot of customers?

SALESPERSON: No. As a matter of fact, he's been able to go after business he used to think he didn't have time to handle.

MRS. COREN: Okay, I give up. Who is he and what did he do to make this happen?

SCRIPT 3.3A. CLOSING FOR THE APPOINTMENT

SALESPERSON: Instead of telling you over the phone when you're so busy, why don't I come by when it's convenient for you and *show* you. I'll bring along the letter he was nice enough to send spelling out the benefits he got.
MRS. COREN: You're really not going to tell me, are you?
SALESPERSON: Of course I'll tell you. I'll tell you the whole story—who, what, why, when, and where. What's a better day 'for you, Wednesday or Thursday?
MRS. COREN: Okay. Make it Thursday morning around ten.
SALESPERSON: Fine. Plan on setting aside an hour so you can get the complete picture and so we'll have time to deal with any questions you have.

> TIP: Our objective was to get the personal appointment that had been eluding us, not to close over the phone or even give our prospect any specific information we didn't have to provide. If we had been unable to get the appointment, we might have provided a little more information—just enough to get the appointment or, failing that, to keep our name in Mrs. Coren's mind to ensure her being receptive to our next phone call.

SCRIPT 3.4. USING CASE HISTORIES TO GET A RFP (REQUEST FOR PROPOSAL)

> OBJECTIVE: Get an invitation to go in and do a Needs Analysis preparatory to submitting a complete systems proposal. Qualify Mrs. Coren as the primary buying influence or find out who is.

SALESPERSON: Good morning, I'm Stuart Davidson with Cardinal Business Services. Mrs. Coren is expecting me. (Hand receptionist your business card.)
RECEPTIONIST: Oh yes. Mrs. Coren just breezed by here on her way out to the shop and said she'd be back in less than ten minutes. Would you like to take a seat?
SALESPERSON: (with a smile so it doesn't sound sarcastic) No thanks. I already have one.
RECEPTIONIST: What? Oh. Believe it or not, I haven't heard that one before.

> TIP: This receptionist is ugly—like a character Charles Dickens or even Edgar Allen Poe would have invented, so she probably doesn't get much repartee from visitors. Your attempt at making a friend and possible future ally will go even further in this case. Remember that she could well be beautiful inside.

SCRIPT 3.4A. MAKING THE RECEPTIONIST A FRIEND

SALESPERSON: Do you know what time it is? (She's not wearing a watch.)
RECEPTIONIST: Not exactly, but there's a clock at the end of the hall over there.
SALESPERSON: Well, let's make it simpler (reaching into briefcase). Here's something that should make things easier for you. You can stick this little digital clock anywhere.
RECEPTIONIST: What's that red bird? Oh, I see. Your card did say *Cardinal* Business Services. "Our systems sing for you." That's cute. Oh, here's Mrs. Coren.

> TIP: No, I don't own an advertising specialties company. I just happen to think that the tremendous cost of personal sales calls justifies spending another 1 or 2 percent to make 10 to 20 percent more of an impression.

SCRIPT 3.4B. SETTING UP THE DEMONSTRATION

MRS. COREN: Do you have something in that big box that's going to solve all my problems?

SALESPERSON: Well, I don't know *all* your problems but there is something there that will solve a lot of them. First take a look at this (handing over Mr. Kristofferson's letter). I promised you I'd tell you the whole story. This is the first chapter.

MRS. COREN: Glen Kristofferson. Wow. I remember him as being about as disorganized as you can get and still be able to find your way back to your office. And he bought a *computer*? Amazing.

SALESPERSON: He *was* a tough sell, but I did some work for another client of his—a C.P.A., Lisa Krisberg. Lisa practically pushed him into this after seeing what we were able to do for her other client.

> TIP: In *one* sentence, we invoked *three* third-party endorsements. Mrs. Coren *has* to be interested.

MRS. COREN: I know Lisa. We both belong to the Shaker Heights Professional Women's Association. You've worked with her?

SALESPERSON: Only on this and one other client so far. It does seem though that she has the kind of clients whom our systems are made for—*companies like yours.*

MRS. COREN: Okay. You've got my attention. How about showing me what you've got in that box of yours?

> TIP: Perfect. Getting an invitation from a prospect to do what you want to do is always better than your having to push for it.

SALESPERSON: Fine. I'm going to plug in this portable computer and run the demonstration disk of the system that Glen, Lisa, and I installed in his place.

> TIP: Run the demonstration and, when it's over, pause to see if you can get Mrs. Coren to break the silence and, by what she says, show you the line to pursue next.

SCRIPT 3.4C. GETTING THE DECISION-MAKER INVOLVED

MRS. COREN: What's the matter? The demonstration was good but not enough to make you speechless.

SALESPERSON: Why did you think it was good?

MRS. COREN: It was aimed right at *my* problems—estimating, entering jobs, keeping track of costs, and then billing them on time. I also like that Daily Activity Report and the way it takes only three seconds to find out where any job stands. How expensive is this system?

SALESPERSON: Most of our clients who are using it figure that it's paid for itself in cost savings in six months to a year. The other benefits you saw come as a bonus. Let me ask you a question, if you were convinced that you'd have the same kind of savings and payback period, what would our next step be?

MRS. COREN: Well, Mr. Granoff has to approve anything over $5,000. He'd have to be involved.

SALESPERSON: You could probably lease the hardware *and* software for a lot less than a $1,000 a month.

MRS. COREN: Mr. Granoff is still involved. He approves *all* leases.
SALESPERSON: Well, let's get him involved *now* while the machine is still warm. This time, *you* take him through the system and throw the ball to me on anything you're uncomfortable with.

> TIP: In one fell swoop we've gotten Mrs. Coren in a position where she will sell herself through the demonstration, she'll do our work for us, and she's become a *third party* who will help us sell Mr. Granoff on the system.

The demonstration was held, Mr. Granoff was impressed, he gave Mrs. Coren the assignment to work with us to come up with a firm proposal, and we're on our way to a closed sale. And, anytime we show up, the receptionist insists on bringing us coffee while she personally hunts up the person we want to see. (See Chapter 2 for suggestions of the kinds of activities that will be necessary from this point to the final close.)

SCRIPT 3.5. HANDLING THE INDECISIVE BUYER—THE *NOW* BENEFIT

The "impending event" close has long been famous (or infamous) in sales literature. This is where the salesperson tries to close the sale on Friday by talking about a price increase effective next Monday. Most prospects have heard this one too many times. Let's be more imaginative:

> OBJECTIVE: Push a buyer whom we've been courting off dead-center by offering a desirable incentive for buying *now*.

SALESPERSON: Good morning, Mr. Johannes. This is Stu Davidson from Cardinal Business Service. I'm calling to learn your accountant's reaction to the proposal we worked out last month.

> TIP: Do *not* say something like "Have you had a chance to . . ." Mr. Johannes promised to check your proposal with his accountant, so start by assuming this has been done. If it hasn't been done, Mr. Johannes will be defensive and you'll earn points by taking him off the hook.

MR. JOHANNES: Well, actually I haven't discussed it with him yet. I was going to give it to him when he came in, but we had to postpone our appointment.
SALESPERSON: He's in Richardson isn't he? I'm going to be out in Grapevine the end of next week. Why don't I send him a copy, call him to set a time, and discuss the proposal with him next week?
MR. JOHANNES: No, that's okay. He'll be here the day after tomorrow and I can talk to him about it then.

> TIP: Well, our first procrastination-banishing try didn't work, so we'll move on from here. We still want to develop a relationship with this third party so we'll stay on the lookout for another excuse to do this.

SALESPERSON: Fine, I'll plan on calling him the end of the week to see if he has any questions.
MR. JOHANNES: That's not really necessary.
SALESPERSON: No problem. It's important to us to know how our proposals are per-

ceived by accountants and other professionals, so the chance to talk with him is really doing us a favor.

TIP: We're being a bit pushy, but our prospect's procrastination would make Hamlet look decisive. It's like authority. Nobody *gives* it to you. Authority is *earned* and *taken*. Here we *are* taking the initiative and are *not* taking "no" for an answer. Maybe some of this will rub off on Mr. Johannes. At least he'll wind up looking less than responsible if he hasn't given his accountant the proposal by the time we call.

MR. JOHANNES: Well, all right.

SCRIPT 3.5A. USING THE THIRD PARTY TO OUR ADVANTAGE

SALESPERSON: Let me ask you a question, Mr. Johannes. If your accountant agrees that the system is the right one for you and verifies that the system will pay for itself in less than a year, can we count on a purchase order from you by the end of the month?
MR. JOHANNES: Well, there are a lot of considerations.
SALESPERSON: Like what?
MR. JOHANNES: We just want to be sure that we're making the right decision. The last time I bought anything this size the price dropped the next month.
SALESPERSON: Yes, I can see your concern. I can assure you that *our* prices aren't going to drop next month. In fact, we're probably looking at a price *increase* next month.

TIP: Corny and overused or not, it's worth a shot as part of our repertory.

MR. JOHANNES: I'm sure you'll let me know in advance if you aren't going to stick to the prices in your proposal.

SCRIPT 3.5B. USING THE *NOW* BENEFIT TO CLOSE NOW

SALESPERSON: Of course. In fact, I can take that a step further. Our fiscal year is ending in five weeks and my boss wants me to get as much business on the books as we can. So, he's authorized me to throw in that spreadsheet package you were thinking about *and* a word processing package *if* we can book your order in the next month. You know you're going to install this system in the near future, so why not take advantage of my boss's need to look as good as possible this year?
MR. JOHANNES: Now you're talking. Say, why don't you come over the day after tomorrow? I'll get the proposal hand-carried to my accountant today so he has a chance to look at it before our meeting. Then we can all discuss it together.
SALESPERSON: Fine. Why don't we plan on lunch?

TIP: It looks like we finally found our prospect's hot button and have a chance to develop a relationship with his accountant.

SCRIPT 3.6. HANDLING THE INDECISIVE BUYER—THE "TAKEAWAY"

Sometimes the most effective way to push a buyer into the sale is to take something away or at least threaten to. There are a couple of obvious examples of this tactic:

SALESPERSON: I have to ask you a few questions now. You understand that I have to get your application approved by our home office and I can't guarantee your acceptance until they have reviewed it.

TIP: This may not be strictly accurate, but can be an effective ploy.

SCRIPT 3.6A. ANOTHER TAKEAWAY—LIMITED DEALERSHIPS AVAILABLE

SALESPERSON: We want only two dealers in this territory. We have already accepted one and I've been given just one more week to recommend a second so it's important that I have your commitment in two days.

TIP: More legitimate but no less effective.

SCRIPT 3.6B. THE "TIME IS RUNNING OUT" TAKEAWAY

Now, *you* may not have an "exclusive club" nor a franchised or preferred territory to offer, but there may be some instances where a similar strategy will work for you:

OBJECTIVE: Push a reluctant prospect into a sale by threatening (in a nonthreatening way) to pull the rug on something that was a part of the proposal and get the prospect to buy *now*.

SALESPERSON: Good morning, Mr. Gambino. This is Stu Davidson from Cardinal Business Services. Do you have our proposal in front of you?
MR. GAMBINO: It's here somewhere. Just a minute. Is there a problem?
SALESPERSON: Yes and no. Would you turn to page 14 under "Installation." You can see that we deviated from our normal terms and agreed to hook up your printers and extra monitors at no charge. We also said we could provide installation with 48 hours notice.
MR. GAMBINO: Yes, I liked that idea.
SALESPERSON: Well, our service director has just told me that we'll no longer be able to do that—the demands on his department are just too many. You remember that the proposal was good for 60 days and we're already past that.
MR. GAMBINO: Does that mean that I can't get this?
SALESPERSON: That's the policy, yes (pause). However, we've been working together on this for so long that I'd like to see us honor the original proposal even if the time *is* past. We know that you're about ready to sign. If you can get your order to me by the end of the month, I'll personally guarantee that I'll get our service director to go along with the original terms.
MR. GAMBINO: Well, we still have some work to do before we can cut a purchase order.
SALESPERSON: I can understand that. Why don't I come over later this week and we can iron out any final questions. I'll hand-carry the order back to our office and make sure that it's understood that we're giving you the original terms.

TIP: Note again ". . . final questions"

MR. GAMBINO: Okay. I guess Friday afternoon will work out pretty well.
SALESPERSON: Fine, why don't we plan on lunch?

LETTER 3.3. THE PRICE INCREASE LETTER

Some people don't mind price increases. Distributors can pass on the increase to their customers, keep their margins in percentage terms the same, and take more dollars to the bank. For most people, however, price increases are painful. Handled properly, much of the pain can be removed.

A price increase can actually provide a good boost to business. I was once general manager of a company that was absorbed by a much larger conglomerate. By the time they added their corporate services "tax" to our budgeted costs and expenses, we had to raise prices almost 30 percent to stay in the black. The accounting department wanted to hold off notice until the last minute as they had in the past. Instead, we gave a full 60 days' notice to all our customers and kept the factory busy working off the backlog for over six months. This kind of increase motivated some customers to order a year's supply. So, consider this strategy, giving fair and ample notice and writing this kind of letter:

Dear (Customers):

Our last 38 letters to you have discussed new advertising programs, new demonstration tools, more favorable freight policies, and increased field service support. Your response tells us that you warmly welcomed these letters and these support activities.

It has been two years since we have had to write a letter on a price increase. This is a price increase letter.

Effective July 1st, the new enclosed price lists will be in effect. The average percentage increase is about 6 percent.

Any orders received in the next 60 days (until July 1st) will be honored at the old prices. We feel that this is ample notice for you to plan accordingly. If, however, you have outstanding commitments extending beyond July 1st based on the old prices, please get the details to your district manager before June 1st. We'll review all requests on a case-by-case basis.

Our next letter to you will contain information on the new video training program which is being completed right now in response to your requests.

We look forward to an even better relationship with you in the future. Let your district manager or me know what we can do to make this happen.

TIP: Let's look at what we did with this letter:

1. We started by reminding our customers of all the good things we've done for them over the past two years.
2. We reminded them that it has been a full two years since the last price increase.
3. We provided (for our industry) an unusually long length of time during which we would accept orders at old prices. We knew what we were doing. June and July are historically slow months. The timing of the increase should make June and July our best months this year.
4. We allowed for the possibility of really legitimate reasons for an extension of the old

prices in special circumstances. This isn't costing us anything—we were going to raise prices 5 percent and went to 6 so we could be generous on a selective basis.

5. We didn't apologize for the price increase by laboriously citing increased costs and other factors. We acted as though we were entitled.

6. Finally, we ended the letter with good news and on a positive note.

SCRIPT 3.7. USING THE PRICE INCREASE CALL TO BOOST SALES

This chapter is about boosting sales, so we're going to look at the price increase as a given fact and beyond our control except for how we can milk additional sales from it. You'll want to call your "A" customers and perhaps some of your "B's" *before* they get the letter from the home office—they are important to you and they deserve to be singled out for this special attention. If there are special considerations—customers who are using your product as a part of theirs, customers who publish catalogs, customers who have rigid captial requisition budgets, etc.—you will want to visit these people personally to work out arrangements for their price protection.

OBJECTIVE: Smooth over the bad news of the price increase without apologizing for it. Use the increase to generate some additional business now.

SALESPERSON: Good morning, Mr. Davies. Stu Davidson How are you today?
MR. DAVIES: I'm great but I'll get better.
SALESPERSON: Good. I have something that will make at least your business life better. I just got word from one of my contacts at the home office that we'll be announcing a price increase next month to be effective 60 days from the announcement date.
MR. DAVIES: That's good?
SALESPERSON: We can make it good. You know that everyone in our industry raises their prices at about the same time. It makes sense. We all have the same problems with material and labor costs. I thought that by working with you well in advance of the increase we could estimate your requirements for the next few months and figure out how much inventory you can afford to carry if you could buy it at the old prices.

TIP: In less than a minute we've turned bad news into a plus-profit opportunity. By referring to "old prices" we get the customer to also accept the price increase as a given.

MR. DAVIES: That sounds good, but what about those bids that I have outstanding. Your product makes up over 30 percent of the cost on some of them.
SALESPERSON: I'm glad you brought that up. All I have to do is get the details of the bid and we'll protect you until the end of the year or four months from the date of the new price lists. I have a summary of all your purchases by product number for the past two years. Why don't we use this to project what you'll need in the next few months and see how much you can afford to order at the old prices.

TIP: The accountants will want you to hold off price increase notification until the last minute so you don't get covering orders. Nonsense! We *want* covering orders. We went with a 6 percent increase instead of 5 to allow for this and we timed the price increase so the covering orders would come in at a slow time of the year.

Covering customers on bids and catalogs won't do our relationship with them any harm.

LETTER 3.4. KEEPING THE FACTORY BUSY DURING SLOW PERIODS

Your company has fixed overhead to carry regardless of the level of business. That is, it costs you money just to open the doors in the morning—rent, depreciation on equipment, basic administrative people, management salaries, etc. Your gross margins minus the variable expenses—sales commissions, postage on invoices, telephone calls, and other expenses that vary with the level of business—may not be enough to cover your fixed overhead during slow periods.

It makes sense, therefore, to offer an extra inducement for customers to place orders that can be filled during these slow periods. Just be sure to plan and announce the program well enough in advance so your customers can make their plans and your factory can take advantage of this peak-and-valley smoothing strategy.

> OBJECTIVE: Create additional business to keep the factory running at normal capacity during the usually slow months of January and February (we supply a product to building contractors in the northeast) by offering a special inducement to place orders in December.

Dear (Customers):

WOULD YOU LIKE A FREE KED-FAST TOOL?

How about a dozen, or one each for all your people?

That's exactly what we're offering from now until December 31st. We will send you *free* of additional charge one Ked-Fast tool for every 1,000 Ked-Fast fasteners you order.

Since its introduction last year the Ked-Fast fastening system has caught on all over the country. Our field studies, however, have told us that the system isn't being used as efficiently as it could be. Many roofers are wasting time by handing the Ked-Fast tool around.

We want to help you eliminate this inefficiency. That's why we're throwing in one tool for every 1,000 Ked-Fast fasteners you order before December 31st.

Talk with your district manager or use the enclosed order form and postage-paid envelope to get your order in and start saving time and money as soon as possible.

> TIP: "Free" and "new" are still the most powerful words in space and direct-response advertising. Let's look at what else we did with this letter:
>
> 1. We offered a pretty good "buy now" inducement. Having all those tools out there that can be used only with our fasteners won't do future fasteners sales any harm.
> 2. We put a time limit on the offer to create a sense of "buy now" urgency.
> 3. We got in a few points on the success and desirability of our fastening system.
> 4. We made the focus of the campaign a response to a need we saw in the field rather than a way to keep our screw machines running.

5. We included a brochure on the system (not mentioned) and an order form and envelope to encourage immediate orders.

The accountants may tell you that you can't afford to do this. A quick look at your fixed overhead and breakeven chart will suggest that you can. They might argue further that you're just mortgaging business that you'll get later anyway. Maybe. But by offering the tool, we're helping to ensure a greater long term market for our fasteners. Also, we don't know what's going to happen next month, tomorrow, or even 5 minutes from now. You may think that you'll be reading this book 5 minutes from now but suppose the roof caves in 3 minutes from now? Better to go for the bird in the hand and come up with another idea to hype sales next quarter.

LETTER 3.5. BOOSTING SALES BY PASSING ALONG EXTRA DISCOUNTS

A similar effort from our old friends, Cardinal Business Services, might look like this:

OBJECTIVE: Take advantage of the extra discount the software manufacturer has given us on the Swan database package and keep our position as a software package supplier in front of our customers' minds.

Dear (Customers):

HOW MUCH TIME DO YOU SPEND EVERY DAY LOOKING THINGS UP?

If your organization is like most, you and your people spend a lot of time every day finding phone numbers, addresses, and other information. You probably also spend a lot of time every week preparing reports that are summarized from raw data or other reports.

You don't have to spend so much time.

The new Swan database package can organize all that material into convenient, easy-to-use computer files that can be accessed in seconds. It will also print out in minutes those reports that take you or your people hours to prepare.

And, for the next 30 days we'll provide:

—A *free* demonstration of this package.

—*Free* training for up to five of your people.

Every business can use this database package to save time and make life a lot simpler. To start enjoying these benefits as soon as possible, return the enclosed card or give us a call *today*.

SCRIPT 3.8. BOOSTING SALES BY ADDING LIMITED TIME BENEFITS

Besides accomplishing the immediate objective, the added benefit call is a good reason to stay in touch with good ("A") customers and (over the phone) renew contact with the "B" and "C" customers.

OBJECTIVE: Create additional business from our roofing contractors to keep our screw machines running during the normally slow months of January and February.

SALESPERSON: Good morning, Mr. Closkey. How are you today?

MR. CLOSKEY: Terrible. It keeps threatening to rain and I don't know whether to send my crews home or not.

SALESPERSON: Well, I can't do anything about the weather, but I might be able to bring some sunshine into your life in another way.

MR. CLOSKEY: Oh, how's that?

SALESPERSON: You remember that you bought one Ked-Fast tool when you switched over to our fasteners. I guess your people have to take turns when more than one wants to use it at the same time.

MR. CLOSKEY: Yeah, but those things are too expensive to give one to every roofer.

SALESPERSON: You're right. But you would agree that it would be neat if everyone *could* have a Ked-Fast tool wouldn't you?

MR. CLOSKEY: Sure, are you going to give them one?

SALESPERSON: Yes. (pause)

MR. CLOSKEY: Okay. What do I have to do? Take you out to dinner? Give you my boat for the weekend? What?

SCRIPT 3.8A. EXPLAINING THE ADDED BENEFIT DEAL

SALESPERSON: Just buy some of our fasteners a little sooner than you normally would. Here's the deal. For every 1,000 Ked-Fast fasteners you buy from us, we'll throw in a Ked-Fast tool. Buy 5,000 and you've got a tool for another five people. Buy 12,000 and you've got a tool for everyone.

MR. CLOSKEY: You're asking me to tie up a lot of money.

SALESPERSON: Sure. But you know you're going to use the fasteners in the next few months, and, as you pointed out, the tools *are* expensive.

MR. CLOSKEY: (after a pause while he does some figuring) Well, I don't need a tool for *everyone*, but we could use some more. Send me 3,000 fasteners. That will give me a total of four tools—just what I need.

SCRIPT 3.8B. CLOSING THE ADDED BENEFIT DEAL

SALESPERSON: Why don't we allow for the fact that your business will grow and make the order for 4,000 fasteners and four tools?

MR. CLOSKEY: Okay, okay. Now you get to take me out to dinner.

SALESPERSON: Go for 10,000 and you'll get ten tools and my cabin for a weekend. And, I'll stock it before you get there.

MR. CLOSKEY: Enough. You can take your time on the fasteners but get me the tools as soon as you can.

SCRIPT 3.9 USING ADDED BENEFITS WITH THE RELUCTANT BUYER

Here's how a phone call from Cardinal Business Services might be conducted:

SALESPERSON: Good morning, Mr. Dennison. How is that new computer running?

MR. DENNISON: Well, some of our people are still a bit slow with it, but it's coming along fine.

SALESPERSON: Do you remember how I had to twist your arm to get you to let us include the word-processing package in the system? You said that you just didn't write enough letters.

TIP: We're leading up to a "Stu knows best" pitch if we need to use it.

MR. DENNISON: Yes. And you were right. Once we learned how to use it we found a lot more uses than we thought possible. In fact, it's running off a selective mailing list right now.
SALESPERSON: Good. I'm glad it worked out well for you. You know, Harry, if you do a lot of work with selected names on a mailing list, you're probably better off with a database package than using the mail-merge section of your word-processing package. Actually you're now ready to go for a database package for more than just mailing lists.
MR. DENNISON: Give us a break. We might be ready for something new in a few months, but we're still trying to digest what we have.
SALESPERSON: Harry, you and your people are really a lot further along with your system than you may think you are. I know it still seems a little mysterious, but you're *there*. Actually, based on the distance you've come so far, a database package is an easy and natural next move. And, do I have a deal for you.
MR. DENNISON: Oh, what's that?

TIP: This is a bit of a sales trick. We answered his objection and then, while this is subliminally sinking in, diverted his attention with a statement that *has* to elicit a question. Normally, we don't advocate answering or meeting objections. We would prefer to ask questions instead to find out the *real* objection and then lead the prospect to answer his own objection. In this case, however, we have to push a little bit more.

We remember from our Account Call Sheet that Harry is more concerned with a $100 bargain than a $10,000 system. (In the initial system installation we threw in an extra monitor to close the deal.) He's sniffing for a bargain now.

SCRIPT 3.9A. CLOSING THE ADDED BENEFIT DEAL

SALESPERSON: For the next 30 days, we'll provide a free demonstration on the Swan database package *and*, when you buy one or more packages, we'll provide *free* training for up to five of your people.
MR. DENNISON: Well, that would sound good if we were ready to add something else.
SALESPERSON: Look, Harry, you didn't think you were ready for the word-processing package. Where would you be right now if we hadn't included that?
MR. DENNISON: Okay, I see your point, but I don't think my people can absorb another software package.
SALESPERSON: I can appreciate your concern. Tell you what: Let me bring the demo disk over and show you and your people what it can do. Then, sound them out about whether they want it and think they can handle it. Does this make sense?
MR. DENNISON: I guess it won't do any harm to learn what the package can do for us whether we're ready for it or not. At least we'll learn something.

Done deal. We didn't sell the package over the phone, but we got the next best thing. Mr. Dennison has underestimated his people. We know that they *can* handle it and *are* ready for it. But, it's a nice situation. Mr. Dennison can tell his people that he thinks they are too busy and overloaded to handle it and they can talk him into letting them get the package and taking on the extra burden. Then, since it was their idea, they'll have to make it work.

LETTER 3.6. BOOSTING SALES WITH THE TRIAL OFFER LETTER

There are times when nothing you do seems to work in getting a prospect to commit to an order or accept your proposal and cut a purchase order. This could be especially true if you have a new or innovative product without a large, established base. That's when a trial offer could be an effective device.

Copy machines are a good example of a product that lends itself to a trial offer demonstration. Once a machine is delivered on a test basis it stays put the majority of the time. As a fastener company, we could offer the loan of a fastening tool and some sample fasteners. Extensive sampling is a part of most writing instrument manufacturers' new product introduction campaigns. It's a little tougher for a company like Cardinal Business Services to use this tactic, but they could offer a demonstration disk on a new software package or let a prospect borrow a laser printer for awhile. The danger, of course, is that the prospect will be sold on our kind of product and buy it elsewhere, but that's always the danger when we get a prospect interested. Let's try something tough—a company that offers carpet dyeing services:

> OBJECTIVE: Get our prospects (apartment buildings and condos) to agree to a test of a room or hallway in order to demonstrate the kind of professional job we can do.

Dear Manager:

DO YOU HAVE SPOTS IN FRONT OF YOUR EYES?

No, we're not suggesting that you have a medical problem. We're talking about those soiled-beyond-cleaning carpets in your building's apartments.

You know that carpet appearance is an important factor to new residents. You don't want to lose a prospective tenant, but replacing carpets is expensive.

Carpet dyeing is the only sensible alternative. Plant stains, sunfade and bleach stains will disappear right before your eyes. And, dyeing will save you up to *75%* of the cost of carpet replacement.

We use only guaranteed DYCO dyes. The are just like the dyes used at the carpet mills and will not wash out.

SPECIAL OFFER: For the next 60 days we'll dye the carpet in one room to show you the difference it can make and the kind of professional job we can do for you.

We'll call you in a few days to set a date. If your need is urgent, return the enclosed card or call us *today* at 282-2802.

> TIP: We honed in on a real problem that all building managers can identify with and provided a logical solution. By saying we would be calling to set a date, we acted as though the acceptance of the offer were a given. Finally, we included a request for action. Our ''I/you'' count (see Chapter 1, page 14) was eleven to seven.

SCRIPT 3.10. GETTING PROSPECTS TO MOVE WITH A TRIAL OFFER CALL

This is a case where the combination of direct mail and telemarketing (letters and phone calls) will produce synergistic (one plus one equals three) results. Instead of making a large mailing and completing the telephone follow-up months or even weeks later, *batch* the prospect list by zip code area and mail only as many letters as you can afford the time to follow through on with phone calls a week or so later.

SALESPERSON: Good morning. This is Sue Irving from Sue's Carpet Cleaning. Do you remember our mailing on carpet dyeing?

TIP: We assumed that the manager *did* get it. If we asked "Did you get it?" we've made it too easy for him to say "no." If he still says "no," tell him that you'll send it out again, make sure the name and address are correct, and put the card in next week's calls to be made file.

MANAGER: Yes, I remember seeing something recently on carpet dyeing. Was that you?
SALESPERSON: Yes. We told you some of the advantages of carpet dyeing—how we can save carpets that you thought were beyond hope and save money on replacement costs of new carpeting.

TIP: We repeated the two biggest customer-oriented benefits—what he would be most likely to remember from the letter. Save the free offer deal until you get more information and are ready to close on the appointment. "Free" is worth little if there is no real customer benefit.

MANAGER: Yes, now I remember. I was thinking about that carpeting in 4C. Half the room, where the furniture was, is blue and the other half, by the south window, is almost white.

TIP: Perfect. Just what we wanted him to say.

SALESPERSON: What were you planning on doing about it?

TIP: "What *were* you planning . . .", not "What *are* you planning . . ." That is, what were you going to do before you were lucky enough to get my phone call this morning? It would have been tempting to jump right in with a sales pitch, but the question gets us more information to tailor the pitch and gets the manager more involved.

MANAGER: Well. I'm not sure, probably replace it.

SCRIPT 3.10A. SETTING UP THE FREE TRIAL OFFER CLOSE

SALESPERSON: Then you have nothing to lose in giving us a shot at saving it. It sounds like an ideal situation for carpet cleaning. Let's use this room for our special 60-day free offer.
MANAGER: What's that?
SALESPERSON: You may remember from the letter that we offered to dye the carpeting in one room so you can see the results and the kind of professional job we do.
MANAGER: You'll do it *free*?

SCRIPT 3.10B. CLOSING ON THE TRIAL OFFER

SALESPERSON: Yes. We're sure that once you see what we can do you'll want to use us a lot more in the future to save those carpets. Let me get my appointment book.

TIP: This is a good excuse for a pause. If there are any reservations or any more questions, the manager will raise them now. If there are not and the manager doesn't say anything else, he's most of the way to committing to an appointment.

SALESPERSON: Let's see. We could make it next Wednesday morning or next Thursday afternoon. Which would work better for you?

TIP: By now the "choice of two yeses" tactic should be a familiar one.

MANAGER: I'll be off next Wednesday. Let's make it Thursday around 1 o'clock.
SALESPERSON: That would be cutting it a bit close for us. Is 2 o'clock okay for you? We can be done by 5.

TIP: It does no harm to indicate that there is a lot of demand for our services whether we have anything going on Thursday morning or not.

MANAGER: Fine.

TIP: We haven't yet qualified this manager. We don't yet know if he has the authority to approve future jobs. If not, we'll want to get the decision-maker involved in the trial. One way to find out is to ask the question, but carefully, since we don't want to offend Mr. Morra.

SCRIPT 3.10C. DETERMINING BUYING AUTHORITY

SALESPERSON: Mr. Morra, can I assume that, if you like our work and our prices, you çan approve the work we'll do for you in the future?

TIP: If we act as if this is just the first of many jobs, we may get Mr. Morra thinking this way.

MANAGER: Yeah. The boss leaves everything to me. He gives me a refurbishing budget for each apartment. You know, spackling, painting, and stuff like that. I tell him when it looks like it will cost more. If I tell him that I've worked out a way to make the carpeting last longer he'll be tickled pink, especially with the freebie you're going to give us.
SALESPERSON: Good. I'll look forward to seeing you next Thursday at 2 o'clock.

Granted, this is an expensive way to get started with a new customer. However, when you consider how effective it can be and the cost of making personal calls to accomplish the same result, it begins to look like a cost-effective strategy. Besides, Mr. Morra probably knows other building managers and can help us spread the word.

If this call seemed fairly easy, remember that we softened up our prospect with our letter. This is one of the best uses of direct mail advertising. The effective, synergistic combination of direct mail and telephone follow-up will usually yield many times the result of either effort by itself.

LETTER 3.7. OPENING NEW MARKETS WITH SEMINARS

Seminars are big business today. With "future shock" accelerating, most aware people involved in any kind of activity are eager to keep up with what is happening. We can turn this phenomenon into a sales boosting venture by thinking through how we can relate our product to a knowledge need in our marketplace. Computer services are too easy and lend themselves too well to this strategy. Let's pick something tough as an example—an art gallery. Our market is professionals—attorneys, C.P.A.s, etc.

Dear (Prospect):

ARE YOUR WALLS WORKING AGAINST YOU?

If you're like most professionals in your field, you gave a lot of thought to your office decor. You picked colors and furnishings that would reflect your professionalism and be reassuring to your clients.

But, what's on your walls? Some professionals spend thousands of dollars on furniture and carpeting in order to convey the right image and then stick calendars or poorly chosen posters on the walls.

Original and limited edition art could solve this decorating problem and cause your decor to accurately reflect your professional image. And, it's an investment that doesn't lose value. In most cases, it actually *appreciates*.

But, art selection can be a difficult undertaking. That's why we would like to invite you to a *free* seminar at our gallery on "Selecting Art for Professional Offices." All the information is on the enclosed brochure and enrollment form.

The seminar will be limited to the first 30 participants who respond. Send in the enrollment form *today* to reserve a place for you or your people.

> TIP: We started the letter with a provocative question that should encourage the reader to want to know what we're talking about. We pointed out benefits to the prospect and finished with the "exclusive club" tactic. (See Script 3.6, page 47, this chapter.)

SCRIPT 3.11. BUILDING SEMINAR ATTENDANCE

We're dealing with professional people who get paid to a large extent by the hour, so it's not going to be easy to get them to listen to a long story and we may have to deal with the administrative assistant or office manager.

SALESPERSON: Good morning, this is Darlene Allan. May I speak with Mr. Guyer, please?

SECRETARY: I don't recognize your name. Are you a client of this firm?

SALESPERSON: Well, I'm a prospective client, but I wanted to talk with Mr. Guyer about something more important. (pause)

SECRETARY: Why don't you tell *me* what that is. Mr. Guyer is due in court this morning.

TIP: Remember our advice from Chapter 1 about the importance of making the secretary your ally. She may be the one to attend the seminar, select art, and approve the purchase order.

SALESPERSON: Of course. Do you remember getting our letter on the *free* art selection seminar?
SECRETARY: I do remember seeing something from an art gallery. Seminar?
SALESPERSON: Yes. You know how important it is that your office decor reflect the professional image of your firm and that art is one of the best ways to do this.
SECRETARY: (interrupting) That's probably true, but I don't think we could afford anything like that.
SALESPERSON: That's the advantage of our limited editions which are carefully produced lithographs made by the artist of his or her original art. You get to enjoy the beauty the artist has created at a fraction of the cost.
SECRETARY: What is this seminar about?
SALESPERSON: I'm sure you know that selecting art can be a difficult undertaking, no matter how much money you have to spend. The purpose of the seminar is to take some of the confusion out of the selection process and provide some practical guidelines on what to do and how to do it.
SECRETARY: While you've been talking, I've found your letter. It looks interesting if Mr. Guyer will let me get away for a morning. Why don't I call you back tomorrow or the next day?
SALESPERSON: Fine. I'll tentatively reserve a spot for you. If I don't hear from you by Friday, I'll give you a call before I give your place away.

TIP: If we had gotten an "Oh Mr. Guyer handles . . ." response, we still would have told the secretary what we were up to so she could pass the word along and would have kept trying for Mr. Guyer. We also used the "exclusive club" tactic again. (See Script 3.6, page 47, this chapter.)

SCRIPT 3-11A. A SEMINAR OUTLINE TO BUILD EXCITEMENT

Just to close the loop, let's look at an outline for a seminar, using this tough example:

Selecting Art for Professional Offices

1. Types of art media:
   Oil
   Acrylic
   Watercolor
   Scratchboard
   Woodburning

2. Types of art production and reproduction:
   Original, including seriographs and etchings
   Lithographs
   Prints

3. Important framing considerations:
   Matting
   Acid-free paper
   Non-glare glass
   Framing material

4. Type of image, atmosphere, environment, and feeling you want to create
   Soothing
   Bright
   Soft
   Electric

The seminar doesn't have to be complicated. This may sound a bit hard-nosed, but your purpose is not to educate your prospects but to boost sales. You will use *your* products (with price tag and order information attached) to demonstrate your points. Each element of the outline should give you the opportunity to tell your prospects why they (in this case) should use art and why they should buy this from your gallery.

SCRIPT 3.12. GETTING IN THE DOOR WITH UNPLANNED CALLS

Most of our efforts in this book are designed to make the expensive and time-consuming, unplanned or "cold" call unnecessary. The use of direct mail letters to soften up prospects, and the telephone to sell, set up appointments, and pave the way for closing, should ensure that most of our calls are *planned* calls where we have been invited in to see our customers and prospects.

There is a danger in unplanned calls—you could give your prospect the impression that you have nothing better to do than drive around and look for someone to call on. There are times, however, when the unplanned call can be an appropriate strategy:

1. When you are going from point A to point C, have a half hour between appointments, and have a prospect whom you've been unable to reach on the phone at point B.

2. When you are in the same building or industrial park as a prospect and have some time.

3. When you haven't been able to make any headway with a prospect over the phone. You just might get lucky if you show up on his doorstep.

4. If you are driving by a prospect's place and see something significant going on like a moving truck parked outside.

OBJECTIVE: Make one more contact to show the prospect we're serious about his business, try to get in to see him to close for the order or another appointment, and keep our name in front of him by leaving some sales literature behind for him to review.

SALESPERSON: Hi. I'm Stu Davidson from Cardinal Business Services. (Hand the receptionist your card.) Is Mr. Hall in?

TIP: This is a little better than, "I'd like to see Mr. Hall," which would invite controlling questions by the receptionist.

RECEPTIONIST: I could check for you. Do you have an appointment with Mr. Hall?

SCRIPT 3.12A. GETTING PAST THE RECEPTIONIST

SALESPERSON: (producing envelope) I have the material he wanted.

TIP: You ducked the question and indicated that Mr. Hall wants to see you. Actually, when you last talked with Mr. Hall on the phone, you suggested that you send him some literature and he agreed to receive it.

RECEPTIONIST: (on phone) Mr. Hall, Mr. Davidson is here to see you. (pause) From Cardinal Business Services. (pause) He says he has some material that you asked for. (pause) Okay.
RECEPTIONIST: Mr. Hall said that he's not expecting you, but will see you for 5 minutes. Make a left through the doorway. It's the second door on the right.
SALESPERSON: Thank you.

SCRIPT 3.12B. AROUSING THE PROSPECT'S INTEREST

SALESPERSON: Hello, Mr. Hall. First let me give you that brochure and spec sheet we talked about on the phone last week. (Hand over envelope.)

MR. HALL: I didn't know you were going to deliver it personally.
SALESPERSON: I usually don't, but I was down on the second floor working with Donovan Creations.
MR. HALL: You do work for Donovan?
SALESPERSON: We have a couple of projects we're working on with them.

TIP: We didn't actually say we had *sold* them anything.

MR. HALL: What are you doing with them?
SALESPERSON: It's fairly complicated and I'm sure you realize I can't go into details. Maybe I can answer you by asking a question. What would you say is your biggest problem with paperwork?
MR. HALL: We don't have time in 5 minutes to go into all my paperwork problems.
SALESPERSON: I can understand. I appreciate your taking the 5 minutes, but if you do have these problems we really should talk when it's convenient for you. (Taking out appointment book) I'm going to be back in your area next Tuesday and Wednesday. Which day would be better for you?
MR. HALL: To do what?

SCRIPT 3.12C. CLOSING THE NEXT APPOINTMENT

SALESPERSON: Well, Swan Software Systems has come out with a new database package that's the best I've seen. It's more powerful and a lot easier to use than anything that has been developed before now. I could get my demonstration disk from the car right now or we could do it next Tuesday or Wednesday. Which alternative would be better for you?
MR. HALL: Okay. Let's make it Tuesday. Can you get here by 8:00 a.m.?
SALESPERSON: No problem. I'll look forward to seeing you then and I'll bring along some more information.

TIP: Mr. Hall could very well have decided to talk about his paperwork problems and we would find ourselves right in the middle of a legitimate first appointment call.

Or, as above, this appointment could be postponed until next week. To determine where we would go from here, you might review the scripts in Chapter 1, Getting the Initial Appointment, particularly Script 1.2, The Initial Call—Prospect, page 4.

It's true that we were a bit lucky to get in and see Mr. Hall without an appointment, especially when we had been spectacularly unsuccessful on the phone. It would also be a bit of luck if we were able to go through our first appointment routine on this call. Somehow, however, salespeople who work hard to take advantage of every opportunity seem to have all the luck. (If we hadn't gotten to see Mr. Hall, we would have left some literature on the database package behind.)

LETTER 3.8. CEMENTING THE UNSUCCESSFUL UNPLANNED CALL WITH A FOLLOW-UP LETTER

We've notched off one more prospect contact on our pistol whether we got to see the prospect or got an appointment, or not. Let's go back to our form letter file and knock off another notch. First, we'll assume that we did *not* get to see our prospect:

OBJECTIVE: Parlay our brief, unplanned call attempt and literature leave-behind into a reason for another prospect contact (turning the heat up just a little more) that will soften him up a little more for our next appointment-seeking telephone call.

Dear (Prospect):

Sorry we weren't able to get together when I stopped by yesterday. As your receptionist may have told you, I was on the second floor doing some work with Donovan Creations and took a chance that you might be free.

The brochure I left for you describes the new database package from Swan Software Systems. You may have seen the new product announcements in the trade press, an example of which is enclosed.

Frankly, the package is so new that we have only one completed installation, but this client is delighted with its power and ease of use.

Based on our previous conversations, it sounds like the kind of package that would be a natural addition to your system.

I'll get back to you in a few days to set a time for us to discuss in more detail what this new database package could do for you.

If we had gotten in to see our prospect, but didn't get the chance to tell our whole story, the letter would be slightly different.

LETTER 3.9. PARLAYING THE SUCCESSFUL UNPLANNED CALL

OBJECTIVE: Get one more contact in, remind our prospect of the appointment scheduled, and provide just enough information to get him looking forward to the appointment.

Dear (Prospect):

Thanks for taking the time to see me yesterday without an appointment. I think the brief time we spent will prove to be worthwhile for both of us.

I've enclosed a review article from one of the trade publications on the new database software package from Swan Software Systems—the one I mentioned in our brief meeting yesterday.

Frankly, the package is so new that we have installed it with only one client, but the feedback we've gotten so far on its power and ease of use is excellent.

I'm looking forward to seeing you Tuesday morning at 8 o'clock and discussing what this package will do for you and your company.

IN CLOSING

We've dealt with a lot of sales-boosting strategies and tactics in this chapter. We've only scratched the surface. The letters and scripts suggested are designed to stimulate your imagination and alert you to the wide range of possibilities that exist.

Two important points should have come through:

1. Use every conceivable reason to keep in constant (weekly or biweekly) touch with a hot prospect. "Out of sight—out of mind" is called a cliché because there's a lot of truth in it.

2. Follow up, follow up, follow up. Too many sales efforts fail or stop short of where they could go because the salesperson gets busy on less important matters and neglects the important few.

Vilfredo Pareto, a nineteenth century Italian economist, made this point well in what you may know as the "80-20 rule." He pointed out that countries, organizations, businesses, and individuals spend 80 percent of their time on what he called the "trivial many" and 20 percent on the "critical few."

The best route to boosting sales is to be sure that we are spending the majority of our time on the 20 percent of those activities that will account for 80 percent of our results.

4

Handling
Price Objections

INTRODUCTION

I've done few sales training sessions or ''obstacles session'' seminars where price is not immediately mentioned as the biggest hurdle to overcome in selling a product. Later on in the sessions, the real obstacles come out. It's the same with buyers. Price is rarely the reason for not buying, but a convenient cop-out indicating that the salesperson hasn't sufficiently sold the *value* of the product during the demonstration phase of the sales presentation. People *do* like to buy. They just don't like making decisions, and a price objection is a good way to postpone a decision unless the salesperson makes it for the prospect and then asks the prospect to agree.

In this chapter, we'll present some scripts to handle the issue of price whenever it comes up in the sales process. Better, we'll present scripts that will deal with the question *before* it even becomes an issue. We'll continue to use a computer system as our product example since it's a difficult sell and incorporates a lot of selling problems—it's new to most people, it's rarely a one-call close, it's a fairly expensive item, and it has tangible and intangible elements.

COMMUNICATING VALUE FROM THE BEGINNING

The concept of value starts from the very first contact with the prospect so you are not dealing with price objections during the close. Let's set the stage with the first person you are likely to talk with, the prospect's secretary or administrative assistant.

SCRIPT 4.1. AVOIDING PRICE ISSUES BY SETTING VALUE STANDARDS WITH THE "SCREENER"

OBJECTIVE: Get an appointment with the prospect, using the screener to help do this. Establish the concept of *value* versus price from the start.

SALESPERSON: Good morning. This is Stu Davidson from Cardinal Business Services. Chris Hundley, please.

   TIP: The informality of "Stu" instead of "Stuart" and the brief request for the person imply that you know the person and that it's only natural that you will be put through, especially if your tone of voice reflects that confidence.

SECRETARY: (carefully screening the call) May I ask what this is in reference to?
SALESPERSON: Cardinal Business Services has developed a system for *companies like yours* that has saved them the kind of money I think Mr. Hundley would be interested in. May I speak with him please?

   TIP: If you take nothing else from this book, remember the phrase "companies like yours." It's an indication that you're not shooting in the dark, a promise that you have something interesting and worthwhile to say, and a sure "hook" or "grabber." In this simple statement you've identified your motive as saving Mr. Hundley and his company money, and not as selling something.

SECRETARY: Mr. Hundley is tied up right now. (This may be the standard answer to all callers.) May I have your name again and your phone number?

   TIP: This may be nothing more than a good way to brush you off. Don't fall for it. Instead:

SALESPERSON: Yes. My name is Stuart Davidson from Cardinal Business Services. My number is (215) 822-1746. I would appreciate it if you would include the words "save money" on your note. Since I may be out of the office, I'll plan on calling back tomorrow. What would be a good time to call?

   TIP: If the taking of your name wasn't just a brush-off, you may actually get a call, especially with the "save money" note. If it was a brush-off, you at least have the secretary's invitation to call back. Make sure you get his or her name so you can use it when you call again. This simple courtesy will go a long way with a potential decision-influencer.

SECRETARY: Well, Mr. Hundley is usually free after 4:00 and usually stays until 6:00.
SALESPERSON: Thank you. May I call you Sherie? Thank you, Sherie. I'll call Mr. Hundley late tomorrow afternoon if I don't hear from him in the meantime. May I ask you one more question? What would you say is your or Mr. Hundley's biggest problem in processing paperwork or in keeping track of what is going on in your company?
SECRETARY: Well, we have trouble keeping on top of our accounts receivable because invoices don't get posted to the receivables ledger cards right away, and payments sometimes never get recorded because the checks go right to the bank.

   TIP: Perfect. You've found at least one possible grabber for Mr. Hundley that hits him where he lives—in the checkbook. It just so happens that your hardware/software system has an excellent accounts receivable module that ties into the billing and cash receipts operations.

Now you've set the stage for a *value* presentation and a money-saving list of benefits that will home in on at least one problem area that is real. Here's how your initial conversation with Mr. Hundley would go with some modification if he actually calls you.

SCRIPT 4.2. AVOIDING PRICE ISSUES BY SETTING VALUE STANDARDS WITH THE PROSPECT

OBJECTIVE: Get an appointment with the prospect, stressing the *value* of your product and service as opposed to price.

TIP: Make the call between 5:30 and 6:00 p.m. There will be less possibility of interruption and people who work late usually appreciate other people who don't split as soon as the minute hand hits 12.

SALESPERSON: Good afternoon, Sherie. This is Stu Davidson from Cardinal Business Systems. I assume that you gave Mr. Hundley my message and that he can't wait to start saving money. (A little humor never hurts.)
SECRETARY: Well, I wouldn't exactly say that he's panting, but he would like to talk with you for a minute or two. I'll put you through.
SALESPERSON: Good afternoon Mr. Hundley. I think Sherie told you that my company, Cardinal Business Systems, has developed a system that has saved a lot of money for *companies like yours.*

TIP: Pause for about 3 seconds longer than you feel comfortable. You don't know whether Mr. Hundley actually got or remembers the message, you don't know what state of mind he is in, and you're not completely sure that the accounts receivable problem will be the grabber that will get you the appointment. Let him make the first move and you'll have your cue about how to proceed. A lot of salespeople make the mistake of trying to sell a buyer before they know why the buyer isn't buying. Get as much information as you can before committing yourself to any one line of pursuit.

MR. HUNDLEY: Well, we're always interested in saving money as long as we don't have to spend a lot to do it.
SALESPERSON: (Pause again to see if Mr. Hundley will expand on this point so you can get a more complete idea of the direction to go in.)
MR. HUNDLEY: (feeling uncomfortable about the silence) You see, we're under some severe budget restrictions because deregulation has encouraged our competitors and caused some slowing down of our business. I don't know what you're selling, but we have a freeze on most expenditures.
SALESPERSON: Mr. Hundley, what I hear you saying is that you are not just interested in saving money, but that you really need to look hard for ways to do this and have to justify all your expenditures on a cost-effectiveness basis.

TIP: Repeat his words back to him but in a way that paves the way for your approach to setting the appointment. Don't worry about the freeze. You've already turned this into an opportunity by starting to talk cost-justification, proving that you are on Mr. Hundley's side and that the freeze and expenditure-approver is the obstacle.

MR. HUNDLEY: You got it. I can't buy a dozen pencils without someone questioning why we need them.

SALESPERSON: Then I think we have a good deal to talk about. Our system has saved *companies like yours* thousands of dollars a year and sometimes that much in a month . . .

MR. HUNDLEY: (interrupting) What is your system?

SCRIPT 4.2A. CLOSING FOR THE APPOINTMENT

SALESPERSON: A way for you to save money that can best be explained in person. It will take you about 15 minutes to decide whether or not you would like to learn more about it. I understand from Sherie (you and she are old friends now) that late afternoon is a good time for you. Which would be better for you—5 o'clock Wednesday or Thursday?

> TIP: Sidestep the explanation of the system. Your objective is to get an appointment, not to sell the system over the phone. Keep the accounts receivable module in your back pocket until you need it to push for the appointment, to develop further interest, or to close.
>
> You also used that tried-and-true ploy of offering a choice of two "yeses" instead of a "yes" or a "no." The "15 minutes to decide" makes the appointment less of a commitment of your prospect's time, but leaves the door open to take as much time as you need after you've developed Mr. Hundley's interest.

MR. HUNDLEY: Well, I'm pretty busy this week . . .

SALESPERSON: Most of our customers are. Once they've seen the value of what we've developed for *companies like yours*, however, they usually agree that the time spent in learning how to save money this way was the best time they've spent. Would 15 minutes on Wednesday work for you?

MR. HUNDLEY: Make it Wednesday at 4:30.

SALESPERSON: Thank you Mr. Hundley. I'll give Sherie a call Wednesday morning to make sure she has this on your appointment calendar. I'm looking forward to showing you how we've been able to save money for *companies like yours*.

> TIP: Talking about how you've *been able* to save money for companies like Mr. Hundley's is more powerful than a vague promise that you *will be able* to do this. Mr. Hundley should feel that he's not keeping up with the times if he doesn't at least explore your system.

Now you've completed the first loop. You're not selling a product or service. You are offering a money-saving benefit. You've put the focus where it belongs from the beginning contact—on value and not cost or price. This will help during the demonstration phase of the sales process (where the real selling is done so the close phase is a natural consequence) as you translate the cost of your system into dollars a day weighted against savings. Let's go on to reinforce that by looking at what you could say during the appointment.

SCRIPT 4.3. HANDLING PRICE OBJECTIONS, FIRST CALL—SECRETARY

Before you make the call, you've learned a little more about Mr. Hundley's company and the situation in the industry so you can reinforce the idea that you are, indeed, on his side. Sherie is the first person you will meet at your prospect's office.

> OBJECTIVE: Begin to develop Sherie as an ally in your value-setting efforts with Mr. Hundley and to help pave the way to a close.

SALESPERSON: Good morning, Sherie. I'm Stu Davidson from Cardinal Business Systems. We talked on the phone the other day. (Hand her your business card.) You're a lot younger than you sound on the phone.

> TIP: This is usually effective unless Sherie is about 18 and wants to be thought of as looking older. In this case you might say something like, "You sound very mature over the phone." I've yet to find a case where even remotely sincere flattery hurt any situation or relationship.

SHERIE: Oh, yes. I remember talking with you. (Of course. You made her feel important by getting her name and making sure she got yours. The "save money" note set you apart from other callers as did your asking *her* opinion about the company's problems.)
SALESPERSON: Yes, you were very helpful in suggesting a problem area where Cardinal's system can be helpful and save your company money. (Keep plugging the idea that you are a money-saver, not a salesperson.) Would you mind if I gave you credit for suggesting the accounts receivable area as one to be looked at?

> TIP: You don't yet know to what extent Sherie can influence Mr. Hundley's decision. The answer to this question should give you some clue. If she says "yes," it's a good indication that she may be involved and you've developed an ally. If she says "no," it's possible that bringing it up as her idea may turn Mr. Hundley off. Better to know that going into the meeting.

SHERIE: Sure. I guess that would be okay. Mr. Hundley can see you now.

Now you've gained an ally who may or may not be helpful to you in the future. At the very least, Sherie will be responsive to putting you through in the future and may even drop hints of information that you could find useful in pursuing Mr. Hundley. Also, you've "warmed up" for your presentation by coming across as friendly, confident, and sincere. Contrast this with sitting in the reception area with your nose buried in a magazine. Now let's go on to the meeting with your prospect.

SCRIPT 4.4. HANDLING PRICE OBJECTIONS, FIRST CALL—PROSPECT

> OBJECTIVE: Establish yourself and your company as value-providers. Get permission to do a needs analysis on the way to a complete proposal and presentation of the products you'll suggest.

SALESPERSON: Good morning, Mr. Hundley. Are you ready to learn how to start saving money?

MR. HUNDLEY: Good morning. I'm *really* ready to figure out how to save money. I just came from another budget meeting. It doesn't look like we're going to be able to buy anything for some time.

SALESPERSON: It looks like I came at a good time. Let me discuss our system by telling you what we've done for a *company like yours*. Incidentally, here's a copy of the recommendation letter they sent us just 2 months after the system was installed. Notice their emphasis on the savings—even after only a month.

MR. HUNDLEY: I know this company. I didn't think they were that progressive.

>   TIP: You started off by homing in on Mr. Hundley's frequency and continuing *his* conversation by picking up on the first point he made. You then disarmed him by unloading the second barrel almost in the same breath but still sticking to *his* point about cost-consciousness and *your* point about how your system will save him money. You are now both on the same side with only the proof of savings as an obstacle. You've done what some people call "neutralizing" the prospect's mind, and you eliminated any adversarial positioning right from the start. You didn't *hear* any talk about his not being able to buy anything.

SCRIPT 4.4A. SETTING UP THE DEMONSTRATION

SALESPERSON: Well, in the beginning, they thought that the system might be too sophisticated for them, but when they found out how much money it would save, they got interested in our training programs that will teach almost anybody how to be proficient in less than 2 weeks. When they found out that the training program really could do that and that the system worked, they locked me in a room until I would agree to take the order they wanted to place.

>   TIP: You're getting ready for the demonstration part of your sales presentation and there might be a little tenseness. This "locking in a room" exaggeration should lighten things up a bit.

SALESPERSON: Before describing what we were able to do for Wendell Company, let me ask you some questions about your operation so I can address those issues that will be of particular interest to you.

>   TIP: It's time for the prospect to handle the bulk of the conversation for awhile. Most people like to talk more than they like to listen so you're making your prospect feel good about you. Also, you'll pick up some more clues about the kinds of grabbers Mr. Hundley will respond to.

Now, you'll go on to ask questions about number of employees, volume of transactions, present equipment which might be compatible, etc. If your company doesn't have a standard questionnaire or information form, you should. It provides discipline for this part of the sales process and makes you look more professional. It will also be useful for future follow-up calls.

As your prospect talks about his problems, you might make *brief* comments that will indicate that your system is, indeed, the right one for Mr. Hundley without actually saying so.

SCRIPT 4.4B. CLOSING THE APPOINTMENT

SALESPERSON: Job costing must really be a problem for companies like yours. I know that this is one of the areas our software engineers spent the most time on.

or,

SCRIPT 4.4C. CLOSING WITH A FEATURE

SALESPERSON: Being able to come up with an aged accounts receivable trial balance *daily* is one of the features our customers really like about the billing module in our system.

or,

SCRIPT 4.4D. CLOSING WITH A BENEFIT

SALESPERSON: It's interesting that keeping track of tools and parts inventories is such a big issue since our system handles it so easily. I guess I've become spoiled by seeing how well it works.

TIP: Now you want to get information on Mr. Hundley's present system—number of employees processing the different kinds of paperwork your system will handle, equipment used, etc. Depending on the specific nature of your product or service, you might also want figures on supplies and energy used so you have the information you need to justify the cost savings benefits.

You know that you're not going to close on this call so your job now is to ensure that Mr. Hundley stays interested. (He has already spent one hour with you, with him doing most of the talking, so you know you've gotten at least some interest.) You also want him to be looking forward to the next appointment where you'll demonstrate the value of your system and possibly close.

SCRIPT 4.5. HANDLING PRICE OBJECTIONS—FOLLOWING UP ON THE FIRST CALL ON THE PROSPECT

SALESPERSON: Well, Mr. Hundley, I think I have enough information for our systems engineers to tailor a system proposal for you. Are there any other questions I can answer for you about Cardinal Business Systems?

TIP: Keep mentioning the name of your company.

MR. HUNDLEY: Yes, what is this going to cost me?
SALESPERSON: I won't have a figure on cost *or savings* until we've had our team do a systems analysis.

or, better

SCRIPT 4.5A. SETTING UP A SAVINGS BENEFIT

SALESPERSON: I'll have a figure on costs *and savings* as soon as we've had our team do a systems analysis—about a week from now. You see, all of our systems are tailored to our clients' needs and our people insist on doing a thorough job.

> TIP: Your whole approach is based on not letting the issue of cost come up. If it does, you put the emphasis on *savings* immediately. You have also paved the way for an effective demonstration to make the close a natural consequence of the work you will have done up to that point.

MR. HUNDLEY: I don't know if you should go through all that work. I'm not at all sure that we can afford any system, no matter how good it is.

SCRIPT 4.5B. CLOSING THE APPOINTMENT

SALESPERSON: We're happy to take that chance. Usually, when a client is able to explain his problems as clearly as you have, putting together a proposal for a system that will more than justify its cost in savings is relatively easy. Would next week at the same time be convenient for you or would you prefer Thursday?
MR. HUNDLEY: Next Wednesday at 4:30 will be fine. Call me in the meantime if you have any questions.
SALESPERSON: Thank you. It's a pleasure to work with someone who has such a good handle on his operation.

> TIP: You are also using the "boil a frog" strategy talked about in Chapter 1. By making the time investment and by having Mr. Hundley make a similar investment, you gradually turn up the heat by increasing his commitment to you step-by-step. Your objective is to get him so used to working with you and your company that going out for competitive bids would seem like an unnecessary duplication of effort.

Now you'll go back to your office (or transmit the information to your systems engineers using your lap-top computer) and get the proposal going, paying particular attention to your prospect's main interests. Your people have done this before so they'll whip it out quickly. In the meantime, say Friday, you call Mr. Hundley again.

SCRIPT 4.6. HANDLING PRICE OBJECTIONS—RESELLING THE FIRST CALL ON THE PROSPECT

> OBJECTIVE: Set the next appointment, resell Mr. Hundley on the value of what you are doing for him, and make sure he hasn't gotten cold feet since the last time you talked with him.

SALESPERSON: (You get put through right away because Sherie knows you are important and you've developed a nice relationship with her.) Good morning, Mr. Hundley. This is

Stuart Davidson from Cardinal Business Systems. Our systems engineers are working on your system. (Not "the proposal," but "*your* system"—always preparing for the close.)
MR. HUNDLEY: Good. Can you tell me how much it's going to cost yet?
SALESPERSON: We're working up the total payback and estimated savings figures and I'll have those ready for our meeting Wednesday. So far, it looks very good. You should begin to realize cost savings almost right away.

TIP: We can't let our prospect focus on costs for a minute. Keep emphasizing *cost savings*.

MR. HUNDLEY: Well, you're going to have to convince our controller of that. She's pretty hard-headed about spending money for anything these days.

SCRIPT 4.6A. INVOLVING THE THIRD PARTY BUYING INFLUENCE

SALESPERSON: I'm glad you mentioned that. Controllers usually get involved in our final discussions so we try to present the information in such a way that they can quickly see the financial advantages of our system. Why don't we include your controller in our discussion? You and I can go through an overview of the system so you are familiar with it and we can then make the presentation together.

TIP: It looks like the controller will be one of the decision-makers, that third party discussed in Chapter 2. You *don't* want your prospect to take your proposal to the controller himself. It won't get the kind of presentation *you* would give. At the same time, you have to let Mr. Hundley stay in control.

MR. HUNDLEY: Let me take a look at it first and I'll discuss it with our controller.

TIP: Well, you don't always win, but let's see if we can get the ball back.

SALESPERSON: I agree that it would be a good idea for us to discuss it together first.

TIP: Get back on the same side or your prospect will start to balk at anything you suggest, including recommending that his company buy your system.

SALESPERSON: However, she may have some questions that I could help you answer since we've done this once or twice before. Let's set up a time for us to meet with the controller when we get together on Wednesday. You and I can discuss it first and then I'll be on hand to help you answer your controller's questions.

TIP: Emphasize the "that I can help you answer," not "that I can answer." Your prospect isn't going to let you loose with a decision-maker who could be his boss, but you want to be there to make sure the proposal doesn't get shot down without a fair hearing. You started this by suggesting that you set up a time for *us* to meet with your prospect's controller.

MR. HUNDLEY: Well, that might work out all right—*if* I like what I see. Our getting together will give me a chance to become really familiar with it before we have to go tackle Big Ann.
SALESPERSON: Big Ann?
MR. HUNDLEY: Yes. Our controller—big in more ways than one, and tough.

SCRIPT 4.6B. UNCOVERING ADDITIONAL BENEFITS

SALESPERSON: Good. I'll look forward to meeting her with you. One final thing for our proposal—there was one question that we had on your receivables. We're working on the cost savings benefits of reducing your average outstanding receivables. Could you tell me what your receivables are running right now?

> TIP: If there was any doubt left in Mr. Hundley's mind about whether or not he is doing the right thing in talking with us, we should have removed the last trace. Accounts receivable are his nemesis so he has to be impressed that *we* are concerned and are working on it.

MR. HUNDLEY: The last report showed an average of 65 days outstanding, down from 67 days at the beginning of this fiscal year.

SALESPERSON: I see. As I recall, that's a bit more than the industry average. The reason I asked is that we want to include in our report an analysis of what the benefits to you would be if we were able to speed up invoice processing and cash receipts posting. We have an idea that this will be one of the immediate benefits of our system to you.

MR. HUNDLEY: Well, it would be a miracle if you could. We've been struggling to knock even a few days off our average outstanding.

> TIP: Great. You've hit on a grabber besides showing your prospect that you are really working on his system. You've also talked benefits to divert attention from the cost issue.

SALESPERSON: Cutting down days outstanding is hard to do with a manual system, but we've done this in almost every case when we've installed the system in *companies like yours*. I'll look forward to discussing with you exactly how the system makes it happen. Are there any other questions that I can answer for you now?

MR. HUNDLEY: Yes, you can tell me how I can afford to buy anything right now.

SALESPERSON: Mr. Hundley, I expect to be able to show you *and* your controller how you can't afford *not* to have us install this system. I'll look forward to seeing you Wednesday at 4:30.

MR. HUNDLEY: Why don't you make it at 3:30 and I'll set us up with Big Ann at 4:30?

Besides reinforcing the points you made during your sales call and keeping the emphasis on benefits and off price, you eliminated any post-cognitive dissonance. This is a term market researchers use to describe the phenomenon that occurs after a buyer has made a decision. (See Chapter 2, Letter 2.4, page 37.) Some salespeople call it "buyer's remorse." Mr. Hundley may have had second thoughts about even considering your proposal or spending more time with you. This phone call should have made him eager to see you again. You've also continued the emphasis on cost savings instead of price.

SCRIPT 4.7. EFFECTIVE PROPOSAL PRESENTATIONS

This step will vary so much depending on the product, the suitability of the proposal to the use of visual aids, and the prospect that a checklist may be more helpful than a detailed script:

1. You keep your appointment, and go through all the benefits of the system, discussing the hardware/software features only as they are necessary to explain the benefits. (If you were selling a technically minded prospect, you might dwell more on bits, bytes, and bauds.)

2. You lead your prospect through the report you've prepared, perhaps with additional visuals. Then you explain in detail the cost savings benefits in terms of manpower saved and benefits like cutting 2 weeks from the invoice processing and cash receipts posting cycles.

3. You wrap it up by showing the less tangible or measurable aspects of improved cost control and more timely statements. The controller is still lurking in the background, but you might as well try for a close now.

SCRIPT 4.8. HANDLING PRICE OBJECTIONS—TRIAL CLOSE

OBJECTIVE: Of course, you want to actually get the order. It may be unlikely that you will on this call, but it's worth a shot. The least that should happen is that you'll find out what obstacles remain before you are able to pull off a final close.

MR. HUNDLEY: I agree that it looks pretty good, but I think I told you from the beginning how tight money is for us right now. How much is it going to cost?

TIP: By now, you've established so much value and so many cost savings benefits that there is no reason not to get right down to the nitty-gritty of the cost of the system. Any further dodging at this point would be a turn-off.

SALESPERSON: On our lease/purchase plan, your monthly investment would be about $650 per month—or about $20 per day, about half what it would cost for a clerk who would do 10 percent of the work.

TIP: *Always* break down the cost into monthly or daily installments and relate it to something else: "About the cost of a pack of cigarettes per day." "About as much as two drinks at the lounge in the hotel down the street per day."

MR. HUNDLEY: But how much is the total cost?

TIP: You're not ashamed of the total cost since you know what the system can do and you don't want to appear to be hedging.

SCRIPT 4.8A. PUTTING PRICE IN PERSPECTIVE

SALESPERSON: The total invoice cost is $12,650, including installation and normal training. We estimate that the payback period for this is about 8 months, not counting the extra benefits of a tighter cost control system and more timely financial reports.
MR. HUNDLEY: That's a lot of money for a big calculator that also turns out paper.
SALESPERSON: Well, Mr. Hundley, I think you can see that this system which has worked successfully for *companies like yours* can work as well for you. You know from the recommendation letters I've shown you that you can depend on Cardinal Business Systems to back up everything that we've said the system will do. Do you feel that we've addressed all of your problems and can save you time and money?
MR. HUNDLEY: Yes, but $12,650 is more than we can afford to spend right now.

SALESPERSON: I agree that it seems like a lot of money, but not if you consider the savings. Mr. Hundley, do you have a savings account or other kinds of interest-producing investments?

MR. HUNDLEY: Yes, several kinds.

SALESPERSON: Would you like to make three times as much from these investments?

MR. HUNDLEY: Of course, if it didn't involve risk.

SALESPERSON: Well, unless you've found some secret, these investments don't pay you one-third of the return that your company could realize from the purchase and installation of this system. Doesn't this sound like a good investment?

MR. HUNDLEY: Well, if you put it that way, I suppose it would be.

SALESPERSON: I think you'd agree that looking at things in this way is what we all get paid for—using the company's resources to get the best return on the money as we can. Your commitment under our plan would amount to only $650 per month. You can authorize this can't you?

MR. HUNDLEY: Oh yes, I can.

SCRIPT 4.8B. GOING FOR THE CLOSE

SALESPERSON: One of our installers can be here next Monday to work with you and your key people to set up the equipment and install the software. We can start a three-person training program by Wednesday. Would that be soon enough for you?

MR. HUNDLEY: (Big pause.)

> TIP: Keep quiet and wait. The worst thing you can do at this point is to open your mouth. If you have something else to say, you can do it after Mr. Hundley shares with you what is going on in his mind during this pause.

MR. HUNDLEY: Yes, I guess it would. Sherie was hoping we'd get the system and she's looking forward to working with it. And, our controller was complaining the other day about how long it took to get monthly statements. I told her I might have a shortcut up my sleeve to get statements out faster.

SALESPERSON: Fine. I'll just need your authorization to go ahead on these three pieces of paper, and a check for the first month's payment, and I can confirm the dates first thing tomorrow morning so you can start saving money as soon as possible.

MR. HUNDLEY: (as he is signing) My kids will be amazed. They've been telling me we should have a computer, but felt I was too old-fashioned to go for it. I can't wait to tell them.

SALESPERSON: Thank you.

SCRIPT 4.9. HANDLING PRICE OBJECTIONS—AND CLOSING

The above script (Script 4.8) showed a favorable outcome. Indeed, most of the scripts in this chapter and in this book show favorable outcomes because of some fortunate circumstance. You may not find identical circumstances, but there is almost *always* a favorable circumstance that can be exploited—a strategy, a tactic, a gimmick, a tool, that will turn a lemon into lemonade. All you have to do is use your imagination to find it. There *is* a silver lining in every cloud, and every problem (read "objection") *does* contain the seeds of its own solution.

In fact, the more objections you get, the better armed you will be to figure out the prospect's "hot button." (Incidentally, Paul Micali of the Lacy Sales Institute in Boston should probably be given credit for the term, "hot button." To the best of my knowledge, Mr. Micali popularized and may very well have invented the term at least 15 years ago.)

Dealing with a prospect who doesn't pose objections but still doesn't buy is like trying to hold on tighter to a wet fish. *Welcome* the prospect who objects even if his objections are specious price objections. Let's look at a few ways to deal with those prospects who still remain unconvinced after all our "value instead of price" pitches.

> OBJECTIVE: Get the prospect off the price kick. Get him to realize, subtly or not so subtly, that *price is not his main concern* no matter how strongly he protests that it is.

Let's look at some mini-scripts that deal with a stubborn prospect's price objections.

SCRIPT 4.9A. "ARE *YOU* THE CHEAPEST IN *YOUR* AREA?"

SALESPERSON: Mr. Tropea, does your company offer the cheapest prices in your market area?

MR. TROPEA: Well, no. We're competitive, but we're not the cheapest in the area.

SALESPERSON: How many competitors do you think you have in your market area?

MR. TROPEA: Oh, I don't know exactly—probably seven or eight, plus some mail order houses.

SALESPERSON: How many of these seven or eight have cheaper prices than you do?

MR. TROPEA: I guess all of them do at one time or another, one special sale or another.

SALESPERSON: Then, how do you stay in business? I thought I heard you say that price was the only thing that counted in making a purchase decision.

MR. TROPEA: Well, we offer a lot of things our competitors don't, especially the mail order houses—free delivery, advice on how to use our products, faster service, and a whole bunch of other things that make us *worth* more.

SALESPERSON: Son-of-a-gun. It sounds like you're talking about *value added*. Wow. That's exactly what *we* do and why we're not only still in business but growing faster every year, probably for the same reasons you are. Now, why don't we talk about what's really important to you with this kind of product?

> TIP: In every market area, any company can usually count about ten competitors. Only *one* of these contenders in the marketplace can be the cheapest. This approach, therefore, should work 91% of the time.

SCRIPT 4.9B. HANDLING THE HOLDOUT

SALESPERSON: Ms. Davis, you have agreed that our system has everything you are looking for. You've seen the recommendation letters from satisfied clients so you know that we can back up every promise I've made to you. You've agreed that our quality is tops. What else could possibly be in the way of your cutting a purchase order today?

MS. DAVIS: It's my job to get the best prices for this company. That's my understanding of what a purchasing manager is supposed to do. I'm not yet satisfied that you have the best prices.

SALESPERSON: Let me make it easy for you. We don't. We're not 5 percent cheaper.

We're 20 percent better, and this excellence difference will save you money in the long run.

MS. DAVIS: Have you ever heard what that economist said, "In the long run we're all dead"?

SALESPERSON: In this case, the "long run" is about 9 months from now when you'll have saved enough money on data processing to *pay* for the entire system. Besides, if you're going to be dead, why not make the rest of your life easier and give me that purchase order I know you have ready to sign in the right-hand corner of the top drawer of your desk?

MS. DAVIS: (looking) It's in the left-hand corner. How did you know that?

SALESPERSON: I'd suggest that that's not as important as why you are holding off saving your company the money that you know this system will. (Respectfully) May I ask why you're doing this?

MS. DAVIS: Okay, I admit that I've been sitting on it and could have signed it a couple of weeks ago. I just figured that if I stalled, you would come down in price in order to get me to sign.

SALESPERSON: That's probably a good strategy with some companies, but we believe in providing a thorough proposal and a fair price on the first go-around. As I said, we're not 5 percent cheaper, but 20 percent better. This doesn't leave much room to cut prices after the proposal is delivered.

MS. DAVIS: You won't bend at all, will you?

SALESPERSON: Pat, I *am* going to *bend*—over backwards—to get you the best, most efficient, and most cost-savings system you've ever seen, just as soon as you sign that purchase order. You see, the way our company operates, this order is just the beginning. I don't just want an order from you. I want a recommendation letter and I want at least three or four referrals. In order to earn this, I have to make sure that you get such a successful installation with the right kind of follow-through that you're going to be a hero to your administrative people.

MS. DAVIS: You want a lot, don't you? And, "hero"? I'm usually the opposite of that.

SALESPERSON: Yes, I do want a lot, but I'm prepared to earn it. As for being a "hero," it looks like it's time for a change in your image. To keep some part of it intact, however, how about if you add the word-processing package that you were thinking about and I'll throw in the training on it for up to five people *free*? That way you can tell everyone that you wrestled it out of me.

MS. DAVIS: How about training for ten people?

SALESPERSON: Boy, you *are* a tough lady.

MS. DAVIS: I know you were thinking "tough *broad*." That's okay. I don't mind people thinking that. It didn't work with you, but it sometimes gets me lower prices and saves the company money.

SALESPERSON: I don't think of you as a tough broad or even as a tough lady. I think that you are a thorough professional—very much like the people we will have working on your installation and training.

MS. DAVIS: (pulling out the purchase order) Okay, you silver-tongued devil, I'm signing this—but I'll break your knees if it doesn't turn out to be everything you promised, and I mean *everything*.

SALESPERSON: Thank you.

SCRIPT 4.9C. PROVING THAT PRICE ISN'T PRIMARY

MS. EHRMAN: You know, Stu, I really like everything you've done so far, but your prices are the highest of the three people I've talked with.

SALESPERSON: Good.

MS. EHRMAN: *Good?*

SALESPERSON: Yes. I would really hate to think that we have offered you a value package worth at least 50% more than anyone else can offer and didn't propose to charge you more for it.

MS. EHRMAN: I appreciate the *value*, but *price* is the most important thing to us.

SALESPERSON: I don't believe you (pause).

MS. EHRMAN: What do you mean, you don't believe me? How can you say something like that?

SALESPERSON: Let me ask you a question. What kind of car do you drive and what kind of options does it have?

> TIP: By now, you're familiar with the "answer a question with a question" bit.

MS. EHRMAN: What does that have to do with this proposal we are talking about?

SALESPERSON: Please just trust me for a minute. What kind of car do you drive and what kind of options does it have or did you get when you bought it?

MS. EHRMAN: Well, I have a 2-year-old black Merkur, and I guess I got almost all the options you can get on a car that comes with a bunch of options thrown in. Now, tell me why you asked that question.

SALESPERSON: I think that you're saying that price isn't the only thing we look at in buying any product or service. If this were true we would all be driving black stick-shifts without radios or air conditioning.

MS. EHRMAN: But, that's different.

SALESPERSON: Why? We're talking about a product, whether it's an automobile that you drive or a computer system that you're installing for your company as a *value package* or a bundle of satisfactions. You got the value you wanted with your Merkur even if wasn't the cheapest car you might have bought. Why should your company deserve less?

MS. EHRMAN: H'mmmmm.

> TIP: Shut up now. You've got her cornered. Anything you say now can and will be used against you.

MS. EHRMAN: (pulling out proposal) You have a point. Let's take a look at some of these extras beyond a bare bones system in your proposal.

SCRIPT 4.9D. UNCOVERING THE UNCONSCIOUS REASONS

SALESPERSON: Mrs. Darden what's the *real* reason you haven't placed your order yet?

> TIP: This is the "last resort" approach. You're ready to give up and walk away, so you have nothing to lose by pushing your prospect a lot further than you would ordinarily feel comfortable doing. Just remember, if you feel really uncomfortable, that you can only lose an order once.

MRS. DARDEN: What do you mean by that?

SALESPERSON: Just what I asked. We've proven that we're a credible company. We've snowed you under in recommendation letters. We've convinced your people that, with our training program, they will *love* the system. Just why are you refusing to do what is right for your company?

MRS. DARDEN: I told you. I don't think I can live with your prices. I saw a system like yours advertised for about 30 percent less.

SALESPERSON: Patty, we've been over that before. We're talking about *value*. You know that you'll pay *60 percent more* for support in order to save 30 percent on the system. C'mon now, what is the *real* reason you're holding out on something you know is right for your people and your company?

MRS. DARDEN: (getting choked up) My husband and I are splitting up. I guess I began to believe him when he said that I can't do anything right. I don't want to make a mistake on this and I'm not sure that I've done everything I should have to check out this system with what has been going on in the past 3 months.

> TIP: Well, we finally got to the proverbial bottom of this somewhat different reason for using price as a cop-out for not making a decision. You don't want to play shrink and you certainly don't want to get in the middle of this (unless Patty is a good friend as well as a prospect). Let's back off our tough "Why not?" approach, be sympathetic, and see where we go.

SCRIPT 4.9E. CLOSING THE REALLY TOUGH PROSPECT

SALESPERSON: Patty, in my opinion, you handled *everything* right with this project. I don't like admitting this, but you have been one of the toughest purchasing managers I've dealt with. By "tough," in this case, I mean *good* and thorough. And, it wasn't because you were being difficult, but because you were being thoroughly *professional*.

MRS. DARDEN: Don't patronize me just because you can see that I'm upset.

SALESPERSON: I'm not. I meant everything I said, just like our company will back up everything in our proposal. Look, if this isn't a good time for you to make an objective decision, let's postpone it.

MRS. DARDEN: Objective? You don't think I can be objective about something that's my job?

SALESPERSON: (softly) I don't know, can you?

MRS. DARDEN: Darn right I can. I learned a long time ago to separate my personal life from my business life.

> TIP: Sure. Sure she did. (Lest this be taken as a chauvinistic remark, let's go on record as suggesting that the same kind of situation could have existed had the purchasing manager been male. The only difference is that the *man* may not have been smart enough to admit it.)

MRS. DARDEN: Let's get back to what we were talking about. You asked me why I don't go ahead and approve this? I guess I don't know. You're right about costs and prices. I've made mistakes before going for the cheapest price instead of what you call the best value. What is it that you told me, you're not 5 percent cheaper, but 10 percent better?

SALESPERSON: 20.

> TIP: This is that point in the dialogue that you may recognize from previous scripts—it is time to keep your mouth shut and let the prospect sell herself, however uncomfortable the pauses and silences may be.

MRS. DARDEN: Oh, (Steve Martin impression) excuse me.

SALESPERSON: (You say zip, as in keep you mouth shut.)

MRS. DARDEN: Okay. You've given us the best proposal. Every one of your clients that we've talked with says that you do a first class job. *You* seem honest and sincere. But, are you going to disappear when you get the order from us?

TIP: These remarks and questions are buying signals. Now you can open your mouth, but carefully.

SALESPERSON: No. I'll be here when your system is installed and when we begin to train your people and whenever else you want me.
MRS. DARDEN: How do I know that?
SALESPERSON: Simple. If I told you that I do this because I really care about my clients and the systems I sell, you probably wouldn't buy it. It's true, but I can't blame you if you didn't swallow this whole. Look at it this way: If everything works out well here, you'll give me a recommendation letter—and, perhaps, three or four referrals. That makes my job a lot easier, so I'll work hard for that.
MRS. DARDEN: Now that makes sense to me. You're going to do a good job for me and my company because there's something in it for you. Neat.
SALESPERSON: Yep. (And shut up.)

TIP: *Anytime* you can give a prospect a self-serving reason for doing something that looks like (and is) for their benefit, you'll get a lot more credibility points.

MRS. DARDEN: Okay, what happens now?
SALESPERSON: What would you like to happen?
MRS. DARDEN: Boy, you're something else. You're supposed to be taking advantage of me and pushing me into the order you want.
SALESPERSON: Really?
MRS. DARDEN: Yes, really. (Now Patty plays the waiting game. You outwait her.)
MRS. DARDEN: Well, aren't you going to offer some final inducement, like going to Tiajuana or at least Catalina Island for the weekend?
SALESPERSON: Nope.
MRS. DARDEN: Good. (Pause—and you don't move.) Okay, I guess I'm supposed to do something now.
SALESPERSON: If you think you should.
MRS. DARDEN: (reaching into her file) How about signing the purchase order for the whole darn system?
SALESPERSON: I think that would be a good move for both you and your company.
MRS. DARDEN: (signing purchase order and handing it over to you) No final inducements?
SALESPERSON: How about this? We said the system would pay for itself in 8 months and you've set up a way to track this. If it pays for itself in *less* than 8 months, you take me out to dinner at Moon Shadows. If it takes longer, I take you out to dinner at Moon Shadows, or the restaurant of your choice.
MRS. DARDEN: You're on.

Another done deal. Sometimes it makes sense to just hang in there, realizing that you've done all of your previous work properly and thoroughly. Keep still and let the client come to an agreement on the decision you've already made for them. As we've said before, people really *do* like buying. They just don't like making decisions. Finally, realize that price *is*, more often than not, a cop-out and excuse for the *real* reason the prospect doesn't want to make a decision. Hang in there, ask questions, and find out the real reason for not buying.

IN CLOSING

Again, all of the above scenarios had a favorable outcome. We still suggest that you *can* orchestrate a favorable outcome, regardless of the circumstances. There will be some times, however, when nothing works. Our advice: Drop it. Put the prospect in the "B" or "C" section of your card file and follow up according to the schedule you've established for direct mail and telemarketing efforts, and go on to your other live ones.

Remember the Pareto time rule. (See Chapter 3, page 63.) Concentrate on what are, for you, the "critical few," consider those "nothing worked" prospects as part of the "trivial many," and put them back in the file for future phone and mail follow-up.

There was a time, a few years ago, when I felt like I was hitting my head against a kind of wall and not getting as far as I thought I should have. I fretted about it and was miserable. My daughter had the answer to pull me out of this. She suggested that I "couldn't win them all." I didn't buy this. At that point, I *wanted* to win them all—and the heck with smelling the daisies.

Finally she got to me with something from Ayn Rand's *Fountainhead*. She said, "Remember, Dad, Atlas too shrugged." She was right. There *is* a time to walk away even if you do this by putting the card back in your prospect file vowing to close them at some point in the future. Just don't sweat it.

5

Turning Price Increases into Sales-Boosting Opportunities

INTRODUCTION

We dealt with this subject to some extent in Chapter 3. In that discussion, we were able to turn the price increase problem into a sales-boosting opportunity. In *this* chapter, we're going to assume that we have a tougher problem. Our customers are not going to be so easily persuaded that our price increase is either fair or logical. We will assume, however, that our company has taken into consideration the necessary lead times for our customers to react without having to absorb the increases themselves.

Our job will still not be easy since we're going to assume that we are working for a company that manufactures electric and bottom-of-the-line electronic typewriters at a time when the industry is going to sophisticated word-processing equipment with full page displays instead of the one-line display we offer. This may not sound like the progressive company that *you* work for, but our founder is ready to retire and just doesn't want to risk his estate on a development project that would enable us to keep up with the rest of the industry. You may have your resumé out on the street, but you still have to deal with the present situation.

SCRIPT 5.1. USING A PRICE INCREASE TO GET AN ADVANCE ORDER

In this case we're going to a script first instead of a letter since it *is* such a sensitive issue. Our dealers and direct customers have been badgering us for a price *decrease*, so we want to talk to them personally before they get an impersonal letter even if we have to take a lot of flak by doing it this way. This script deals with the *personal* call—what you will want to do with your "A" customers and prospects. The approach suggested will work with dealers/distributors as well as with direct customers:

SALESPERSON: Good morning Mrs. Darden. How are you today?
MRS. DARDEN: Good morning. Busy. I only agreed to see you because you said it was important. What's up?

TIP: At this point the old "sandwich" routine is appropriate. That is, intersperse the bad news with good news. Start with the good. (Any price increase that may spell bad news for customers should be acccompanied by some kind of good news.)

SALESPERSON: I wanted to show you how that new display that we talked about on the phone works. You recall that some of your people were asking about when we would be able to make it react faster to mistakes.
MRS. DARDEN: Yes, I remember. Can you make it fast?
SALESPERSON: Sure. I set up the demo model in your secretary's office. Let's go take a look at it now.

The demonstration is completed satisfactorily since you got to the secretary a half hour before your appointment and made sure it worked.

SCRIPT 5.1A. BREAKING THE PRICE INCREASE NEWS

MRS. DARDEN: Great. It does everything you said it would. Thanks for coming in.
SALESPERSON: There is one other thing we should discuss. As you know, we've made a number of improvements in the past two years besides what you just saw. This has cost us money. I know you don't have a lot of time to play games, but what would you guess these improvements have added to the value of the basic model your people are using?

TIP: We've set the premise—improvements cost money. We've talked *value*, not price, and we've asked a question instead of making a statement—all nonthreatening moves.

MRS. DARDEN: Oh, I don't know. It seems that recently most of the changes wind up costing us less money because of technological improvements.
SALESPERSON: Yes, that's sometimes true. We've been able to do that in the past, as you've seen. But this improvement really does add value. How much do you think that's worth?

TIP: *You* want an answer and want to control the interview, so don't give up on the question.

MRS. DARDEN: Okay. Let's say that it's worth about $100. What's it going to cost me?

SCRIPT 5.1B. TURNING THE PRICE INCREASE INTO AN ORDER

SALESPERSON: Nothing.

MRS. DARDEN: Nothing?

SALESPERSON: Nothing until September 1st. I got special permission from our marketing department as soon as I found out about the price increase to let you place orders for up to 500 machines with the new improvement at the old price.

> TIP: In one breath you've provided a benefit to your customer, made her feel special, and suggested a really neat purchase commitment.

MRS. DARDEN: Five hundred machines will last us a whole year, and who knows what kinds of improvements your competitors will come up with in that time?

SALESPERSON: Yes, that's just about a year's supply—locked into *last* year's price.

> TIP: Keep pushing *benefits* and get her mind off the price increase she's eventually going to have to pay for your machines. Your company, of course, has figured the cost of customers taking advantage of the "old price" deal in the determination of the amount and timing of the price increase.

MRS. DARDEN: That's not a bad deal, but what about the chances that one of your competitors will come up with a beautiful machine at half the cost?

SALESPERSON: Technological improvements are always possible and always happening. *But*, your people are used to our machines and will still want to use them for at least another year rather than going through a relearning process. You remember that we found that out last year when you introduced a competitive machine to the sales department. It wan't a bad machine, but your people preferred *our* familiar machine.

MRS. DARDEN: That's because you had them brain-washed.

SALESPERSON: Can we call that effective training and effective follow-through. Or, better, *value added*?

> TIP: Keep pushing the *intangible*, value-added benefits of dealing with you and your company to overcome the effects of the price increase and your nonindustry-leader position. *But*, get back to your objective—you want to, as discussed in Chapter 3, turn this possible obstacle into an order-obtaining *benefit*.

MRS. DARDEN: Okay. Your machines do the job. They may not be the latest or the best, but my people like them. Where do we go from here?

> TIP: Great. As we've discussed before, the best thing that can happen in a sales interview is for you to create the circumstances or environment for the customer or prospect to ask this kind of "buying" question.

SALESPERSON: Here's a printout of your purchases, by model, over the last two years, weighted by your purchases in the last six months to reflect the latest trends. Based on this, I've worked out a purchase schedule for the next year of the improved machine, all at last year's prices.

> TIP: *Always* have an order worked out in advance and make it as ambitious as you can. If you shoot for the moon, you may miss and fall back to earth. If you shoot for the sun, you still have a shot at the moon.

MRS. DARDEN: You seem to have thought of everything.

TIP: Oops. If we've thought of everything, we haven't allowed Mrs. Darden to participate in and *own* the purchase. Let's back up a bit.

SALESPERSON: Well, this is a tentative order. I think it needs some of your personal
judgment. After all, it's based on a computer projection. I'm sure you'll want to make some
modifications.

MRS. DARDEN: (now somewhat mollified) Well, let's go with your projections for the
first three months and make adjustments after that. Now (sharp purchasing agent skills
showing) what kind of deal can we make to pay for these machines? You are, after all,
asking us to make a pretty substantial commitment.

TIP: Being a sharp salesperson, you've already thought of this and have a 90-day
dating plan (usual terms plus 90 days) in your back pocket already approved by
your boss and the credit department. Bring it out gradually so Mrs. Darden can
feel that she won a concession.

SCRIPT 5.1C. CLOSING THE ORDER WITH A LOW-COST BENEFIT

SALESPERSON: Well, I don't know what I can sell the home office on. What do you think
is fair? (As though the thought that she would want something else hadn't occurred to you.)

MRS. DARDEN: How about 60 days dating?

SALESPERSON: (Whew! I can handle that.) Well, you know how important a customer
we feel you are. I think that if you're ready to sign a blanket purchase order today, I can get
our marketing department and credit department to go along with the dating.

TIP: Save the other 30 days dating that you might have given so you're a hero to the
credit department. Remind them of what you did when you need a favor from
them. Notice that we're also getting our customer in the most natural and comfortable way possible to commit to an order.

MRS. DARDEN: Mr. Davidson, I think we have a deal.

We do, indeed, have a deal. As in Chapter 3, in the section on price increase letters, we
turned a possible negative (price increase) into a positive (a year at the old prices for an
"improved" machine). We parlayed our fairly weak position in the industry into a strength
by reminding our customer of what we've done in the past to make her job easier and really
provide value-added benefits.

Now, this was an "A" customer who deserved personal treatment. For our "B" customers, we'll use the telephone-call approach and we'll notify our "C" customers and prospects by mail:

SCRIPT 5.2. USING THE PRICE INCREASE TO GET A BLANKET PURCHASE ORDER

As in the case with your "A" customers who rated a personal call, you want as many of
your "B" customers as possible to hear from you about the price increase before they get

that letter in the mail. You may want to use a similar technique with your "A" customers whom you can't reach before the letter arrives. No matter what happens during the interview, you don't want to apologize for the increase. The only position you can take is that it's justified and a given, and you want to turn it into an opportunity to get closer to your customer.

OBJECTIVE: Turn the bad news of the price inrease into a sales-increasing opportunity. Every cloud has a silver lining and every problem contains the seeds of its own solution.

SALESPERSON: Good morning Mr. Ehrman. How was your vacation in Boca Raton?
MR. EHRMAN: Well, it rained one afternoon, but I managed to average about 18 holes a day and finally began playing to my handicap.

TIP: You have your Account Profile and Call Sheet (see Chapter 1) in front of you so you were able to pull out this handy tidbit of information.

SALESPERSON: That's great. One of my customers was there earlier this year. He really enjoyed it but talked about how much prices have gone up since he was there two years ago.
MR. EHRMAN: Yes, they have. Prices are going up all over the place.

TIP: Not very subtle, but at least we have Mr. Ehrman thinking our way. Be careful of cutesy traps, however. They can backfire when your customer finds his neck in the noose.

SCRIPT 5.2A. GETTING AGREEMENT ON *VALUE*

SALESPERSON: Mr. Ehrman, I'm calling about our XR4 machine. Our engineering department feels that we have come a long way with customer-responsive improvements since it was first introduced. As an important user (even a "B" customer should be made to feel that he is as important to you as *he* thinks he is) would you agree with their assessment?
MR. EHRMAN: Well, some of the changes haven't come along quite as fast as we would have liked and the retrofit kits don't always work as easily as they should. But, on the whole, I guess I'd say that you've done a good job.

TIP: As we suggested in Chapter 4, if you set the value standards first, you'll have an easier time dealing with price objections.

SALESPERSON: You know that despite these improvements, we haven't raised our prices in almost two years . . .
MR. EHRMAN: (interrupting) Uh oh. I think I hear something coming up that I'm not going to like.

SCRIPT 5.2B. BREAKING THE PRICE INCREASE NEWS

SALESPERSON: You're too sharp for me. I confess. *One* of the reasons I called is to be sure that you would hear about the price increase directly from me before you got a letter.
MR. EHRMAN: (getting a bit upset) You know, you already have the most expensive machine on the market for its features. And now you're *raising* prices?

TIP: He didn't even hear your point about "*one* of the reasons" so he obviously has something else on his mind. This would be a good time to keep quiet. This question he raised is a rhetorical one, so let's see if he'll keep talking and give you a clue to the specific reason he got so upset so quickly. You will then know which way to go with the rest of your conversation.

MR. EHRMAN: Hello. Are you there?
SALESPERSON: Yes, I was waiting for you to finish.
MR. EHRMAN: Well, what I just finished was our office machines capital budget for the rest of the year. A price increase is going to throw it out of whack *if* we continue with your machines.

TIP: Good. Now we know which way to go, but let's let it be Mr. Ehrman's idea. Remember to ask questions and get as much information as you can. Don't provide answers until you know what the *real* questions are.

SALESPERSON: (sympathy, empathy) I can see where that would cause you some problems. Let's see if we can't find a solution. You could always, of course, go to a competitor . . .
MR. EHRMAN: What? And throw away all the training time we've invested with your machines?

TIP: Nice move. The competitor question *had* to come up sometime. Isn't it nice that *he* is telling *us* why this isn't such a good idea?

SCRIPT 5.2C. DEALING WITH THE CUSTOMER'S PRICE INCREASE PROBLEMS

SALESPERSON: You're right. That wouldn't be smart *or* fair. Let's see if we can't find some other solution. Someone once told me that every problem has the seeds of its own solution. I think you can see that the improvements *have* cost us money and that, sooner or later, we would have to find a way to pay for them. Besides not raising prices, what would be the *ideal* solution for you?
MR. EHRMAN: (now a little calmer) Well, I've given the board the budget. If I go back with different figures it will wave a red flag and they'll tell me to go out for more quotes. They won't listen to the retraining and other problems.
SALESPOSER: I can see your situation. Suppose I could work a deal with the factory where they would take a blanket purchase order for your needs from now until the end of the year at the old price? Can you estimate your needs that closely?
MR. EHRMAN: I already have for the budget.

TIP: Isn't that neat? "Allowing" a blanket purchase order for a specific quantity of machines and winding up looking like we are doing our customer a big favor.

SCRIPT 5.2D. TURNING THE PRICE INCREASE INTO A BLANKET ORDER

SALESPERSON: Hmmm. It looks like that would be the best solution for you and I certainly agree that it would be a fair one. Let me check with our people and see if I can work it out. I'll need to tell them how many machines we're talking about.

TIP: Mr. Ehrman has always been very careful to keep his purchase plans to himself to keep his options open. Now we have a good reason to have him share this information with us.

MR. EHRMAN: We were planning on 50, but (hastily) that was a minimum figure. Maybe we should be looking at 60. We can always use them the first month or two of next year.

TIP: Now, wasn't that neat? Not only did we slide in the blanket purchase order, but we got the quantity increased by 20 percent because Mr. Ehrman is going to "take advantage" of us. Remember that we already anticipated the need for covering orders and built the cost into the price increase amount and timing.

SALESPERSON: Okay. I'll check with our people and get back to you either this afternoon or tomorrow morning.

TIP: You didn't have to check with your people. You already had the deal approved *and* with dating but without the extra bonuses of a blanket purchase order and an increase in quantity. "Checking," however, makes it clear that this is a special concession to Mr. Ehrman.

MR. EHRMAN: Try to make it this afternoon. I have to be out of town tomorrow.

TIP: Nice. A customer is asking us to get back as quickly as possible so he can place an order.

We succeeded in this case mostly because we *listened*. As it turned out, embarrassment and not the price increase was the real issue. If we had rushed right into a justification, or, worse, an apology for the increase, we might never have found the real reason and might not have that gratifying blanket purchase order. Find out the questions before providing answers.

It's true that the price increase interview might not have gone that easily. Here are some additional script lines that might be useful:

SCRIPT 5.2E.

SALESPERSON: (only if you already know the answer) Mr. Ehrman, hasn't your company had to raise its prices in the past two years?

SCRIPT 5.2F.

SALESPERSON: You should continue with us because we're giving you a $1,000 machine for $800.
MR. EHRMAN: How's that?
SALESPERSON: With *our* machine you get $800 worth of machine and $200 worth of support and insurance that we'll be there to solve any problems that come up.

One final note: You may not always get through to your customer before he gets the letter. Be sure, on your first call, to leave word with a responsible person that there is something important that you want to talk with the customer about. This way the customer may put two and two together when he gets the letter and you will at least get points for trying to have the discussion before the letter arrived.

SCRIPT 5.3. HANDLING THE REALLY "TOUGH" PRICE INCREASE CALL

In the above two examples, we assumed the luxury of ample time for customers to cover. That is, to make plans to adjust their operations to the extent necessary. We also assumed that your management realizes the necessity for this kind of flexibility and will have built it into the price increase planning process. Sometimes this isn't true and sometimes it isn't possible. Your division may have just been taken over by someone who doesn't understand your market and wants immediate profit improvement, no matter what the cost in long-term relationships. You may be in a volatile market where *your* costs change too frequently for you to give your customers adequate notice. This is not ideal, but, if it were an ideal world, the gypsy moths would come in the fall and eat the leaves on the ground. Let's look at some ways to handle the tough increase notification:

SALESPERSON: Good morning. Mr. Glaser. Did you get those extra catalog sheets you asked for?

MR. GLASER: Yep. They're already in our people's hands. What can I do for you? We placed our order early last week.

SALESPERSON: I know and thank you. I got the shipping notice this morning. Incidentally, I notice our business with you is up 20 percent over last year and I want you to know I appreciate that.

MR. GLASER: You didn't call just to tell me that.

SALESPERSON: No, I didn't. Do you want the long story or the short story of why I called?

> TIP: Admittedly, we're stretching to get back into our questioning mode, but it's a start.

MR. GLASER: Make it short, I have about a foot of paper work on my desk.

SALESPERSON: Okay, May I ask you a quick question first? (Don't wait for an answer.) What would you say is the number-one reason you buy from us?

MR. GLASER: I don't have time for surveys.

SALESPERSON: I understand. How about a quick answer in that case?

MR. GLASER: Service. And *you're* usually right on the job when we have a problem. Why?

SCRIPT 5.3A. ESTABLISHING VALUE

SALESPERSON: Is this worth something to you?

MR. GLASER: What's this all about?

SALESPERSON: I guess it's about *value*, or, more specifically, about value-added. You see, those extra things that we do to try to make your job easier cost us and those costs have been going up even faster as our material and labor costs have.

> TIP: We're trying to steer the conversation away from price alone and towards *value*. It's easy to compare our prices with our competitor's but more difficult to compare value-added components.

MR. GLASER: I think I'm beginning to get the point of this conversation.

SCRIPT 5.3B. BREAKING THE PRICE INCREASE NEWS

SALESPERSON: I think you have. The short story is that our prices are being increased an average of 7 percent effective yesterday.

MR. GLASER: *What*? If I had known that I'd have doubled up on my last order.

SALESPERSON: I suppose our company knew that and figured that we just couldn't afford it if we were to keep offering those extra value-added benefits. Have you ever figured out what that's worth to you?

TIP: Again, the question to keep in control.

MR. GLASER: That's not going to mean very much if you force us to go somewhere else so *we* can stay competitive in *our* market.

SCRIPT 5.3C. USING THE "ARE YOU THE CHEAPEST?" PLOY

SALESPERSON: About how many competitors would you say you have in your market?

MR. GLASER: Oh, I don't know—eight or ten maybe.

SALESPERSON: Are you the cheapest?

MR. GLASER: Of course not. We use your stuff, don't we?

SALESPERSON: (ignoring this little dig) As I understand it, your products are generally the most expensive. May I ask, then, what the secret is of your staying in business?

MR. GLASER: We have a better product, our salespeople do more for their customers than our competitors do, and our order turnaround time is the best.

SALESPERSON: And, it costs money to do this but because you turn out a better value package, you're able to get a higher price and still benefit the customers you're serving. Is this a fair explanation of why you're successful?

TIP: Most companies can name eight or ten competitors, and only one can be the cheapest so this strategy should work 80 to 90 percent of the time.

MR. GLASER: I'd say that you have a pretty good understanding of what makes us tick.

SALESPERSON: And it's important to maintain this high quality, high service level isn't it?

MR. GLASER: Okay. Enough. You've made your point. I just wish you'd given us more notice.

SALESPERSON: (Silence. This is another time when the odds are ten to one that you'll say the wrong thing. Let Mr. Glaser have the ball—there is only one way he can run with it unless he wants further discussion. If he does, better that you know *his* direction and take your clue from this.)

MR. GLASER: When can you come over to explain the increase to our people and show them how to adjust their price schedules?

SALESPERSON: How about next Tuesday at eight?

Lets review some of the several things we did to bring this tough situation around:

Summary—Handling a Tough Price Increase Situation

1. We did not apologize for the increase. We started out with the position that it was justified

and stuck with that position even though we, ourselves, were disheartened by the lack of notice.

2. We controlled the situation by asking questions that would let us know where Mr. Glaser was and let him appear to have the ball instead of rushing into a (possibly off-base) justification pitch.

3. We talked *value* and compared (or, rather, had Mr. Glaser compare) our situation to his in order to drive the point home.

LETTER 5.1. THE PRICE INCREASE NOTIFICATION LETTER

This is the letter that will be sent to *all* customers, including those "A" and "B" customers you talked with in person or on the phone. It can also be used for inactive customers and prospects since we are going to stress the buying opportunity over the price increase.

OBJECTIVE: Announce the price increase to all customers and prospects and turn the increase into a sales opportunity at a time of the year when the factory needs work.

Dear (Customer or Prospect):

WOULD YOU LIKE A 28 PERCENT TO 42 PERCENT RETURN ON YOUR INVESTMENT?

You may find this an unnecessary question. Who wouldn't want a return like this?

Let me explain: As you know, we've made dozens of product improvements in the past two years on our XT4 machine. These have been costly, but we haven't raised prices in this entire two-year period.

In order to continue making improvements, producing a quality product, and providing the kind of service you've told us you appreciate, prices will be increased approximately 7 percent, effective June 1st.

Now, here's the ROI (Return on Investment) opportunity: I've gotten special permission from the president to extend the old prices for up to 3 months' worth of purchases at your current volume level!

If you bought 2 month's worth of products, you would get the equivalent of a 42 percent return (12 months ÷ 2 months = 6 × 7 percent = 42 percent). If you bought 3 months' worth, your return would be 28 percent (12 ÷ 3 = 4 × 7 percent = 28%) but the dollar amount of your savings would be higher.

You have until June 1st to place your order. I expect to be talking with you before then, but please call if you have any questions or would like to work out your order sooner.

P. S.: The new 4TI retrofit kits will be available by the end of the month and we'll start shipping back-orders right away.

TIP: We've covered all the bases succinctly and turned the increase into a buying opportunity for our customers and a sales opportunity for us. At the same time, we've opened the door to go back to our inactive customers and prospects with a reason to talk with them. We closed with good news in the P. S., the most-read part of any sales or business letter.

Okay—admittedly, this one was fairly easy since we had a clear-cut business opportunity to present. But, as we've stressed throughout this book, you can *create* opportunities if they don't exist naturally. Consider, or try to talk your management into considering, the following for your next price increase:

FIVE PRICE INCREASE TACTICS THAT WILL BOOST SALES

1. Anticipate the need for a price increase at least 3 or 4 months ahead of time so you'll have time to plan your strategy properly.

2. Determine the time of year when you most need a big influx of orders—your slowest months—and make the increase effective (depending on your manufacturing lead times) on a date that will coincide with the desired receipt of orders.

3. Provide enough notice of the increase so there will be plenty of time for covering orders. Your customers will appreciate the opportunity and forget most of the negative implications of the increase.

4. Add a point or two to the percent increase to allow for the covering with no sacrifice of profit and make this a sales strategy rather than trying to sneak by apologetically with the increase, hoping to get more orders at the new prices.

5. Consider dating or some other way of providing extra time to pay for the merchandise purchased and build the cost of this into the increase.

Now let's look at a tougher letter to write—the situation where, for any number of reasons (including top management being unaware of the importance of the above five points), there is no notice or covering possibility.

LETTER 5.2. SMOOTHING OVER THE NO-NOTICE PRICE INCREASE

This letter will be sent to *all* customers, including those "A" and "B" customers you talked with in person or on the phone. Because the timing of the notification may be short, it's possible that this will be the first notification many of your "B" customers and, because of their unavailability, some of your "A" customers will receive, so we want to take more care to sell the increase.

OBJECTIVE: Announce the price increase to all customers, soften the blow of a no-notice increase, and turn the increase into a positive customer relations effort if not a sales opportunity.

Dear (Customer or Prospect):

Enclosed are new terms and price sheets, effective August 1st. (The letter is dated August 1st.) There are two significant changes:

1. Prices for the basic models have been increased about 6 percent and components, peripherals, and retrofit kits about 8 percent.

2. The $1,000 minimum order requirement no longer exists, meaning that you no longer have to hold orders for components and peripherals until you have a machine order.

As you know, we've made dozens of improvements in the past two years in our XT4 series product line and in our training and other backup support. These have been costly, but we haven't raised our prices to you in this entire 2 year period.

As you may also be aware, the recent and sudden drop in the dollar's rate of exchange has caused some of the high-quality component parts used in the machines to just as suddenly become significantly more expensive.

We could have taken the route that some of our competitors have taken and substituted lower cost (and lower quality) components. We could have cut back on some of the training and other services we provide. Our recent market research survey, however, showed that you listed consistent product quality, training, and other backup support as the most important reasons you prefer our machines.

We also listened to you when you told us the problems you have when you find you need a part or component the day after you just placed a machine order and don't want to put together another $1,000 order. Waiving the $1,000 minimum order requirement makes order processing more expensive, but we want to maintain your high service and quality level.

We look forward to continuing to provide to you the kind of total *value package* you've told us you want.

P.S.: Also enclosed is a postpaid card you can return to order the new salesperson pocket guide outlining the prospect survey steps.

SEVEN WAYS TO IMPROVE CUSTOMER RELATIONS DESPITE A PRICE INCREASE

Let's review some of the things we did in this letter to accomplish our customer relations objectives:

1. We didn't apologize for the increase. We didn't "regret" the necessity of it. We didn't empathize with the potential problems this might cause our customers. This can be done in person, fitting our responses to the particular situation or complaint raised by the customer and the way he does it.

2. We combined the notice of the increase with a sure crowd-pleaser—the waiving of the $1,000 minimum order. It's important always to provide some good news, however insignificant, with the bad.

3. We reminded our customers of all the good things we have done and continue to do for them. We appealed to a total *value package* and *quality* concept by mentioning the lower cost and quality alternative.

4. In a way, we made the price increase *their* idea since we referred to the market research survey as the reason for going the price increase route instead of cutting back on quality or services. ("If you want it, you have to pay for it. There ain't no free lunch.")

5. We put some other good news and yet another *value-added* benefit in the P.S. This is important. Survey after survey have shown that people look at whom the letter is addressed to, whom it came from, and the P.S.—in that order. Always save some good ammunition for the P.S.

6. Our "I/you" count is more than acceptable. You remember that this is an index of the number of times we use "I," "we," and "our" versus the number of times we use "you," "your," and "yours." The "you's" should always outnumber the "I's," and the greater the margin the better. (You could say that this is one case where the "I's" *don't* have it.)

7. Finally, we didn't mention any possibility of making exceptions in the letter. Actually, we added one percentage point to the planned price increase to allow for unusual situations which will be looked at on a case-by-case basis. We won't accept any more orders at the old prices, but we have some other, equally valuable benefits in our back pocket that we can offer in the case of real hardship—sample or demonstration models, extra training support, handling a service problem that rightly belongs to the customer, cooperative advertising allowances, etc.

SCRIPT 5.4. GETTING INACTIVE CUSTOMERS ACTIVE WITH A PRICE INCREASE

So far, we've been able to turn this price increase bad news into sales-boosting opportunities, or at least customer relations improvement efforts for current customers. If it works for current customers, it should be yet another tool to get those former and inactive customers back in the fold.

OBJECTIVE: Use the price increase and the covering (place an order at the old prices) opportunities we've wisely built into the increase program to reactivate inactive customers. Find out why inactive customers are inactive.

SALESPERSON: Good morning Ms. Bogue. This is Stuart Davidson from Cardinal Business Services.

TIP: Go on a little from here to give Mr. Bogue a change to remember you and avoid any possible embarrassment on her part.

SALESPERSON: It's been awhile since we've talked, 2 years in fact. That was just after we'd completed the training of four of your people on our XT4 machines.
MS. BOGUE: Oh, yes. As I recall, that conversation was about the problem we were having with the machines, and your company refused to replace them but gave us those funny retro-fit kits instead.

TIP: You knew that from your Account Profile and Call Sheets which you consulted before making the telephone call or visit and have worked out what your *tentative* reply will be. (We'll explain "tentative" and the reasons below.)

SALESPERSON: Yes. I remember that clearly. May I ask you a question? (Don't wait for an answer.) Have you been getting our technical update bulletins?
MS. BOGUE: Yes. I pass them on to the word-processing center manager.

TIP: No help here, but we're on the right track by starting with a customer-oriented question. The unenlightened salesperson (one who has not yet read this book) would plunge right into a pitch about how the problems Ms. Bogue felt she had previously have been solved, or, worse, get defensive about the situation and start explaining. We're going to be smarter.

SALESPERSON: And?

TIP: We don't yet know the lay of the land. That is, Ms. Bogue may know exactly what the bulletins have contained and that they have solved any problems that may have existed or she may be unaware of what is going on. Let's find out before we go further.

MS. BOGUE: And? (Salesperson pauses to outwait Ms. Bogue.) Well, I'm not sure what she does with them. (Salesperson pauses again.) I guess they're helpful. (Keep waiting.) I have to admit that we have fewer complaints these days about your machines than the competitor's that we installed a few months ago.

TIP: Isn't it amazing how much you can learn by keeping your mouth shut? It would be tempting to jump in with an "I told you so," but let's hold back and make sure we're on firm ground.

SCRIPT 5.4A. RE-ESTABLISHING THE RELATIONSHIP

SALESPERSON: Tracy (we were on a first-name basis before), I'm sure you remember our discussing Cardinal's commitment to after-sales backup service. It's very important to us and it would be important to both of us, I think, if we knew exactly what is going on with the machines and how satisfied your word-processing center manager is with them.

TIP: Notice the "we." Ms. Bogue is now our partner and not our adversary.

MS. BOGUE: Well, I guess it would be. You know, I'm so busy putting out fires I don't have time to go looking for problems when so many find me.
SALESPERSON: I understand. (Always a great line to use in a lot of situations.) I wonder if we (notice the partnership again) could do this: Why don't you call the WP manager and see just what is going on. I know you're busy, but I can help you do an even better job if we know exactly what the situation is.
MS. BOGUE: What will that accomplish?
SALESPERSON: It will show that you're doing a good follow-up job and are concerned about your departments. If you find a problem, I want to help you fix it.

TIP: We've obviously taken a detour, but a sensible and logical one. This is what we meant by "tentative" above. There's no sense in using the price increase notification to boost sales if there is an existing problem. If everything is great and Ms. Bogue has that brought to her attention, we're in much better shape to pursue our original line than we would be otherwise. Remember that we want to find out why someone isn't buying before we try to sell.

MS. BOGUE: Why weren't you interested before?

TIP: Here's a trap if there ever was one. We have to defend our company's position and can't cop out with an "I can't help company policy—it was them that did it, not me'' approach, but we can't afford to get into an argument. So, as usual when we're stuck, we go to a question.

SCRIPT 5.4B. DEALING WITH OLD PROBLEMS

SALESPERSON: It's always difficult to know exactly what is the right thing to do in this kind of situation. I'm not sure how we would handle it today. (A fairly innocuous comment.) Looking back on it, what do you feel now would have been the fair thing to do—besides (subtle reminder) the retro-fit kits, the additional training, and the other support?

TIP: We are, of course, using the old "throw the hot potato back" ploy.

MS. BOGUE: (she doesn't want to handle it either now that it's in her hands) Well, I'd have to think about it. Anyway, that's in the past and I have enough of today's problems to deal with without digging into what happened then.
SALESPERSON: I agree. Let's see what *we* can do to look at today. First, we need to know how the word-processing center people feel about the machines today. Could you find out from the manager?

TIP: Now we're back on the subject with an agreement, a partnership proposal, and a request put in the form of another question.

MS. BOGUE: Well, okay. I'm still not sure what good it will do, but at least the manager will know that I'm interested in her problems.
SALESPERSON: Good. Do you think you could do it this morning? That way, we can discuss it this afternoon and figure out the best route to take.

TIP: Again, the partnership idea which gives us a good reason to be pushy—we're concerned about solving *our* (Ms. Bogue's and ours) problem. We have also paved the way for a commitment to another phone call that should be more welcome than this one.

MS. BOGUE: I'll call as soon as we hang up and get it out of the way. Don't call back until after 3:00.
SALESPERSON: Fine. I have a meeting at 3:00. Why don't I plan on calling you at 4:00?

What more could we want?

1. We've turned an adversary into a "partner" by refusing to get defensive, by asking questions, and by appealing to her self-interest. We played the "We're on the same team" game effectively.

2. We've gotten some information on what is happening in the company and the word-processing center—they have bought competitive machines that they're not completely happy with. This news doesn't exactly bring tears to our eyes.

3. We've shown some unusual post-sale interest even if it *is* some time later. Ms. Bogue doesn't know why we called since we were smart enough to ask questions instead of plunging into a pitch.

4. Ms. Bogue will be expecting if not looking forward to our phone call later today. If the news is good, she should be very receptive as long as we stay away from "I told you so." If it's not so good, we still have a sales opportunity because we have a problem that we can work on remedying. (See Chapter 9, Using Customer Complaints as an Opportunity.)

This detour that we took means that we will have to spend more time with this inactive customer, but we can postpone our pitch until later in order to enjoy a more favorable environment. Better two effective calls on one prospect than five calls that might not be as effective. Selling may be a "numbers game," but it's a *quality* numbers game.

Now let's pick up the conversation with Ms. Bogue this afternoon at 4:00 with the next script.

SCRIPT 5.5 FOLLOWING THROUGH WITH AN INACTIVE CUSTOMER (NONDETOURED)

SALESPERSON: Hi, Tracy. Stu Davidson. I'm calling to learn what our friends in word processing think about the XT4 machines today.

MS. BOGUE: Hi, Stu. Thanks for calling back right on time. I have to leave early today. Well, they're still complaining about word-processing machines in general. I think some of those people would be happier if the *electric typewriter* hadn't been invented.

SALESPERSON: Well, I know I don't have to sell *you* on the cost-effectiveness of this kind of equipment. You've always been on the lookout for all kinds of ways to save your company as much money as possible even if it meant investing some dough up front.

> TIP: As long as we're so friendly, we might as well lay it on a little. I don't ever remember *anyone* ever complaining sincerely about a little flattery. And, we've paved the way for a pitch on additional machines as an "investment."

SALESPERSON: Anyway, given the inevitability of the use of word-processing equipment, what's the verdict?

MS. BOGUE: This should make your day. They voted that your machines are "less worse."

SALESPERSON: What does that mean?

> TIP: We *know* what it means, but let's pull as much information out of Ms. Bogue as we can before deciding on our approach.

MS. BOGUE: Well, they don't really like *any* of the machines, although they're getting used to them, but said that if they *had* to have them they would rather have yours than your competitor's. The manager thinks that your technical bulletins are very helpful.

SCRIPT 5.5A. TRIAL CLOSE FOR NEW BUSINESS

SALESPERSON: Well, that's good news. How soon will you be ready to talk about our super, new, improved model that is even easier to use?

> TIP: Sometimes a direct approach, no matter how lightly expressed, can be effective. After all, this *is* an *inactive* customer.

MS. BOGUE: You never stop, do you? Well, here's a surprise, Mr. Davidson: We do need to add three more machines in the next 3 months and we're going to give you a second chance.

SALESPERSON: That's great—*and* proves once again how smart and professional you are.

MS. BOGUE: Are you Irish?

SALESPERSON: No. English. (innocently) Why?

MS. BOGUE: Never mind. We'd like to set up a meeting with our buying committee and the WP manager sometime around the end of next month for you to come in and do your thing and then put a quote together.

SALESPERSON: That sounds fine. I think you'll be surprised and pleased at all the improvements we've made in the machines—a lot of very expensive ones.

> TIP: We're starting to set the *value* stage now so the price increase coming up will be perceived in as positive a way as possible.

SALESPERSON: How would you like to save even more money on the machines?

> TIP: Now that we've established *value*, we'll turn the price increase that would ordinarily be bad news that we might be tempted to defend into the good news of a *savings* opportunity.

MS. BOGUE: I said that we would give you a chance, not buy any machines. Anyway, what's the catch?

SCRIPT 5.5B. CLOSING FOR A SELLING APPOINTMENT *NOW*

SALESPERSON: Well, those improvements we've made in the last two years *have* cost a lot of money. So far we've been able to hold prices, but there *will* be an increase next month. If I came in later *this* week, we might be able to wrap up a commitment at the old prices before the price increase is effective.

MS. BOGUE: But we won't have space. And, we won't have the people hired. I don't want to put the machines in storage after I've paid for them.

> TIP: Because of the effective and positive way we positioned the price increase, it got no attention at all and became a nonevent.

SALESPERSON: No problem. I'm pretty sure we can work something out that will get you the machines at the old prices *and* on your terms.

> TIP: Now, *we* know very well that we can agree to deferred payment terms and deferred delivery for a reasonable period, but there's no point in giving it away now. We'll save it for a later negotiating point *after* we've found out what it will take to close the sale. Also, buyers love to hear the phrase, "No problem."

MS. BOGUE: You sound like a different company from the one I bought those first machines from.

SALESPERSON: We're the same company with the same high standards, but I think we have learned a great deal. We've improved our service, training, and backup support as much as we've improved the machines. Would next Tuesday afternoon or next Wednesday morning work best for you and your people to get together?

Our calls on inactive customers for any reason will not always work out this fortuitously, but this is the objective. Unless you are taking time away from more important calls, you may pave the way for an order or learn something new about your market environment. The least that will happen is that you will have logged in one more contact on your Account

Profile and Call Sheet and paved the way to future calls and sales. Now we'll look at a letter that can be sent to those inactive customers whose potential indicates that they are not worth a phone call.

LETTER 5.3. REACTIVATING INACTIVE CUSTOMERS WITH A PRICE INCREASE NOTIFICATION

Since we have set our priorities well and are using our time properly, there will be some inactive accounts that will not be worth a phone call. These are in the ''C'' and ''D'' sections of our prospect file. (To learn how to properly stratify customers, inactive customers, and prospects, you might check out Howard Bishop's *Master Guide to Field Sales Management Tactics and Techniques* published by Prentice Hall in 1987.)

> OBJECTIVE: Announce the price increase to inactive customers, try to get a ''beat the increase'' order, provide information about improvements in the machines, and provide a vehicle for the customer to tell us anything he wants to.

DEAR CUSTOMER:

It has been a while since we've been in touch, but I wanted to alert you to an opportunity you may want to take advantage of.

In the past two years we've made dozens of improvements in our model XT4 machine and have similarly upgraded our training programs and other backup support. This has cost our customers nothing since the increased popularity of the machine and the increased sales have enabled us to absorb the costs.

Effective July 1st, however, prices will be increased approximately 7 percent. (The letter is dated May 1st.) Because you are a preferred customer, we're getting this notice to you in plenty of time for you to place orders for additional machines at the *old price*.

The XT4 machine you bought some time ago was an excellent product—at the time. If you haven't seen the new enhanced XT4T, you'll be amazed at how much we've added to the original features in just two years.

If you are considering any kind of expansion in your word-processing areas, it would be well worthwhile to check out this machine. Just check off the box on the enclosed postpaid card or call me at (215)-555-7218 and we'll arrange for a no-obligation demonstration.

P.S.: Use the space on the enclosed card to tell us how you feel about the machines you bought and we'll send you a free keyboard template identifying the special function keys and their uses.

Let's look at some of the things we did with this letter to accomplish the objectives we spelled out.

> TIP: It's important to mentally, if not in writing, spell out your objectives before beginning to write and then check your final letter against the objectives.

SEVEN STEPS TO EFFECTIVE WRITING

All writing (including this book) consists of the following seven steps:

1. Think
2. Plan
3. Organize
4. Write
5. Revise
6. Revise
7. Revise

Anyway, here's what we find we did after completing step 7:

NO-NOTICE PRICE INCREASE LETTER REVIEW

1. We stressed a positive buying "opportunity" instead of the negative of a price increase.
2. We sold our total value package—improvements in the machine and our total *value package*.
3. We gave our "preferred" customers (not our *inactive* customers) the opportunity to buy at the old prices. Don't *you* get a little more interested when your favorite or not-so-favored department store sends you a "preferred customer sale" notice?
4. We set up the opportunity to demonstrate and sell additional machines by stressing "new" and "improved" (enhanced). These words take a back seat only to "free" in terms of capturing a prospect's attention.
5. Finally we saved a goodie for the P.S., which may also give us some of the reasons our inactive customers are inactive and other information.

SCRIPT 5.6. HANDLING THE "I'M GOING TO A COMPETITOR" RESPONSE

No matter how clever and skillful we are in turning a price inrease into a sales-boosting opportunity, there are bound to be *some* disenchanted customers. Their usual response will be to threaten to or actually "go shopping." We're better off with those who voice their threats since we then know what we're dealing with. This is why we should visit or phone our important ("A" and "B") customers. Unless they actually do return a reply card or call us, we won't know their reaction with a letter. Here's a script that will work, with some modification, for telephone calls or personal visits:

OBJECTIVE: As before, turn the bad news of the price increase into a sales-boosting opportunity. Get the customer's immediate reaction to the price increase so we know what avenue to pursue. Handle the "I'm going to a competitor" reaction if this happens.

SALESPERSON: Good morning, Mr. Knight. Stu Davidson from Cardinal Business Services. I want to talk with you about an opportunity.

TIP: Mr. Knight has told us in the past (as we remember from the note on the Account Profile and Call Sheet entry) that he doesn't like discussing the weather, his health, or last night's game with salespeople, so we plunge right in (or at least make it look like that's what we are doing).

MR. KNIGHT: When someone tells me about an opportunity I've learned to grab hold of my wallet.

SALESPERSON: Good point. I know what you mean—and if it weren't for the fact that all of the opportunities *we've* worked on together have turned out to be just that, I wouldn't blame you for reaching for your wallet. Let me ask you a question. (Go right on with a pause long enough for Mr. Knight to grunt "okay" but not long enough for him to say anything else.)

TIP: In one breath we've agreed with Mr. Knight's little tidbit of wisdom, made him a *partner*, and reminded him of past favorable experiences with us.

SCRIPT 5.6A. ESTABLISHING VALUE

SALESPERSON: Why *were* our machines such a good opportunity for you and your company?

MR. KNIGHT: You want *me* to tell *you* that?

SALESPERSON: Yes. (Pause and remember the Miranda Decision: Anything else you say here could and will be used against you.)

MR. KNIGHT: Well, the machines work right, the price wasn't too bad, and you've always been there when we had a problem or needed some information. Now will you get on with this so-called opportunity?

TIP: Mr. Knight is not exactly eating out of our hand, but we at least have agreement that our machines do, indeed, provide *value*.

SALESPERSON: As you know, we've made dozens of improvements in the machines over the past two years and we've even further improved our training. With the retro-fit kits, you've been able to take advantage of most of these improvements and we've used our new training programs for your new people. Would you agree that the machines you have now and your people's ability to use them are even better than when you bought them?

MR. KNIGHT: Yeah, I'd buy that. What's the point?

TIP: It would be very tempting to jump in here and answer the question with "The point is . . ." If we did, Mr. Knight would be in control and we'd be following *his* script. Let's see if we can get back the control over this interview.

SALESPERSON: Cost . . . and value.

MR. KNIGHT: What does that mean?

TIP: Mr. Knight has also learned to control interviews by asking questions. He got this out of a book called "Purchasing Scripts That Work" (fictional title). At this point we had better answer.

SALESPERSON: These improvements have cost us money and provided value to you. Aren't the machines working even more effectively than when they were installed?

MR. KNIGHT: You didn't call for an endorsement or recommendation letter. I've already given you that. What's the point?

TIP: He *is* tough. It looks like we had better play his game—for awhile. We'll get back into our "control through questions" mode later.

SALESPERSON: After two years of absorbing the extra costs involved in this total *value package* you mentioned we're going to be raising prices.
MR. KNIGHT: *What*? Your machines are already the highest priced in the market. I can buy machines from Priestly for 20 percent less than yours.
SALESPERSON: (Pause. It can't hurt.)
MR. KNIGHT: (He, too, pauses having learned the value of this from *his* book. Better continue to play his game.)

SCRIPT 5.6B. RAISING DOUBT ABOUT A COMPETITOR'S PRODUCT

SALESPERSON: Why do you think they can afford to sell their brand of machine for less than ours?
MR. KNIGHT: Probably because they're more efficient.
SALESPERSON: Do you mean more efficient in terms of not providing the quality and support we do?

TIP: You've made the point, but in the form of a question that is tough for Mr. Knight to dodge and made a stab at getting back control.

MR. KNIGHT: No. I mean more efficient in terms of manufacturing and distribution of their machines.
SALESPERSON: Do you remember the last time we discussed your needs, and, at your request, I showed you a point-by-point checklist demonstrating just why our machines were of higher quality?
MR. KNIGHT: Yes, I remember. It was very cleverly put together to maximize your advantages.
SALESPERSON: Do you have a copy of that handy?

TIP: Again, we're refusing to be drawn into a defensive argument but may be able to accomplish the same thing in a syllogistic way.

MR. KNIGHT: No.
SALESPERSON: I do and I'm looking at a line on the bottom that you may find interesting. It says "Prepared by AWN Independent Testing Laboratory." Do you recall that it was an independent study?

TIP: Here's that *third-party referral* bit again. You may not always have an independent testing laboratory report, but there is *always* some sort of third-party endorsement you can call to your aid.

MR. KNIGHT: Okay. I remember. Maybe your machines are better, but there's only so much we can pay for them to get the job done.

SCRIPT 5.6C. PROVING THAT PRICE ISN'T ALWAYS PRIMARY

SALESPERSON: Mr. Knight, what kind of car do you drive?
MR. KNIGHT: You know what I drive.
SALESPERSON: Right. And it's not a black stick shift without radio or air conditioning is

it? You paid a lot for the extra features because they meant *value* to you. Isn't it like that with word-processing machines?

MR. KNIGHT: Cars are different.

SALESPERSON: Sure they are. But, you and I both know how conscientious you are about getting the best *value* for your company in everything you buy.

> TIP: Again, flattery never hurts, even with a "Mr. Knight." In fact, it's surprising how effective it is where you would least expect it to be.

MR. KNIGHT: Priestly provides value too.

SCRIPT 5.6D. UNCOVERING THE *REAL* OBJECTION

SALESPERSON: Right. And that's why they deserve business from companies that aren't interested in *the best* value package as you are. Mr. Knight, what is your *real* objection to a 7 percent price increase?

> TIP: Ordinarily, we might hold this question as a final resort for fear of offending on the basis that we can only lose a customer or order once. In Mr. Knight's case, however, he responds well to this kind of direct approach.

MR. KNIGHT: The buying committee isn't going to like it. I went out on a limb recommending your machines when young Jacobs was pushing for Priestly's. Now he has another arrow in his quiver to point at me.

> TIP: Okay. Ask a direct question and you sometimes get an honest and direct answer. Now we know what the real reason is and how to proceed. But, let's go slowly so the final answer is not ours, but Mr. Knight's.

SALESPERSON: Suppose we could make you look like a hero to the buying committee?

MR. KNIGHT: Just how would you do that?

SALESPERSON: I'm not sure. On the one hand we *have* to pass our costs along in the form of a price increase. On the other hand, I can see your point and would like to find a way out of this dilemma. Do you know what your usage will be in the next say, 3 months?

MR. KNIGHT: Well, I could come up with a fair estimate. What did you have in mind?

SCRIPT 5.6E. TURNING THE OBJECTION INTO A BLANKET ORDER

SALESPERSON: I know I'm taking a chance here because I might not be able to sell it, but what about a blanket purchase order for your next 3 months' requirements at the old prices?

> TIP: Obviously, you've gotten some indication that you can make some sort of deal, but we don't want to give everything away in the opening salvo.

MR. KNIGHT: Well, it's May 10th and your new prices aren't effective until August 1st. Three months really doesn't give me very much. (Pause.)

SALESPERSON: (pausing while ostensibly thinking it over) Yes, I can see your point. Okay. Suppose I try to sell 3 months from August 1st? Can you get me a list of your requirements in the next couple of weeks?

MR. KNIGHT: How about 6 months' requirements?

SALESPERSON: Well, I could *try* to sell it, but I doubt they'd buy it. What else is important to you?

TIP: We can't go along with *all* Mr. Knight's requests even if we have the authority to do it. If we give him everything he asks for, he'll think he should have asked for more. If we hold something back, he'll know he made the best deal he could. At the same time, we want to round out the package with some goodies that won't cost us as much.

MR. KNIGHT: Well, I never did like the way you push so hard on 30-day terms. I can keep other suppliers waiting 60 days before I even get a phone call.

SALESPERSON: Well, you know that our training programs and support are the best in the industry and they cost us, so we have to get our money. Suppose, on this one deal only, I could work out an extra 30 days to pay for the machines you take each month under this blanket deal? You're doing us a favor by letting us forecast production so I think I could sell this.

TIP: A concession with a logical, self-serving reason is always more credible than a concession alone.

MR. KNIGHT: It sounds like we have a deal *if* you can sell this to your people.

We do, indeed, have a deal because everything we grudgingly agreed to is within the parameters of the program our management was smart enough to put together. *And*, it was Mr. Knight's idea. By asking questions and keeping quiet as long as we could, we found the *real* reason for his reaction to the increase. By being patient and not launching into a defense we worked on a *same team* basis as *partners* and made an adversary out of Jacobs and the buying committee instead of each other. Finally, we came up with a plan that gives us what we want and lets Mr. Knight feel good and be a hero to the buying committee.

IN CLOSING

Price increase notifications are never an easy nor pleasant chore to deal with. As we have seen, however, they *can* be turned into sales-boosting opportunities with the proper planning. The most important elements of the planning effort for management are:

1. To the extent possible, build in enough notice and enough of an increase to provide covering (letting your customers place orders at the old prices) and to provide for special situations where the old prices should be made available to customers.

2. Plan the increase for a slow time of year so the influx of covering orders will be welcome.

6

Increasing Sales by Changing the Discount Structure

INTRODUCTION

Many of the same sales-boosting principles that we used in Chapter 5 on price increases will apply to changing the discount structure for dealers, distributors, and wholesalers as well as direct or end-user customers. For the sake of simplicity, we'll call indirect distribution channels (we sell to someone who resells to someone else) "distributors" and direct channels (we sell directly to someone who uses the product) "end-users."

Changing the discount structure for distributors usually means that they will change *their* discount structure unless you're in an unusual industry where distributor discounts are so small that they always sell at retail. Changing the discount for end-users is tantamount to a price increase so a lot of the points made in Chapter 5 will be directly applicable. In either case we have a selling job to do that we will turn into an opportunity to increase sales and improve relations with our customers.

We'll assume that we're selling a microprocessor called the 4TI series whose retail price ranges from about $2,000 to $10,000. We sell it with its business-oriented software packages through distributors, and, with it's engineering-oriented CAD/CAM (Computer-Aided Design/Computer-Aided Manufacturing) packages, direct to end-users. To make it tougher, we'll assume that our distributors are nonexclusive and are sought after by our competitors. There are separate sales forces and a separate marketing organization for both channels.

The same basic principles will apply to other businesses. For example, changing the discount structure for computer distributors is similar to changing the "mark-down money" policy for manufacturers who sell to soft-goods retailers.

SCRIPT 6.1. SELLING DISTRIBUTORS ON A DISCOUNT STRUCTURE CHANGE

We'll assume that we have an even more difficult assignment since our distributors have been telling us that they need wider margins in order to support the inventory, training, and support requirements of the product line. We, on the other hand, after listening to our distributors, have concluded that a more centralized training and support effort, supported to a much greater extent by us, would be more effective.

We don't want to raise the sensitive retail price, so the money has to come from the distributors' discount. We also found that, at the present 40 percent discount level, distributors are giving part of it away and providing discounts to their customers ranging from 10 percent to 25 percent. In some cases this kind of "footballing" has made the marketplace for our product unnecessarily messy.

> OBJECTIVE: SELL the discount structure change to our distributors as being a part of a total *value package* that will make our product line easier to sell, more attractive, and more profitable.

SALESPERSON: Good morning, Mr. Morra, Stuart Davidson from Cardinal Business Services. Did you get those training manuals I sent you?

> TIP: One of the ways we're going to sell the discount structure change is by pointing out the advantage of a centralized training and support effort so we start by reminding Mr. Morra of what we are doing for him from square one. (We've already talked with his sales manager so we know that they are already being used.)

MR. MORRA: Yes and I got them right out to our people.
SALESPERSON: Good. As I recall, you had two reasons for wanting the manuals. One, you wanted to use them for training your own sales force, and, two, you wanted to see if you could develop a prospective end-user seminar program. How are these programs going?

> TIP: Again, with a question, we've introduced the way we are going to sell the discount structure change but without tipping our hand. Also, our approach will have to be different if the programs are going gangbusters than if they are rusting on the launching pad. We need a bit more information and asking questions is the most effective way to get it.

MR. MORRA: Well, we've had a couple of sessions with our in-store sales staff, but it's hard to pin down our outside salespeople. They move around so much and always seem to come up with an important appointment for the times we schedule training sessions.
SALESPERSON: And the seminar program?
MR. MORRA: Well, we haven't really gotten this off the ground but Glen (Mr. Morra's sales manager) has been putting some ideas together.

SALESPERSON: (all sympathy) I guess this is a pretty difficult thing to do on a local basis.
MR. MORRA: It sure is. Glen's a good salesman, and the salespeople respect him as a manager—but when it comes to training, well, I guess there's only so much one person can do.

SCRIPT 6.1A. ESTABLISHING THE REASON FOR A CHANGE

SALESPERSON: You know, Mr. Morra, we just might have an answer for you. First, let me ask you a question. How important are these programs to you?

> TIP: Obviously, we want Mr. Morra to practically *beg* us to handle this chore for him, so laying the discount structure change on him will be a lot easier. But, we want him to think that it is *his* idea as much as possible, so we go slowly and build our case brick-by-brick.

MR. MORRA: Why, they're *very* important. This isn't like the office products business I used to have where you could always hire someone from another company or train a salesperson by giving him a day with the catalog. Our people have to talk to everyone from the highly skilled and computer-literate techie to business people who have specialized needs but have never even plunked their fannies down in front of a monitor.

> TIP: Perfect. Mr. Morra is making it easier for us to sell the benefits of a centralized training program that we'll provide. We're working the AIDA (Attention, Interest, Desire, Action) formula with *Conviction* included between Desire and Action. Mr. Morra is convincing *us*. This is not exactly an unwelcome situation.

SALESPERSON: And the seminar program?
MR. MORRA: Look, Stu, as you know, computers and even microprocessors have been around for a long time. Yet, 80 percent of our potential customers don't yet have a computer and at least half of these prospects have never even used one. They're computerphobes who would rather be run over by a Sherman tank than put their fingers on a keyboard. Getting them to come to vertical market "problem solving" seminars and then introducing the computer as part of the solution is the best way to sell these recreants. Trying to sell them a computer system without a lot more education is like trying to hold on tighter to a wet fish.
SALESPERSON: That's a nice image. You certainly have a way with metaphors.

> TIP: Our Account Profile and Call Sheet reminds us that Mr. Morra is an English Literature major who is very proud of his command of the language so this bit of blarney busses the stone properly.

MR. MORRA: Yes, "It was not in the open fight
          We threw away the sword,
     But in the lonely watching
          In the darkness by the ford."
SALESPERSON: Is that Kipling?
MR. MORRA: Beoni Bar. Kipling quotes it in "The Rout of the White Hussars."
SALESPERSON: Wow. It always amazes me that you can remember stuff like that.
MR. MORRA: Thanks. "Breathes there a man with soul so dead . . ." (Sir Walter Scott). But do you see our problem?
SALESPERSON: I do, indeed. And, I just might have an answer for you. Do you remem-

ber the last Distributor Council meeting when we discussed the kinds of training programs we were working on?

MR. MORRA: Certainly. I was leading the charge into *that* valley. We don't have the time or resources to do the job ourselves out here.

SCRIPT 6.1B. SELLING THE VALUE OF THE CHANGE

SALESPERSON: Would you be willing to *pay* for an in-house training program already packaged, tested, and proven put on by *our* people.

MR. MORRA: Well, if it were reasonable, I suppose so.

SALESPERSON: How about a packaged, tested, and proven seminar program where our people would train your people to hold them?

MR. MORRA: That's even more interesting, but until sales on your systems take off, I'm not sure how much we could afford.

SALESPERSON: Suppose we could work out a pay-as-you-go arrangement—so much per machine that you buy?

MR. MORRA: That certainly quickens the blood. (grandly) 'Tis a consummation devoutly to be wished.

SALESPERSON: Well, we've worked out a way to do just that, but it will cost you.

MR. MORRA: There ain't no free lunch. What's the deal?

SALESPERSON: You're currently getting a 40 percent discount on the 4TI and 40 and 10 on the periphs. On a $3,000 system that gives you $1,200. You then turn around and give $300 to $500 of that away if you're like most distributors in order to provide an inducement for the prospect to buy the system. Right?

MR. MORRA: Okay. I don't like to admit that we have to give those discounts, but I'm with you so far.

SALESPERSON: Would you have to give those discounts if you had the kind of training and seminar programs we've been talking about?

> TIP: It's tempting to rush right in with the revised discount proposal, but smarter to continue to build the case block-by-block. It's the old "boil a frog" approach. You don't throw a frog into hot water—he'll just jump out barely warmed. Instead, you put the frog in tepid water in which he is comfortable and gradually turn up the heat. Before he knows it, Mr. Frog is cooked. We're turning up the heat with Mr. Morra.

MR. MORRA: Well, Glen and some of our salespeople might argue with this, but I think we could get away with lesser discounts if we had well-trained and knowledgeable people selling the system, and, as you're always saying, "add even more value" to our total value package offering.

> TIP: It's time to cap off our building. We want to stop before we peak so let's not draw this out any further. We'll lay on the deal and then ask questions to handle objections later.

SCRIPT 6.1C. GETTING AGREEMENT ON THE CHANGE

SALESPERSON: Our proposal is to reduce the discount from 40 percent to 35 percent, which would mean that you would make $100 to $200 less on each $3,000 system, given the present discounting. Realistically, since there would be less discounting, you would wind up making a greater gross profit than you do now. It would be like taking $200 back and then giving you $400 in training and other support. You would be ahead of the game on each system and you should be able to sell a lot more systems.

> TIP: We have some other points to make, but let's wind it out slowly and deal with bite-sized chunks of information. Also, we want to tailor our presentation to Mr. Morra's specific concerns.

MR. MORRA: Hmmm.

SALESPERSON: Do you see how this program would work to your advantage?

MR. MORRA: Yes, but how do you propose to drag our outside salespeople into the office to participate in the training program, no matter how good it is? This has been one of the biggest obstacles we faced in what we've done so far to get training off the ground.

SALESPERSON: We had the help of an outside sales training consultant in putting this program together. At our sales meeting where we learned about the program we raised the question and found that she had faced this problem before and has some ways to solve it included in the total program package. *Will* this program work to your advantage?

MR. MORRA: Well, I don't like the idea of your cutting our discount like that, but I can see your point about the discounting we do—and we certainly need a training and seminar program that we can't afford to do ourselves. But, will you really come through on this?

SALESPERSON: The discount structure change is scheduled for August 1st (it's now May) and the training and seminar programs will be tested, cleaned up, and ready for field use, including all the visuals, handouts, and videotapes by July 1st.

MR. MORRA: What if you slip your date? I know how much work it is to put together these kinds of programs and how many revisions it takes.

> TIP: Our home office is smart. They've already thought of this, thanks to a pre-introduction sales meeting with key people which we attended. This is one of the points that was brought up at the meeting. The postponing provision was not a part of the original program plan, but our Vice-President of Marketing wisely listened to us salespeople and changed the program.

SALESPERSON: The videotapes are already in the can. I saw them at the home office meeting we had to discuss the program. If we slip with any part of the rest of the program, we will postpone the discount structure change to 30 days after the training and seminar programs *are* ready for field use.

MR. MORRA: That sounds fair. But that means that we get the programs and still have a month to order machines at the old discount level.

SALESPERSON: Gee. I never thought of that.

MR. MORRA: I'll just bet you didn't. Just out of curiosity, why did you allow that 30 days? You *know* dealers are going to order two or three months' worth of machines just before the change is effective.

SALESPERSON: What month do you think is our slowest month from a production stand-point?

MR. MORRA: I see. I guess I should know better than to underestimate you fellows. Having that sales meeting so you field people could poke holes in the program before it was finalized was smart.

> TIP: Now let's make sure all the bases are covered. We don't want any PCD (Post-Cognitive Dissonance) showing up later. This is the phenomenon that is some-times called ''buyer's remorse.'' It's that feeling that sets in after a course of

action is taken and you start biting your knuckles agonizing over whether you've made the right decision. This is why a lot of automobile advertising is aimed at the new purchaser and why smart marketers spend a part of their budgets promoting post-sale satisfaction. It promotes favorable word-of-mouth advertising—still the best kind of advertising.

SALESPERSON: Well, we try pretty hard to anticipate our distributors' needs and problems. Our home office people really mean that "Partners in Progress and Profit" slogan they coined. Can you see any flaws in anything we've discussed?

MR. MORRA: Not so far. There is one thing. *All* your distributors will be getting a lower discount, but not all of them will take full advantage of your training and seminar programs.

SCRIPT 6.1D. DRIVING HOME THE POINT OF THE CHANGE

SALESPERSON: Right. Is that all bad? We *want* well-trained distributor salespeople representing our product and we want to help you hold the kind of vertical market seminar programs we discussed. We feel as you do that this is tremendously important.

MR. MORRA: Well, I'm certainly with you there. It really sounds good. We have plenty of notice to cover outstanding commitments made with price concessions and we certainly need the programs. I'm glad you're spending your money this way instead of on expensive mass consumer television advertising like some of your competitors are. It may look good on TV but doesn't solve the kinds of problems we need solved.

SALESPERSON: Thanks. I'm sure our marketing people will appreciate the vote of confidence. As we discussed, this is one of the reasons we formed the Distributor Advisory Council in the first place.

> TIP: We're throwing the credit back to Mr. Morra and the Council. Not only do we want this to look as much as possible like our distributors' idea, but it seems that the more you try to give away credit to others, the more it comes back to you.

MR. MORRA: Well, speaking on behalf of the Council, I think I can say that you've got the support of your more enlightened distributors.

Summary—Selling the Discount Structure Change

Another done deal. In this case we used the need for a centralized training and seminar program that our distributors told us they needed as the (proper) justification for the discount structure change. Similar reasons can be found in any business. The important thing is to offer some kind of goodie when you're taking something away, especially if it is in response to a perceived or communicated need.

If your home office hasn't provided a built-in benefit, you can make up your own. For example, with the new discount structure, your customers continue to get *you* and the support and help you provide. If you can't honestly say that you're worth the difference, you might consider giving yourself some career relocation guidance.

Like a price increase, a discount structure change doesn't have to be a negative. It *can* be positioned as a modification of the *value package* components when presented properly by an effective salesperson who refuses to get defensive about it or apologize for it.

In an indirect or distributor channel, changing the discount structure is really reassigning percentages of the total retail sales dollar based on who is doing what. In the above example, we took a burden from the distributors, so it was only fair that we take back a small piece of the pie.

LETTER 6.1. SELLING THE DISTRIBUTOR DISCOUNT STRUCTURE CHANGE

If you have a small number of distributors, you will probably have talked with them all either on the phone or in person. It's still a good idea to send a letter confirming your conversation and to make sure there are no misunderstandings about the new terms. If you have a large enough number of distributors to have grouped them "A", "B", "C", you may not want to or be able to reach them all personally. To be on the safe side, assume that you've talked to no one as we will in this letter.

If the number of distributors is small enough to make it feasible, you might want to use individually word-processed letters to make it seem more personal than a printed letter. You won't fool many people into believing that they are all individually typed, but you'll get credit for the effort.

OBJECTIVE: Formally notify all our distributors of the specific terms of the change in the discount structure and sell it as being a part of a total new *value package* that will make our product line easier to sell, more attractive, and more profitable.

Dear (Distributor):

At our last Dealer Advisory Council Meeting, you or your representatives identified two topics as your main concerns—your top priorities and the areas in which you would like help from us:

1. Training of your in-house and outside salespeople.
2. Development of seminars for prospective customers in specifically identified, vertical markets—attorneys, doctors, CPA's, etc.

Subsequent discussions with many of you have confirmed that these are, indeed, the priorities.

You pointed out the difficulty of putting together an effort like this on your own even though you agreed that this is a part of your responsibility as a 4TI distributor and part of the reason for the distributor discount. You told us that you'd be willing to pay for such programs if they were available.

Well, we listened to you. We developed for you a complete training program that *we* will put on for your salespeople, and a seminar program that we will teach your people to conduct. I think both these programs will knock your socks off when you see them. It was, however, and will continue to be expensive.

Something had to give, so we have worked out a pay-as-you-go program to make these available to you. Right now our discount to you is 40 percent. You told us that, partly because of the lack of such programs, you are discounting the system from 10 to 25 percent to your customers in order to get the sale. This is not a good situation for you and means a less-than-orderly market for us.

So, effective August 1st, the distributor discount will be 35 percent. The programs will be available July 1st. The videotapes are in the can and most of the other material is in the final printing stages. Since this will enable you to sell at lesser discounts from list price, your gross profit per system should be higher and you should sell more systems.

After much persuasion from my (perhaps I should say *your* sales force), we've provided this 30-day gap so you can continue to order at the old discount even while you're enjoying the benefits of these new programs. If there is any delay in making the programs available, the old discount will apply for 30 days from the date they *are* available.

Your district managers will be talking with you soon if they haven't already, explaining the details of our training team's national roll-out schedule and showing you some samples of the videotape programs.

We consider this a very important step forward in our growing "Partners in Progress and Profit" efforts. So far, your preliminary comments indicate that you do too. I look forward to hearing from you if there is any way I can personally make the 4TI product line a more successful one for you.

P.S.: We're still working on a formal cooperative advertising program. In the meantime, I've authorized your district manager to match your local promotional dollars with ours, up to 3% of your purchases in the next 90 days (June 1st through August 31st). Details are on page 5 of the enclosed terms sheets.

DISCOUNT STRUCTURE CHANGE LETTER SUMMARY

Let's look point-by-point at some of the things we did in this letter to accomplish our objectives:

1. We started by positioning the letter as a new program announcement, and, more importantly, a program that *our distributors asked for*.
2. We set the stage for the discount structure change by discussing *their* reports of the difficulty and expense of putting the programs together.
3. We built our case step-by-step much the same way we did in the longer and more elaborate SCRIPT 6.1, recognizing the limitations inherent in a mass-distributed (even if word-processed) letter.
4. We provided some convincing reasons (based on distributor input) on why the new discount structure won't take any money out of their pockets on each system and will enable them to sell more systems.
5. We anticipated one possible objection and dealt with it—the matter of being late with the programs. (Our preliminary discussions with distributors identified this as a concern.)
6. Finally, we saved a goodie for the P.S. That has to win us kudos, especially since it has been asked for in Council meetings and other discussions.

This letter is admittedly written from the viewpoint of a vice-president of sales and marketing, but could also be from a regional manager. It's natural and logical that it should come from this source, but *your* home office may not provide this kind of support to you. With some adaptation, the letter could just as easily come from a district manager or local salesperson. For example, in the P.S., the line could read "I have been authorized by our vice-president to match your advertising dollars . . ."

The important thing to remember is the points that are made. These points, no matter what the home office activities and support may be, need to be driven home by the local salesperson. Besides, you want to begin thinking on this level so you'll get there sooner.

SCRIPT 6.2. SELLING DISCOUNT STRUCTURE CHANGE TO THE END-USER

As shown above, it was relatively simple and logical to suggest to distributors that it made sense to reallocate percentages of the retail price of our product based on the respective contributions made by the manufacturer and the distributor. The distributor will, quite justifiably based on the additional *value added* through training programs, pass on the additional cost of the reduced discount to his customers. His customers will have a better total *value package* and the distributor, because of this, will have more systems sales.

With the end-user, however, a reduced discount *is* a price increase—no ands, ifs, or buts. This gives us a more difficult, but not unsurmountable, problem to deal with. We will stick with the position we started to develop in Chapter 1 and brought to full blossom in Chapter 4: *establish value for your product and price becomes a secondary consideration.*

In this situation, we are selling a CAD/CAM (Computer-Aided Design/Computer-Assisted Manufacturing) system to manufacturers who do from $5 million to $50 million in annual gross revenues. We had been giving them a 10 percent discount on any quantity of product and 20 percent on quantities of five or more systems. Now, we want to go straight list with a possible quantity discount on orders that amount to more than $100,000.

> OBJECTIVE: Sell the discount structure change to our end-users as part of a total *value package* that will enhance the worth of our product line to our engineering and manufacturing customers.

SALESPERSON: Good morning, Mr. Leenay. This is Sherie Kristel from Cardinal Business Services, CAD/CAM division . . . How are you this morning?

MR. LEENAY: Uh . . . Oh, Hi Sherie. You're the young lady who graduated from the same school I did—one or two years later—aren't you?

SALESPERSON: The same, but it just might have been three or four years later.

MR. LEENAY: I might even admit to five or six years later. Anyway, it's nice to hear from you again.

SALESPERSON: (in a very pleasant tone) Why is that?

> TIP: Sherie, as a bright, young engineering graduate, can get away with a lot of stuff that us old, gray pro's may not be able to. We might as well use it as long as it lasts.

MR. LEENAY: (a little stunned) Well, we're fellow alumni or is it alumnae, aren't we?

SALESPERSON: (Pause—our favorite ploy when we're not sure about the "hot button" or direction to pursue.)

MR. LEENAY: And, for someone new to Cardinal and not familiar with *our* situation, you did a great job in straightening out those problems we had with the 4TI CAD system in Department 174.

SALESPERSON: I appreciate your saying that. As you know, I'm new to Cardinal and new to the industry. That kind of feedback is probably more important to me than it would be to an experienced salesperson.

TIP: We need to use all the assets at our disposal. If Mr. Leenay wants to take on the role of father figure, let him, as long as we don't go over the ethical boundary. The customer or prospect should get what he wants and this includes the perception of the salesperson's role.

MR. LEENAY: Well, Sherie, you just tell me what kind of feedback you want and I'll give it to you.

SCRIPT 6.2A. ESTABLISHING VALUE IN THE CUSTOMER'S MIND

SALESPERSON: If you don't mind, I'd like to share with you something I'm wrestling with. I know you can buy a product similar to ours at a lower price even with the discount we've been offering while we've been getting the 4TI CAM system off the ground. Could I ask you why, if this is true, you are buying our product?

TIP: Step-by-step, we're building to the realization that the *value package* we're offering is worth something beyond the product's intrinsic value. We also positioned the discount as a somewhat "temporary" measure.

MR. LEENAY: Sure, little lady. (We swallow this—it goes with the territory.) Your product is top-drawer in terms of quality and you folks have always taken care of any problem I've had. *That's* important. It's comforting to know that someone like you will show up when I have any kind of problem.
SALESPERSON: I appreciate your telling me that. That's what my manager keeps telling me—that we offer a lot more than just the basic product. I'm not quite sure how to ask you this next question . . .
MR. LEENAY: Well, why don't you just go right ahead and ask it any way your little heart pleases?
SALESPERSON: Well, there's no question that we have a very good product. What I was wondering was how much the kind of extra service and support we provide is worth in real dollars?
MR. LEENAY: What are you getting at, little lady?
SALESPERSON: Well, my company tells me that we were able to give all this support *and* provide those extra discounts while we were getting the product off the ground. Now that it's launched, they say we have to begin making money on it.

TIP: This is another step in setting the value stage and a logical reason for the change.

MR. LEENAY: I think I'm beginning to hear something I don't want to hear.
SALESPERSON: (innocently and keeping in the questioning mode) Oh, what's that?
MR. LEENAY: Well, the last time someone told me something like that, he was fixing to raise my prices. Is that what you're up to?

SCRIPT 6.2B. ESTABLISHING REASONS FOR THE CHANGE

SALESPERSON: (a little defensively and just a tad angrily) What I think our company is "up to" is trying to find a way to preserve those expensive services we provide that you said you appreciate, while at the same time getting enough money for what we offer so we can continue to offer it and stay in business.

MR. LEENAY: What's wrong with the way things have been going? We've been satisfied.

SALESPERSON: Nothing at all—as long as we were getting the product off the ground and our customers were helping us get the bugs out of the system. Now that that has happened, we need to get to a more realistic basis of doing business. May I ask you again if you feel that the extra services we've offered have been worth anything?

> TIP: We've again positioned the services cum discount as a *temporary* strategy and made the point that logic dictates that a change is appropriate. Again we went back to the questioning mode to keep control of the interview.

MR. LEENAY: Why, of course they have, honey. (We grit our teeth.) We could have bought a system from a mail-order house for half what we paid you folks and the good people at Priestly's Computer Services even offered me a better deal.

SALESPERSON: (sweetly now) That's really what I wanted to know, Mr. Leenay. May I ask you another question? Why *didn't* you buy from a mail-order house or someone else (we won't even mention the name of our biggest competitor) if their prices are that much lower?

> TIP: The question and Mr. Leenay's alternative sources are there whether we bring it up or not. If *we* bring it up we take the teeth out of it and stay in control. This also gives Mr. Leenay the opportunity to sell *us* on the benefits of dealing with our company rather than a competitor—always more effective than anything we could say to convey the benefits message.

MR. LEENAY: Why, if I had done that, I never would have gotten to meet you.

SCRIPT 6.2C. GETTING AGREEMENT ON OUR PRODUCT'S VALUE

SALESPERSON: (getting things back on track) And, pray tell, what has that done for your *company*?

> TIP: It's important in this interview to get Mr. Leenay absolutely committed to an appreciation of the added value of our extra support services. The more times we can get him to articulate this the more he will actually convince himself of the value. This will make our job of removing the discount while keeping the customer that much easier and more likely to succeed.

MR. LEENAY: Okay. We've gotten an excellent what you folks call *value package*. Yep, that's it—value package. Why, all your help has made your package worth a lot more than that bundle of hardware we could have bought from a mail-order house. Is that what you wanted to hear?

SALESPERSON: Yes. (pause)

MR. LEENAY: Well, darlin' why didn't you just say that in the first place? We could have saved all this hootin' and hollerin'.

SALESPERSON: (back to the innocent bit now) Mr. Leenay, I'm new to this industry and I don't know what the rules or values are. All I know is that our company has been providing a lot of services that are expensive and we don't get paid for them, so I guess the new policy makes sense.

MR. LEENAY: (alarmed) What new policy?

SALESPERSON: Well, effective August 1st, the 10 percent discount will no longer be available except for large-quantity purchases. But, we're going to provide even more in the way of those extra services you told me you appreciate.

MR. LEENAY: Does that mean that I get to see more of you? Just kidding. You know I have to do a professional job for my company.

SALESPERSON: As a matter of fact, it means just that. All of our salespeople have been stretched pretty thin recently because of a tight budget. With the removal of the discount, we've been able to start hiring a crew of tech reps that will provide support to us salespeople and our customers. This means that I can spend more quality time with you and we'll be able to provide even better support than in the past.

SCRIPT 6.2D. DEALING WITH THE *REAL* OBJECTION

MR. LEENAY: Well, that sounds good, but I figure that this next system we're looking at is going to cost us about $1,000 more than we were planning and I've already sent in my capital requisition.

SALESPERSON: (sympathetically) I guess that creates some kind of problem for you.

MR. LEENAY: Darn right it does. I have enough problems with those young turks on the plant floor gunning for my job as it is. This makes me think that I should go back to Priestly's for another quote. I'll bet that they would be *thrilled* to give me an even better discount if I let them in the door.

SALESPERSON: Wouldn't that create another problem for you with two different systems and two sets of support people running around your departments?

> TIP: Rather than get defensive or allow ourselves to feel offended, we stayed calm and met this slap with a question that addresses Mr. Leenay's own interests. Many salespeople make the mistake of taking things like this personally. "How can he do that after all I've done for him?" In the first place, he's not *doing* it, just threatening. In the second place, it's probably an idle threat. If not, we can idle it by keeping our cool and sticking with our script.

MR. LEENAY: Yes, I suppose it would—but nothing we couldn't handle after awhile. You've already created a bunch of problems for me by taking away my discount. What's one more?

SALESPERSON: Well, maybe there's something we could work out. Do you remember my showing you a letter from Harkins Machining that impressed you?

MR. LEENAY: Sure. That's what got you in the door in the first place. I figured if that old dinosaur would use your system, it had to be good.

SALESPERSON: Do you also remember that *you* were going to write a letter telling us how pleased you are with our systems and the support we provided?

MR. LEENAY: Of course I do. I have the note to do that right in front of me.

SCRIPT 6.2E. CUTTING THE LEAD TIME ON THE NEXT ORDER

SALESPERSON: Well, if you could get that letter off to me today, I could take it to my sales manager and try to get the old discount to apply on the next system as long as we can wrap it up in 60 days or less. If you'd like, I could work out a draft of a suggested letter, bring it to you for changes and we could have your secretary type it up while we talk.

TIP: Mr. Leenay has been promising this letter for three months so we have a fairly decent bargaining chip. The letter is important to us since it will be an entre into ten other companies that we can count right now. (The effective third-party referral.) Making the letter part of the deal isn't playing unfairly since it makes the discount concession worth more. An *earned* reward is always perceived to have more value than an *unearned* reward. Mr. Leenay may even feel good about "taking advantage of us" in getting the discount concession by *only* writing a letter.

MR. LEENAY: You don't have to do that. I'll write the letter as soon as I can get to it.
SALESPERSON: It's up to you. I'd be happy to help since the sooner I can bring it to my manager, the better chance I have of getting the discount to apply to your next system.
MR. LEENAY: Okay. Why don't you come over this afternoon and help me write it?
SALESPERSON: No problem, although I'm booked for this afternoon. I already have an outline of what I think we've accomplished with you. I'll bring a suggested letter with me when we *can* get together. At the same time, I'll ask the tech rep assigned to your account to come along so you and your people can meet him.

TIP: This should defuse the cozy letter-writing session Mr. Leenay may have had in mind and accomplishes other objectives at the same time—we get the tech rep in the door and can spend the time revising our letter rather than starting from scratch on a new letter.

MR. LEENAY: All right. When can you make it?
SALESPERSON: I know that you're so conscientious that you like to get in early. How about tomorrow morning at 7:30? I'll bring doughnuts.

TIP: This time not only makes the best use of our day, but avoids, for now, a cozy lunch or cozy after-work drink. It also effectively demonstrates to the technical representative we will be working with that our job is not a nine-to-five deal and gets him started on the right foot.

MR. LEENAY: Make it 7:45.

End-User Discount Change Summary

It's true that we relied on the *pobracita* or "poor little girl" approach to an extent, but we didn't lower our professional standards in doing so. This approach is not limited to recent female graduates. I've seen a lot of experienced pros play the "I'm just a po' country boy" game with equal effectiveness.

It's also true that you may not have anything as dramatic as a technical representative staff to offer as a giveback in exchange for the elimination of the discount, but there's always *something* you can provide. And, as we were able to position this, the customer gets the additional service *today* with the price increase effective with the *next* system. Most customers will be concerned about *today's* problem. Solve this and you pretty much have carte blanche for the future. Our strategy here was:

1. Communicate the bad news (take something away).

2. Provide the good news (give something back that you can position as having equal or greater perceived value to the customer).

3. Listen sympathetically to the problems the change will cause and promise to *try* to do something about it but only when we already know that we can actually solve the problem either because it's a part of the program or we have already anticipated problems and gotten approval on exceptions.

4. Get another concession from the customer that is worth its weight in gold to us but won't cost him anything in exchange for our efforts to solve the problem. In this case we got *two* concessions—the recommendation letter and a tentative commitment for an order for the new system within 60 days. Mr. Leenay has a bad procrastination habit so this will be some kind of accomplishment.

5. Pave the way to an even better relationship in the future. After all, we went to bat for Mr. Leenay with the big, bad wolves in our management and all he did was write a letter. We also gave him a double benefit—the discount on the next system *and* the additional support services of a technical representative at the same time.

LETTER 6.2. ESTABLISHING END-USER VALUE WITH THE CHANGE NOTIFICATION

If we are doing our job properly, we have somewhere between 500 and 1,000 cards (pages) in our prospect file. We have coded them "A", "B", "C", and even "D". The "A's" will be those 20 to 30 percent of the total that account for 70 to 80 percent of our potential sales to all customers and prospects. We may be able to call *and* visit all the "A's" and at least make a telephone call to all the "B's" but we'll need a letter for those "C's" and "D's" we want to stay in contact with.

> OBJECTIVE: Formally notify all our CAD/CAM system end-users of the elimination of the discount and sell it as part of an even more valuable *value package* that will make our product line even more desirable.

Dear (End-User):

EVEN MORE SUPPORT AND SERVICE FROM CARDINAL IS ON THE WAY!

The results of the last market survey conducted for you to tell us how you feel about our products and our company pointed out two important things:

1. You like the extra *value-added* support and services we provide with our systems.

2. You would like even more at a time when we're pushed to keep up with current requirements.

Well, we listened and have started hiring a whole new staff of technical representatives. They will work with me to handle the nitty-gritty problems for you and your people enabling us account executives to spend more quality time with you on the bigger issues.

How can we afford to do this for you and still maintain the high level of product quality? Good question. While we were working together to iron out the bugs in the system, we were able to provide a 10 percent discount on all systems. Now it is no longer appropriate, nor can we afford it if we are to maintain your service level.

So, effective August 1st (about a month after you will have a tech rep available to you), the discount is eliminated. If you have any proposals in the works, I urge you to call me at (205)-822-1746 and we'll see what kind of arrangements can be made.

EXTRA BONUS: We will include our "Engineering Table Organizer" software package (a $195 value) *free* with any system ordered after August 1st.

In the meantime, please let me know if there is any way in which we can be helpful to you.

P.S.: You can ask for help by checking the appropriate box on the enclosed postpaid card. If you will give us a brief comment on how you feel about the system you have, we'll send you a *free* keyboard template explaining the special-purpose keys.

This letter will be sent to our "A" and "B" customers as well as our "C" and "D" customers, whether we've contacted them by phone or in person or not. The *free* software package will be a nice surprise to those customers we've talked with and teach them to read our mail. Let's review what we did to meet the objective we spelled out before we started writing the letter:

END-USER CHANGE NOTIFICATION LETTER SUMMARY

1. We positioned the change as something that had been asked for by our customer base through their answers to our market research survey. (Surveys, don't have to be elaborate or expensive. You could do one yourself in your own territory with an appropriate questionnaire, pencil, and telephone.)

2. We started out with the customer-oriented and asked-for benefits of the new program and reminded our customers that an undertaking like this *is* expensive.

3. We positioned the present 10 percent discount as a "temporary" measure while the system was being debugged, justifying its being dropped now.

4. Right after unloading the elimination-of-discount bomb, we provided a nice goodie to take our customers' minds off the dropping of the discount—the *free* software package. Actually, this package hasn't gone over very well yet and we need more installed bases out there if we are to ever market it successfully, but it *is* a $195 value. *And*, it costs us about $16.17 to do this. If customers who order before August 1st ask for this package to be included, we can grant this generous concession and have a chance to either close the order more easily or get our own concession in return.

IN CLOSING

In this chapter, we've demonstrated again that adversity can be turned into opportunity and that every problem contains the seeds of its own solution. All we have to do is abandon old patterns of reacting and find new, more positive ways to seek out that silver lining. Seemingly negative changes will be accepted by our customers if:

1. We position the change positively and as *their* idea.

2. We give something back while taking something away. Ideally, the giveback costs us less and has a greater perceived customer value than the takeaway.

3. We solve the customer's *today* problem in a way that looks like we are making a real concession just for that customer.

4. The concessions we make are perceived to be *earned*. We do this by getting a small concession for us.

5. Without making any promises, we left the door open for any hardship cases. This may prompt some inactive, bargain-smelling customers who have been thinking about a new system to call us with the news that they were just about ready to make a decision and a plea to extend the discount. Why not? It could be a sale we might not have made otherwise.

6. To get some more market intelligence and sweeten the package even further, we offered a *free* goodie for the return of the card. Once we have a customer or prospect filling out a card, it's easy for him to check the box that says "Please call me for a demonstration on your *new* model." This costs us 84 cents, including postage, and is imprinted with our name and that red bird.

7

Dealing with Competition Effectively

INTRODUCTION

Next to pricing, competitors' activities, "superior" product line, terms, and discounts are the most often-mentioned nemeses of salespeople in the sales training meetings and "obstacles sessions" I've held over the last 30 years of listening to salespeople either voice legitimate objections, complain speciously, or try to justify sub-quota performance. The other guy always has something better.

An interesting thing happens, however, when these obstacles are examined in detail. All of a sudden, it dawns on the people in my groups that the competitive obstacles are not so formidable. In playing the competitor of my trainees in role-play or other situations, I find myself overwhelmed with reasons why *their* product is better and finally have to retreat, beaten down, with my tail between my legs. Why didn't they think of those reasons before they became, in their minds, insurmountable obstacles? Why, indeed?

In this chapter we'll look at some of these situations and at some modified (in order to make the points more clearly) versions of the solutions my trainees have come up with over the years. As in past chapters, we'll use *questions* to turn these obstacles into sales-presentation and sales-closing opportunities.

SCRIPT 7.1. HANDLING THE "YOUR PRODUCT ISN'T AS GOOD" OBJECTION

We can usually be certain that this comment or objection is a cop-out, masking the *real* reason the prospect doesn't want to make a decision to buy. (Remember that people *do* like to buy—they just don't like making decisions.)

Very few prospects who use this dodge have actually undertaken a serious study and test of product features comprehensive enough to say with authority that one product is better than another. *But*, we can't assume that we can use testing laboratory studies or other facts alone to refute that argument. That just leads to endless and fruitless debate. Most people don't make decisions that logically, so we have to find the emotional obstacles that are in the way of the buying decision.

> OBJECTIVE: Get behind the "your product isn't as good" objection to find the *real* reason the prospect isn't making a buying decision without putting down the prospect and his judgment. Find a way to have this process lead to the prospect's selling himself.

For simplicity's sake, we'll pick up this next discussion in the middle, right after the final presentation we made that we thought had gone so well.

SALESPERSON: Well, it seems that we've covered all the bases. (Trial close.) Were you more interested in our leasing program or the 90-day purchase program?

MR. LINDERMAN: Not so fast. I agree that your product is pretty good and that it will probably meet our needs at a reasonable cost, but the decision is far from made.

> TIP: Uh-oh. We thought we had it made until today. We did all our homework and followed through just as we should have. What's happening now? Time to start asking questions.

SCRIPT 7.1A. UNCOVERING OBSTACLES TO THE SALE

SALESPERSON: May I ask what your reservation is?

MR. LINDERMAN: Well, there are a lot. You don't just rush into buying something like this.

> TIP: What is happening? Our friend and ally is suddenly acting adversely. Let's continue to make our selling points and keep on with the questions to see if we can discover why.

SALESPERSON: Mr. Linderman, as we've discussed, you'll start saving money the *day* you start using our laser card system. Isn't that a good enough reason to "rush" into a decision?

> TIP: Obviously there is some hidden objection here that we weren't able to uncover in the discovery and presentation stages of our efforts. We have to get this pinned down before we can go any further with the interview.

MR. LINDERMAN: Well, yours isn't the only system on the market. It's not even the only laser card system.

SALESPERSON: That's true, but it does seem to be the one that most effectively meets your needs. Isn't that what we've found out over the past month?

TIP: We *do not* want to ask about another system that Mr. Linderman may be thinking of. Our competitors have enough notoriety without our helping. With this question, we're still probing to find out what is on Mr. Linderman's mind, and we've subtly reminded him of the time and effort we've put in on this project.

MR. LINDERMAN: Well, what we really found out was that *some* kind of intelligent card system will fulfill our needs for a low-cost, convenient way to handle and update our field service manual records. That doesn't necessarily mean that we found *your* system to be the best way to handle them.

SALESPERSON: Oh! (Pause as though dumbstruck and wait for Mr. Linderman to reveal some additional information that will give us a clue on how to proceed.)

MR. LINDERMAN: Look, Kylie, we've got a lot riding on this decision—the integrity of our whole service operation is at stake here.

TIP: As if we didn't know that. There is something else going on here and it looks like mere questions aren't going to tell us what. It's time for a challenge.

SALESPERSON: I thought it was clear that we both recognized that. I thought that was why I spent so much time checking out all those possible exceptions that you asked me to look at.

TIP: Guilt has always been a powerful motivating factor. It may not get us the sale, but it won't hurt to remind Mr. Linderman in a nice way that we've done everything he asked us to do since we started working on this project.

MR. LINDERMAN: Yes, Yes. You've done everything we've asked you to do. It's just . . .

SCRIPT 7.1B. UNCOVERING THE REAL RESERVATIONS

SALESPERSON: Yes, just what?

MR. LINDERMAN: Well, King Optical Corp. also has a pretty powerful system that I understand is better than your system and cheaper.

TIP: Now, we know that King's product is not as good as ours. Their service may at times be better, their salesperson more charming or persuasive, and their literature more colorful. Their product, however, is *not* objectively better. We have to find the *real* reason for this objection. (Of course, even if King's product *were* better, we would still proceed much the same way and point out how our total *value package* would meet our prospect's needs better.)

SALESPERSON: Well, anyone can be cheaper just by taking out some of the quality or service features of our *value package*. But better? What do you mean by that? How do you feel they are better?

MR. LINDERMAN: Well, the word I have is that their cards will last ten years while yours are only guaranteed for five.

TIP: Now we're getting closer. *Our* cards could last 20 years or longer if they didn't have to survive the "wallet test." That is, the constant bending and flexing if carried in a wallet which prompted us to suggest a policy of every-five-year replacement of the cards. Now we could argue the point logically and get nowhere. We could "prove" conclusively that our cards have passed life tests better than King's, but what would that prove? Instead, we could find the *real* reason for the objection.

SCRIPT 7.1C. DEALING WITH COMPETITIVE COMPARISONS

SALESPERSON: Mr. Linderman, how often do you update your service records?
MR. LINDERMAN: Well, we provide supplements every month and redo whole sections every three months.
SALESPERSON: And how many sections do you have?
MR. LINDERMAN: Eight.
SALESPERSON: So, as I understand this, the entire card will be completely redone in two years?
MR. LINDERMAN: Well, yes—I guess so.
SALESPERSON: (Pause—let Mr. Linderman be the one to voice the conclusion so it's *his*.)
MR. LINDERMAN: Ha-ha. I see your point. I guess it really doesn't make any difference whether a card lasts ten years or 80 if we update that often.
SALESPERSON: I guess not. (Pause—it's his move.)
MR. LINDERMAN: Okay, so card life isn't as important as it might be. But there are so many other factors . . .

> TIP: We're on the right track. In the past 5 minutes Mr. Linderman has not voiced a single logical argument. We have to keep questioning to find the *real* reason for the reservation.

SALESPERSON: Like?
MR. LINDERMAN: Well, like how long you've been in business, what your factory looks like, how quickly we can get shipments, whether or not you'll be around after you make the sale. A lot of factors.

> TIP: Mr. Linderman is weakening, but isn't about to tell us the real reason, at least not yet. We're beginning to suspect that he's on the take from King. Since we can only lose an order once and it looks as if we have nothing to lose at this point, let's go "last resort."

SCRIPT 7.1D. EXPOSING THE HIDDEN REASONS FOR STALLING

SALESPERSON: Mr. Linderman, we don't know each other well, but we've been working on these specifications together for over a month. They make sense for you. What is the *real* reason for your reluctance to place this order with us? (This would be an appropriate time for us to hold our breath.)

> TIP: In most circumstances we might ask a few more questions and drag this out a bit further to make sure we're on sound ground. But, we notice that Mr. Linderman is no longer making eye contact with us and is obviously upset about something. So, we go for it now.

MR. LINDERMAN: (big pause, but we outwait him) Okay, Kylie—you're right. We did work this up together and it does make a lot of sense to me. Let me tell you what happened. Last week our new engineering manager, Francois Lefebvre, came to me with the news that the King system was going to become *the* standard in the laser card industry. I can't buck the engineering manager without a pretty good reason.

SALESPERSON: Francois Lefebvre? Hmmm. French. (The wheels are turning.) May I ask you where he worked before he came here?

MR. LINDERMAN: Some engineering company in Montreal as I recall. The company is supposed to be very good.

SALESPERSON: Montreal? Isn't that where King has its home office and manufacturing facilities?

MR. LINDERMAN: Why, yes. Oh, wow. You don't suppose there's any connection do you?

SALESPERSON: Of course not. Coincidences like that happen all the time (pause). What do you think we should do now?

> TIP: Now we really have a hot potato. Let's toss it back to Mr. Linderman and put him on the hook before we find a way to (with his everlasting gratitude) take him off.

MR. LINDERMAN: Well, I don't know. I can't really confront him with this.

SALESPERSON: Of course not. It's probably just a coincidence even if Mr. Lefebvre *is* knocking our system without, as far as I know , knowing anything about it.

MR. LINDERMAN: Okay, Kylie—what do we do now?

> TIP: Well. Now, instead of being adversaries, we've become partners on the same team. Let's keep it "we" from now on to cement this.

SCRIPT 7.1E. DEALING WITH THE NEGATIVE THIRD-PARTY INFLUENCE

SALESPERSON: Why don't we assume that Mr. Lefebvre is just not well-informed. He may be pushing King's system because that's the only system in Canada and the one he would be most familiar with. (Pause—let's get Mr. Linderman involved so he thinks this is *his* idea.)

MR. LINDERMAN: I'm with you so far, but I can't exactly walk up to the engineering manager and suggest that he's doing something unethical.

SALESPERSON: Of course not. And he probably isn't. You know, Paul, you've never seen our factory. Why don't I set up a tour and a brief meeting with our president for you and Francois so you can both feel more comfortable with us?

MR. LINDERMAN: That sounds pretty sensible.

SALESPERSON: In the meantime, why don't you sound out Mr. Lefebvre a little? In a subtle way you could draw some inferences between his being from Montreal and the source he's recommending being from the same city.

MR. LINDERMAN: I can't accuse him of anything.

SALESPERSON: Of course not. It may be nothing more than the fact that he is more familiar with the Canadian system since he may have seen it in operation. Let's show him our system and let him see our company's operation. He will probably then agree with us that *our* system is the one for you to install.

MR. LINDERMAN: And if he doesn't?

SALESPERSON: Why, then we'll do what I've been doing just now with you.

MR. LINDERMAN: And, what's that?

SALESPERSON: Asking questions until we find out what the *real* reason is for his feelings.

MR. LINDERMAN: You're a bit over my head right now with all this strategy. What do we do if he still pushes King over your system?

SALESPERSON: What do *you* think we should do?

> TIP: Remember that we want to ask questions and make what we are doing Mr. Linderman's idea. We'll be on hand to bail him out or to change course if he's not sailing in our direction. Let's see how he handles the next move.

MR. LINDERMAN: Well, I suppose I'll have to spend some more time looking into the King system. But, I'm still the purchasing manager. It's my decision as long as I meet their specs. Come to think of it, Lefebvre had no business coming into my office like that. I'd like to put that guy in his place.

> TIP: Now that we've accomplished our purpose (attorneys would call this "discrediting the witness"), we can move on to a peacemaker role.

SALESPERSON: Maybe he'll be on our side after the tour. Let's give him the benefit of the doubt for the time being and assume that he's just mistaken because he doesn't as yet know enough about our company and our product. We can fix that.

MR. LINDERMAN: Okay. I'll talk to Francois this afternoon and find out his schedule for next week.

SALESPERSON: Fine. I'll check out *our* available dates and give you a call-back this afternoon. Would you try to get an alternative time in case our availability times don't match up?

MR. LINDERMAN: Sure. Talk with you tomorrow.

Here was a situation where that *third party* got in the way of what we were trying to do. It happens. We still don't know what the circumstances were, but by hanging in there and getting more information, we turned an adversary into a partner and kept our prospects with this prospect alive.

SCRIPT 7.2. DEALING WITH ENTRENCHED COMPETITION WHEN YOU ARE A STRANGER TO THE PROSPECT—FIRST CALL

We will probably lose about 20 percent of our customers each year. Customers go out of business, they drop product lines, they merge, they move, people change, and some may actually start buying from competitors—through no fault of ours, of course. This means that at least 20 percent of our time should be spent prospecting, getting referrals, and finding other ways to develop new customers. Unfortunately, unless we have a brand-new product, most of these prospects are already someone else's customers just as our customers are someone else's prospects.

This script will deal with the situation where we've identified a good prospect and found that they are very happy with their current supplier. Instead of giving up, we'll take a three-step approach. The script is based on an actual approach an Atlanta stockbroker used with me, but could apply just as well for insurance products, other intangibles, and even for tangible products.

> OBJECTIVE: Introduce ourselves and our services to our prospect. Confirm his interest in investment products and determine his present situation with a brokerage house. If we're lucky enough to find a prospect who has some newly found money and no broker, we'll go for a close.

SALESPERSON: Good afternoon, Mr. Nemlich. This is Gene Muscarella from Graham Securities. I have your name as being someone who would be interested in unusual investment opportunities.

> TIP: We'll pause now and wait for the *prospect* to tell us where we should go from here. We've told him who we are and have given him enough information to let him qualify himself if he *is* an investor. The term "unusual" should also arouse some degree of interest on his part.

MR. NEMLICH: Well, I'm into stocks, bonds, covered and naked options, gold, silver, platinum, coins, and stamps. What did you have in mind?

> TIP: Okay. I guess we could say that Mr. Nemlich qualifies as an investor, but let's not get too specific until we know a little more.

SCRIPT 7.2A. INTRODUCING YOURSELF TO AROUSE INTEREST

SALESPERSON: Well, we're a fairly small but well-established regional brokerage firm out of Atlanta. From time to time we come across special situations that we like to alert our clients to. I'd like to put *your* name on our mailing list so you can get these notices from time to time.

> TIP: This investor probably deals with large houses, so let's position ourselves as an alternative.

MR. NEMLICH: I'd be happy to get your material, but I have to tell you that I'm already dealing with three brokerage houses. The last thing I need is to open up a new file for another broker.
SALESPERSON: Mr. Nemlich—uh, may I call you James?
MR. NEMLICH: Jim.

SCRIPT 7.2B. GETTING MORE INFORMATION

SALESPERSON: Thank you. Jim, may I ask which brokerage firms you're now dealing with?

> TIP: Some prospects will be turned off by the use of their first names by a stranger on the phone. Asking permission to do this shows that we have class and still permits us to get a little closer to the prospect.

MR. NEMLICH: I have a cash management account with Merrill Lynch, do most of my trading with Brown & Company for the discounts, and use Smith Barney or Primark for special situations.

TIP: If Mr. Nemlich has *three* brokerage accounts, what's one more? For the time being we'll consider him an ''A'' prospect and make a note to put him on our free newsletter distribution list. That ''special situations'' caught our ear. We'll have to use that as the wedge that will pry open this door, but slowly and patiently.

SCRIPT 7.2C. KEEPING THE DOOR OPEN

SALESPERSON: You certainly *are* an experienced investor. Mr. Nemlich—uh, Jim—I don't want to take up any more of your time this afternoon. Just let me confirm your address and I'll make sure you get notice of any situation we think looks interesting and may even call you if something really looks hot. Would that be okay with you?
MR. NEMLICH: Well, sure—but no guarantees that I'll be interested in buying anything.
SALESPERSON: Understood. Then, I'll be talking with you when something interesting comes up and make sure you're on our mailing list. Thank you for your time.

TIP: Mr. Nemlich was expecting a big sales pitch but we stopped before we peaked and left him wanting more. We weren't about to do a one-call close on this experienced investor who probably gets a call or two a day from people like us. The way to stand out from all those other callers seeking Mr. Nemlich's business is to take it slow.

The Follow-Through to Close

As a matter of fact, I did get four or five newsletters before I heard from the broker again. By now the name of his firm was familiar to me and I had some idea of the kind of approach they used and what their investment strategy was. They became ''real'' in my eyes.

I received one more phone call alerting me to a special situation that I declined. Rather than pushing for an order on this, the broker thanked me and promised to get back the next time he had something interesting. I continued to receive the newsletters. On the next call, about three weeks later, he did try for an order. It had been two months since the first contact, so I listened. It went something like this.

SCRIPT 7.3. DEALING WITH ENTRENCHED COMPETITION— TRIAL ORDER CALL

OBJECTIVE: Break the ice and get the prospect on the books with an attractive offer even for a small ''trial'' order. At least continue the contact with the prospect.

SALESPERSON: Morning, Jim. This is Gene Muscarella from Graham Securities. I promised to call you back when I had something else that looked interesting.
MR. NEMLICH: Yes . . .
SALESPERSON: Jim, we did a joint underwriting project a few months ago with Quest and Hamilton on a North Carolina company called IOS Industries. We brought it public at $5, and it went to $7 in two weeks. Their third quarter earnings were off, so it's backed off to just under $5.

MR. NEMLICH: It makes sense that it backed off. What did they do, dress up the financials for the IPO (Initial Public Offering)?

SCRIPT 7.3A. GETTING ATTENTION

SALESPERSON: No. It's their normally slow time of the year and this was explained in the prospectus. Also, they've moved into a facility *four times* the size of their old plant. Of course, this slowed production and meant extra costs. Just looking at the figures, the market doesn't realize that this will mean a lot of good things for the future of the company.
MR. NEMLICH: What do they do?
SALESPERSON: They are in the plumbing fixtures business. The unique thing here is that they have contracts with several large hotel chains, particularly those that are going to all-suite facilities. As you know, this is one of the fastest growing segments of the hotel business.
MR. NEMLICH: What was last year's EPS (Earnings per Share), and what are you projecting for this year?
SALESPERSON: They earned 15 cents a share last year, and we're projecting 20 cents this year with the start-up costs of the new plant and 25 to 30 cents next year.
MR. NEMLICH: That's over 20 times this year's earnings and almost 15 times next year's. It sounds a bit rich for me. How much stock do the original owners still hold?
SALESPERSON: About 60 percent—but, as you know, it's tied up for over two years.
MR. NEMLICH: Yes, but it still means that they control the company. Gene, this doesn't sound like something I'd be interested in.

SCRIPT 7.3B. AROUSING INTEREST

SALESPERSON: I can appreciate your analysis. You're obviously a lot more sophisticated than most of my clients. But, as you know, emotion rules the stock market more than fundamentals. In this case, one big mutual fund wanted to buy into the initial offering, but there wasn't enough stock left by the time they made the offer. The word we get is that they are still interested and are buying on the open market when the stock gets below $5.
MR. NEMLICH: Well, I'm sure they have their reasons, but they're probably not my reasons for investing. Let me know the next time something interesting comes up.

SCRIPT 7.3C. GOING FOR THE TRIAL ORDER

SALESPERSON: You know, Jim, my business depends on my making money for my clients. I would like the chance to show you I can do this for you. How about placing an order for just 200 shares? You know I won't make enough on that to pay for this phone call but I want to prove to you that we can work together.

The actual conversation went a bit longer, and Gene (not his real name) continued to stress the importance to *him* of doing well for me on this first trial order. Well, I placed the order, the stock did make money, and I continued to do business with Gene and his firm even though I've never met him except over the phone.

This kind of "give me a try and see how I do" trial offer to get a reluctant client on the books will work with almost any product. If it's insurance, it could be a small-term life policy or a specialty product like a mortgage disability policy that could lead to automobile and homeowner's policies. With other intangible services like consulting, it could be a free hour or two. With tangible products it could be free samples or freebies included with a basic product (free disks or software packages with a computer, for example).

OTHER SCRIPTS

By now, the pattern for handling competitive and other situations has been established. The most important thing to remember is to *find out why the prospect isn't buying* or where his head is before you start selling. You do this by *asking questions* and then determining the direction of the interview. In the next few sections, we'll look at some excerpts of more complete scripts. These excerpts or mini-scripts will be directed at specific competitive situations that could arise.

SCRIPT 7.4. TRYING THE LOGICAL APPROACH

Since people behave psychologically and not logically, and make their buying decisions emotionally more often than factually, this approach should be used very sparingly. You may, however, be dealing with a hush-puppies-shod, pipe-smoking engineer with whom you have to deal on a logical, factual basis to overcome an obstacle.

PROSPECT: Our tests so far have shown us that King's laser cards product has more of the features and benefits we're really looking for than yours.
SALESPERSON: May I ask what kind of tests you conducted on both products?

> TIP: The "tests" may be a bluff masking some other reason for not buying. If they are real, our purpose is to attack the methodology used and the relativity of the tests to the actual market use of the cards. Of course, we can't do this directly. Our prospect runs through the testing procedure used and we say:

SALESPERSON: Well, it looks like you've been pretty thorough in your evaluation. I'd like to take this back to our engineering people and see what they say. Can we set an appointment for 8:00 Tuesday?

> TIP: We could have addressed the issue at this point. "Taking it back to our engineering people," however, will make us more points with this engineer. A two-step process also provides more credibility for our report on the results.

SCRIPT 7.5. HANDLING THE "I CAN GET . . . FREE" OBJECTION

PROSPECT: Well, I like the features and price of your machine, but Cohen's Copy has offered me free paper for six months if I buy *their* machine.
SALESPERSON: Why do you suppose they offered to do that?
PROSPECT: I guess because they want my business.
SALESPERSON: And, of course, we do too. Let's look at what this really means. I'm sure you gave them your estimate of 3,000 copies per month, so they have figured on 18,000 sheets or 36 reams of paper. Right?

PROSPECT: Yes, that's what it would work out to.

SALESPERSON: Now, at $5 per ream, that works out to $180. Suppose I said that I'd either match the paper offer or even *give* you the $180 if you buy our machine?

PROSPECT: What's the catch?

SALESPERSON: I would give you the same kind of machine they have offered you— without the enlarging feature included with the machine we quoted on.

PROSPECT: But, that's worth $300.

SALESPERSON: Is it really worth $300 to *you*.

PROSPECT: Yes.

SALESPERSON: What would you like to do now?

> TIP: The six months of free paper *sounded* great and the prospect was caught up emotionally with this deal. By boiling it down to what it *really* meant, we let the prospect come to the conclusion that the extra feature our machine offered has represented a better total *value package* to him than the free paper or the $180.

SCRIPT 7.6. HANDLING THE MISSING FEATURE OBJECTION

There will be times when our competitor really does have something that we don't that is of interest and real value to our prospect. We can't downgrade the importance of the feature since it *is* important to our prospect, but we *can* push an alternative feature of our product or service that is related to the one we don't have.

> PROSPECT: Well, what it boils down to is that Cohen's Copy will give us a full one-year guarantee on parts and service and your deal is only three months.
>
> SALESPERSON: Why is that important to you?
>
> PROSPECT: Because I know I won't be nickled-and-dimed to death with the cost of service calls.
>
> SALESPERSON: Did you have many service calls with your last copy machine?

> TIP: We don't yet know exactly what our prospect's *real* objection is. So, we keep asking *questions* to zero in on this. One of the most important questions deals with his past experience.

> PROSPECT: Yes. It seemed like their service person was in here almost every week.
>
> SALESPERSON: Did that cause you any problems?

> TIP: We *know* what the problems have been. We want the prospect to admit that there *were* problems so we can know how to position our machine as a way to solve them. To accomplish this, however, we have to play it out slowly.

> PROSPECT: Of course it did. I had 12 people on my back every day asking about when the machine would be fixed. I don't want to go through that again.

SCRIPT 7.6A. UNCOVERING THE REAL OBJECTION

SALESPERSON: I guess, then, that prompt service is important to you.

> TIP: Here's where we begin to zero in on the *real* concern our prospect has. We can't threaten in any way, so we have to let the prospect convince himself. The service

contract wasn't the issue. Getting the other people in the office off his back (providing dependable copy service) is.

PROSPECT: Of course it is. That's why Cohen's deal looks so good to me. Their service calls are free for the first year.
SALESPERSON: I can understand why that would be important to you. May I ask you a question? Where is Cohen's place of business from where we are right now?
PROSPECT: Well, they're no more than 20 miles away. (Pause) Oh, I see what you mean. *You're* only 3 miles away.

SCRIPT 7.6B. PROVIDING A SUBSTITUTE BENEFIT

SALESPERSON: What does that suggest to you?
PROSPECT: Well, I guess you're going to make the point that you can be here on the spot to solve our service problems quicker.
SALESPERSON: Is that important to you?

> TIP: Again, we avoid the temptation to jump in with what we think might be a sales-closing clincher. Instead, we ask yet another question that will get us closer to the sale and the close without running the risk of blowing it.

PROSPECT: Of course it is. If your people can get here sooner and get the machine up and running, that means that there is less time for the office manager to be on my back.

SCRIPT 7.6C. CLOSING FOR THE ORDER

SALESPERSON: And, that's important to you?
PROSPECT: I just said that it is. Do you want me to engrave it on a card and send it to you?
SALESPERSON: No, just sign this purchase order so we can start as soon as possible on saving you headaches.

SCRIPT 7.7. HANDLING THAT DEAL-KILLING "THIRD PARTY"

As we have found, the third party can be a valuable asset or a royal pain in the neck. If they like our stuff, they are fantastically perceptive people. If they don't, they are obviously misinformed. Like them or not, they exist and exert buying influence on our prospects. We've dealt with them before, but not so directly as we will now:

> SALESPERSON: Well, Mr. O'Kane, we've covered all of the questions you've raised and it does, indeed, look like our system is the best one for you. It looks like the only question that is left is about leasing or outright purchase.
> MR. O'KANE: Well, that's not the only question left. It's true that your studies have shown us an excellent way to use your system in a way that would be advantageous to us, and you've shown us the cost-effective benefits that we would enjoy if we bought your system . . .

> TIP: Sometimes not hearing objections works. Sometimes it doesn't. It's worth a try,

especially if the objection is an obviously specious one, and with those prospects that you *know* don't really want to postpone a decision if there is an easier way.

SALESPERSON: Then, (pulling the paperwork out of his briefcase and ignoring the objection) I guess you're ready to have me get the ball rolling with the home office. All you have to do to make this happen is to sign where I've placed the "X".

MR. O'KANE: No, wait. It's true that I said that I was satisfied with everything we discussed—but Tracy, our office manager, is still giving me a hard time.

SALESPERSON: Oh, in what way, Martin?

MR. O'KANE: Well, she keeps reminding me of the problems we had with our last copy machine and she thinks that I haven't spent enough time on researching this purchase. Your proposal makes sense, but you were only the third person or firm I talked with.

SALESPERSON: Martin, *every* office I've been in in the past three months or even past three years has had a "Tracy" who wanted to make sure everything was okay with *every* piece of office equipment.

MR. O'KANE: Yep. That sounds like our Tracy.

SALESPERSON: Yes. But, do you know what, Martin? *They* don't like to make decisions. The way you get them off your back is to push them into a decision-making mode.

MR. O'KANE: How do we do that?

SALESPERSON: Well, the first thing we do is to recap the specifications all the managers told us were important in a copy machine. You already have that information in the proposal I gave you a month ago.

MR. O'KANE: But, I already circulated that to all the staff managers three weeks ago.

SALESPERSON: True, but they won't remember if they haven't gotten back to you by now. You can *force* a decision by sending out a listing of our features and benefits versus those of the second-best competitor.

MR. O'KANE: How do I do that?

SALESPERSON: Get out that proposal I gave you and add a second column for a competitor. That will give anyone enough information to make a decision.

MR. O'KANE: Aren't you worried that they will want me to go to a competitor when they see the comparison?

SALESPERSON: No.

MR. O'KANE: No?

SALESPERSON: Mr. O'Kane, I wouldn't have gone this far with you if I weren't convinced that *our* machine was *the* best one for you. A competitive analysis will just demonstrate this with more conviction.

MR.O'KANE: You really want me to send this out to our people and have them *vote* on which machine to buy?

SALESPERSON: Yes.

> TIP: We already have the votes. It's just that no one, including Mr. O'Kane, wants to make a decision. This suggestion and analysis puts it on the line with little risk to us.

The bottom line, of course, is that most everyone voted for our machine (including Tracy), so Mr. O'Kane had no more reason to hold off signing the purchase order. Tracy was off the hook since the decision was endorsed by almost everyone else, and the dissenter never wants to agree with anyone anyway.

IN CLOSING

We could probably develop more than 100 different competitive situations. The essential point is to find out why the prospect is throwing this red herring up to us. If we handled the presentation phase well and found that our product is, indeed, the best *value package* for the prospect, competition shouldn't matter. In almost every case, we need to get beyond the mostly specious objections and find the *real* reason the prospect is hesitating to sign with us. Naturally, we need to do this in a way which will keep the prospect's ego intact.

There will be times, of course, when the competitor's *value package* really is perceived by the prospect as being better than ours. The advice here is to make our final case and then go on to the next prospect whom we *can* sell. Too many salespeople are determined to sell a given number of (or all) prospects, whatever it takes. They are called "time-wasters" and don't usually show up at the top of the sales performance lists. It really is true that "You can't win them all," so play the percentages wisely.

8

Renewing Contracts Fearlessly

INTRODUCTION

Have you ever had it happen to you? About 2 to 3 months before a contract with a major account (an ''AA'', not just an ''A'') is going to be renewed, you begin to sweat over it. You don't sleep as well. You're more irritable than usual. You begin to review in your mind all the mistakes you've made with the account during the last few months. You calculate what the loss of this account will mean to you in commission dollars. You wonder what effect spilling the drink on his wife at the convention cocktail party is going to have.

It doesn't have to be this way.

You (your company) signed the contract with the account because there were *mutual* advantages. During the past year, if you've been handling the account well, you've shown him that there were more advantages to the contract than he first thought, because he had *you* to deal with problems and show him opportunities. This is worth a lot. He should recognize that—but, more important, *you* should. You're in a better position than you were last year regardless of price increases, competitive inroads, or changes in terms. Your customer has had a whole year of dealing with *you* and you're worth a lot of *value added*.

SCRIPT 8.1. HOW *NOT* TO RENEW A CONTRACT—COPING WITH FEARS

Our own mental attitude is, of course, the most important factor in selling. It gets us in trouble more than any company policy or competitor can and gets us more success than any degree of charisma or product knowledge. Before we look at some positive scripts, let's take a look at the *wrong* way to approach contract renewal. You may recognize this as a version of the old ''Keep your d--- jack'' story.

> OBJECTIVE: Meet with our customer, discuss the ''preliminary'' terms of next year's contract, resolve any small differences, and walk away with the assurance that we have this account sewed up for another year.

SALESPERSON: (while shaving in the morning) This is going to be another *great* day, starting with discussing the new ACS contract. I've done a super job for Adler Communication Systems during the last year. Johnny knows this and appreciates it. We want to make a few small changes in the contract, but they're based on his changing business needs and should work out to be better for him as well as us.

SALESPERSON: (to spouse or SO [significant other] over coffee) Yep, today's the day I wrap up another one. I'm meeting with Johnny Adler at ACS to work out any last details of next year's contract. Piece o'cake. Johnny knows what I've done for him and his company so it'll get the day started right.

SPOUSE/SO: Isn't he the one who insisted on reaching us at the shore over our vacation weekend because of a problem with that desktop publishing job?

SALESPERSON: Well, sure. But, we got that resolved during the next week and the job turned out great.

SPOUSE/SO: He seemed pretty upset at the time.

SALESPERSON: I told you. We got it resolved, and there's been no problem anything like that in at least the last three months.

SPOUSE/SO: I'm sure you did. The two-week delay in the annual report for one of his clients was the typesetter's fault, wasn't it?

SALESPERSON: That was resolved. Johnny realizes that it wasn't our fault that the typesetter was closed down by a strike when he needed the job.

SPOUSE/SO: I'm sure he does. Have a nice meeting. I'm sure that everything will go very well.

SCRIPT 8.1A. WATCHING THE FEARS BUILD

SALESPERSON: (driving to the expressway) Johnny knows that the few minor problems we've had could happen to anyone. We're still the best printing firm in town to meet his needs.

SALESPERSON: (getting on the expressway) The problem with that computer software company wasn't anybody's fault except the company. We did give them a proof to review. It wasn't Johnny's fault or mine that they didn't review it carefully enough.

SALESPERSON: (getting off the expressway) I'll bet Johnny has forgotten just how much we scrambled to get him out of trouble on that computer software company job to say nothing of the annual report. Why, I had to *beg* my boss to authorize the overtime to get it done.

SCRIPT 8.1B. SEEING THE NEGATIVES TAKE OVER

SALESPERSON: (pulling into ACS's parking lot) Maybe he doesn't realize how much we did. Johnny has a way of thinking only of what *he* needs to get done without thinking of everything guys like us have to do to make sure it happens.

SALESPERSON: (waiting in the reception room) Okay, so I'm a little early. Does that mean that the jerk has to keep me waiting after all I've done for him?

MR. ADLER: (coming out personally to the reception area after 4 minutes) Hi, Dave. Sorry to keep you waiting—problem in the art department. How are you?

SALESPERSON: Why don't you keep your d--- contract. It's not worth all the problems.

Okay, so the scenario may be a little exaggerated, but isn't this similar to what we often do in and to our heads? As we said on the first page of this chapter, "It doesn't have to be this way." Let's try it differently using the same situation and the same facts:

SCRIPT 8.2. RENEWING A CONTRACT SUCCESSFULLY

> OBJECTIVE: Review the past year's activities with our account in a way designed to show that renewing the contract on the new terms is the *only* way to go.

SALESPERSON: (after having gone through the first few steps above) Okay. I've gone through all of the major jobs we've done with ACS during the last year and I have them listed in descending order of value. I've given us an "A", "B", or "C" depending on how I think we performed on each one. Our overall score is a "B plus" and I have the facts about what happened on those "C's" that pulled our average down from an "A". I think I'm ready to review everything.

MR. ADLER: Morning, Dave. Sorry to keep you waiting—problem in the art department.

SALESPERSON: No problem. It gave me a chance to go over what we've done last year again.

> TIP: Remember that clients and customers love to hear those words "no problem." Also, we don't want our customer or client to feel guilty about a small delay, so we tell him we used our waiting time effectively, thereby taking him off the hook for the delay. If the client is a chronic "keep salespeople cooling their heels" person, we've cured that situation for us by walking out, pleading a tight schedule or another appointment after 10 to 15 minutes of waiting.

MR. ADLER: Well, let's go into my office. I'd like to discuss some changes I'd like made in our contract.

SALESPERSON: (seated in Mr. Adler's office with coffee served and other amenities out of the way) Johnny, before we go into next year's arrangement, I'd like to review with you some of the highlights of our working together last year and use that as a basis to figure out how we're going to have an even better relationship during the next year.

> TIP: We *need* to have control, but can't take it over overtly. Mr. Adler's wanting to discuss changes means that *he* wants control. We smooth this over by client-friendly terms like "working together" and "better relationship." We talked about an "arrangement" rather than the possibly threatening term "contract."

MR. ADLER: Good. There were a lot of things that happened last year that I wasn't too happy about.

> TIP: It looks like he's going to try to use those few problem areas we had as a ploy to negotiate a better contract or some other concession. We can't confront this di-

rectly because that would be ego-threatening, so let's turn this opening gambit around to a move that will benefit us both.

SCRIPT 8.2A. TAKING CONTROL OF THE INTERVIEW

SALESPERSON: (handing over a copy of a report in a nice proposal cover) This is an analysis of all the jobs we've worked on together in the past year. You'll notice that I've rated our performance on each job "A", "B", or "C". Now, this is just *my* evaluation. I'm really interested in what *you* think.

> TIP: *We* have a formal report *and* a formal rating system. This automatically gives us the upper hand. Written reports, especially when contained in proposal covers, can always be counted on to mean a lot more than conversation, no matter how significant the conversation. The phrase "worked on together" does no harm.

SALESPERSON: Look, Johnny, I have to get some information on the Heidi report from Sue. Why don't I give you a minute to review this report while I spend a couple of minutes with Sue?

> TIP: One of the worst mistakes salespeople can make is to hand someone something to read and then go on talking. The second most serious mistake is to give someone something to read without giving them uninterrupted time to read it. Having to check with Sue on something also reminds Mr. Adler of our ongoing relationship and activity with current jobs.

SCRIPT 8.2B. DEALING WITH PROBLEM ISSUES

SALESPERSON: Well, it looks like we're on track with the Heidi brochure. Would you like to discuss the analysis of jobs and the ratings?
MR. ADLER: I didn't realize we'd given you all that much business in the past year.
SALESPERSON: (Silence. Let's see where Mr. Adler goes from here so we know how to proceed.)
MR. ADLER: Well, I think you've been fair about rating your performance. And, it's true that those troublesome jobs were among the smaller ones.

> TIP: Now that we have the problems in perspective and know that they won't dominate the conversation, we can move on to eliminating this as an obstacle to the contract renewal.

SALESPERSON: Thank you, I appreciate the kind words. I have a couple of recommendations on how I can work with you and your people to avoid that kind of trouble in the future. First, here's a project planning chart I think will work well . . .

We could go on from here to ask additional questions and use silences to make sure that there are no reservations remaining before Mr. Adler suggests that the contract be signed. The closing techniques would be similar to those already discussed in other chapters—hardly noticeable. That is, by doing our job well and being *prepared*, the close will almost take care of itself.

SCRIPT 8.3. GETTING THE CONTRACT RENEWED—TELEPHONE CALL NUMBER ONE

The personal visit is appropriate for our largest accounts or if our customer base consists of a few large accounts. For our smaller accounts, where our customers are spread over a wide geographic area or in situations where there are a large number of contracts to get renewed, a telephone call might work. The basic techniques will be much the same. The most important thing is to be *prepared*.

OBJECTIVE: Answer any questions that may remain before the contract will be renewed, uncover any obstacles that may exist and get agreement that the signed contract will be returned.

SALESPERSON: Good morning, Mr. Fuller. This is Wendy Ryan from Cardinal Business Services. I'm calling to discuss the letter I sent you recently on continuing your service agreement.

TIP: By using the term ''continuing'' we're implying a benefit that we are willing to confer. Also, ''agreement'' is much friendlier than ''contract.''

MR. FULLER: Oh yes. I think I have that here, but haven't had a chance to look at it.
SALESPERSON: Well, I think it's important that we answer any questions you have that may not have been spelled out in the letter. You'll see that the increase in the monthly fee is only 6 percent and still a good deal less than you would pay for even a minimum number of service calls. And, you'll see that we've expanded the preventative maintenance program making the service arrangement an even better value.

TIP: The increase is there, so let's not pretend that it is not. The issue will come up sooner or later and we have more control over the interview if *we* bring it up. At the same time, we're throwing in two benefits and placing the emphasis on *value* rather than cost.

MR. FULLER: I would have thought that, with our service history, the price would go down. I don't remember seeing you people around here very much.

TIP: We have the answers to this, including the fact that we deal with Mr. Fuller's office manager most of the time and get a lot of problems worked out over the phone especially with the newer employees who haven't been properly trained on the machines. Let's wait, however, not give it all away and make this a two-step process. We've sensed that Mr. Fuller isn't in a very good mood, so we can only gain by waiting.

SCRIPT 8.3A. DEALING WITH PROBLEM ISSUES

SALESPERSON: Usually the low number of service calls is a testimony to the quality of our machines and our preventative maintenance program. But, why don't we do this: Why don't you take some time to go over the letter I sent and the agreement. In the meantime, I'll go back through our records and recap the number of calls and whatever other information I find. May I call you back tomorrow morning?

MR. FULLER: Sounds fine.

> TIP: Actually, we are prepared with the exact record of calls made and what they would cost if there were no service contract. We'll get more credibility, however, if we promise to check out a request Mr. Fuller has seemed to initiate.

Sometimes a two-step process is necessary to let the customer feel that he is in control. Better a win with two calls than a possible loss resulting from trying to do everything with one call.

SCRIPT 8.4. GETTING THE CONTRACT RENEWED—TELEPHONE CALL NUMBER TWO

We've let enough time go by so it will be clear to Mr. Fuller that we've done some work in checking out "his" question and request. Now we're ready to call back.

> OBJECTIVE: Resolve the issue of the number of service calls that have been made over the past year and demonstrate the *value* of the service contract. Get the contract renewed.

SALESPERSON: Good afternoon Mr. Fuller, Wendy Ryan from Cardinal Business Services. I'm following up on our conversation yesterday afternoon. Have you had a chance to review the letter and contract?

> TIP: This is not exactly a smooth approach—but it's open-ended, meaning that we have a chance to gauge Mr. Fuller's further reaction to the new contract before we start pushing for a close.

MR. FULLER: Yes I have and I want to tell you that I'm pretty unhappy about the increase. I was looking forward to a *decrease* based on our experience.
SALESPERSON: Oh, and why is that, Mr. Fuller?

> TIP: We'll gain nothing by immediately shooting down Mr. Fuller's arguments. Let's stretch it out a bit and let him sell himself if we can.

MR. FULLER: Well, I signed that first agreement expecting to have the same kind of problems with your machine that we've had with previous machines. The fact that we haven't means, it seems to me, that we should get a lower price on next year's contract.

SCRIPT 8.4A. DEALING WITH PRICE INCREASE OBJECTIONS

SALESPERSON: (innocently) Oh, is it a disappointment to you, Mr. Fuller, that you haven't had the kinds of problems with our machine that you've had in the past?

> TIP: This is, admittedly, not very subtle, but we've made our point and gained the upper hand in a nonthreatening way by asking a question instead of an "I told you so!" statement. We also turned the focus from the cost of the new service contract to the value of our total package.

MR. FULLER: Well, I guess not. I guess it's been pretty refreshing to have had so few

problems and so few times that people have been on my back (recovering and trying to gain control). But, that has nothing to do with my service contract.
SALESPERSON: Right.

> TIP: Again, no argument, but a disarming statement that agrees with Mr. Fuller when he expects to be argued with. This also puts the ball in his court so *he* has to decide where to go, and we have the ability to deal with his direction.

MR. FULLER: Right?

SCRIPT 8.4B. EXPLAINING ADDED VALUE TO JUSTIFY INCREASES

SALESPERSON: Yes, *right*. You see, what made it possible for you to have so few problems was not just the quality of our machines, but the preventative maintenance calls that are part of our agreement. And, as we discussed yesterday, we've even expanded these calls with the new agreement.

> TIP: This is a good time to pause and wait. We've hit home with our point on the expanded preventative maintenance program part of the new service contract which the home office was smart enough to give us knowing that the cost of this benefit was well-covered in the price increase. It would be tempting to go on with our pitch, but it's a lot more effective if we do it on Mr. Fuller's timetable and in response to his questions.

MR. FULLER: Well, doesn't that mean that you should lower the cost of our contract for next year?
SALESPERSON: Mr. Fuller, what are you paying for in working out this service agreement?

> TIP: Again, as in previous chapters and scripts, we don't answer the question that is asked except with another question that will keep us in control in a nonthreatening way and tell us where Mr. Fuller's head really is, and give us the ideal platform from which to make our points.

MR. FULLER: What do you mean?
SALESPERSON: Well, you signed the agreement last year. You obviously expected that it would provide some benefit to you or you wouldn't have signed it.
MR. FULLER: Yes. I expected to have a good handle on what my service costs would be and have someone there whenever there was a problem. I didn't really expect that the PM (prevention maintenance) contract would be of a lot of value, but I bought it as a part of what you people called a total *value package*.
SALESPERSON: Did you get this?
MR. FULLER: Yes. You know I did. You people have been great on handling all our problems and I'll admit that there have been fewer of them. But, I still don't understand why our cost for the contract will increase instead of decreasing.

SCRIPT 8.4C. SELLING THE TOTAL VALUE PACKAGE

SALESPERSON: Mr. Fuller, let me ask you another question. How do you really measure the worth of a service contract?

MR. FULLER: On the basis of the kind of service I really get and how much it would cost me to get the same kind of service any other way.

SALESPERSON: What "other" way is there?

MR. FULLER: Well, I could just pay you or an independent service firm to make service calls on a call-by-call basis as problems arose.

SALESPERSON: So, the way to judge a service contract is to measure the cost of the contract versus the cost of individual calls?

> TIP: This is where we begin to close. We don't try to overpower our customer or come up with slick techniques to "trick" him into a close. We ask questions that identify with his self-interest and let him close himself.

MR. FULLER: Sure. That's the *only* way.

SALESPERSON: Then, why don't we take a look at the actual number of calls during the past year?

MR. FULLER: That sounds like a good idea to me. Do you have your information?

> TIP: Now we're dealing on what Mr. Fuller thinks is his turf. It's really *our* turf, but we are in the position of responding to Mr. Fuller's questions. Of course, we knew the answer to his questions before we made the first phone call because we were *prepared*.

SCRIPT 8.4D. LETTING THE CUSTOMER SELL HIMSELF

SALESPERSON: Yes. Would you like to jot this down?

> TIP: *Anything* a prospect puts down in his own handwriting is going to be more convincing than *any* proposal we could send. Mr. Fuller is about to convince himself on his own pad.

MR. FULLER: I'm ready to write.

SALESPERSON: Okay. Your service contract costs you $500 per year. Put that in the lefthand column of your pad if you don't mind.

MR. FULLER: Done.

SALESPERSON: Our service calls are $70 minimum and $70 for each hour after one hour which, as you know, is competitive with all other service firms. Right?

MR. FULLER: Right so far.

SALESPERSON: During the last year you had six service calls. Would you like the exact dates?

MR. FULLER: No. I'll take your word for that, but that adds up to only $420.

SALESPERSON: True. *If* those calls only took one hour or less. Two of the calls took two hours, so the real cost would have been $560. Right?

MR. FULLER: (reluctantly) Well, I guess so.

SALESPERSON: Did you write the extra $140 down on the righthand side of your pad?

MR. FULLER: Yes.

SALESPERSON: Now, let's come up with some other things to put in the righthand column. Our logs show that we received 32 calls from your people about problems that we resolved over the phone.

MR. FULLER: *What*? That's impossible.

SALESPERSON: No, not really. Our people carefully log in every call so we can pinpoint problems that might exist and so we can refine our training program based on any misunderstanding our customers might have about how to get the maximum value from our machines.

TIP: Isn't that neat? We not only answered the question but chalked up a couple of bennies for us that show how conscientious we are and called attention again to our great training program—another *value added* benefit of dealing with us.

MR. FULLER: You really had that many calls?
SALESPERSON: Yes, we did. They averaged from 5 to 10 minutes in length. Let me ask you this question. What do you feel this is worth?
MR. FULLER: Not much. I make phone calls all day long.

SCRIPT 8.4E. CLOSING THE CONTRACT RENEWAL

SALESPERSON: Mr. Fuller, if you were not on a service contract, you would have been charged $20 for each call. Can we say that they were worth $10 each?
MR. FULLER: I guess so. My lawyer charges me $50 every time I call him even if it's just to say that the alimony check really is in the mail.
SALESPERSON: Then, what figure do you think you should put down on the righthand side of your pad?
MR. FULLER: I suppose that works out to $320. Okay, I think you've made your point.
SALESPERSON: (just as innocently as before) But, Mr. Fuller, we haven't even discussed the value of the expanded preventative maintenance services that come *free* with our new service agreement.
MR. FULLER: Never mind, Wendy. You've made your point. What do you want me to do now?

TIP: This is how a close should work. We've handled Mr. Fuller's objections and questions *at his request* and came back with the right answers. Instead of ineffectively blurting out our case prematurely, we developed it *with* him, step-by-step. By the time we're through or even almost through developing this case, our customer is suggesting the close.

SCRIPT 8.4F. CEMENTING THE CLOSE

SALESPERSON: Sign the contract and put it in the mail today so we can start you on our new, expanded preventative maintenance program as soon as possible—unless you have any further questions.
MR. FULLER: No, no. You win.
SALESPERSON: Mr. Fuller, may I suggest that we have *both* won? *You* have a service agreement that makes an awful lot of sense for your company and I have you as a customer. Having you as a customer means a lot to me. I look forward to working with you on an even better relationship on even more machines.

TIP: "You win" is too often a euphemism for "I'll get you later." We don't want this to happen. The only "winning" deal is when *both* parties to an agreement walk away as winners. Also, expressing appreciation for having a person as a customer is a good move, especially when it is sincerely motivated. Too few salespeople remember to do this. Since *we're* smarter than most salespeople, we *always* take every opportunity to tell our customers how important they are to us.

MR. FULLER: Wendy, you are a *joy* to deal with. I have a friend in the moving and storage business who may need a copy machine. Is it all right with you if I give him your name?
SALESPERSON: Mr. Fuller, I'd really appreciate that. Why don't you give me his name and phone number so I can log it in my records now?

TIP: Referrals are great, but only if you can be sure that they are real. Mr. Fuller *may* remember to call his friend or he may be just making a nice gesture. Let's not take that chance. We have a new "A" for our prospect file and let's make sure we sew it up *now*.

Wow—an extra bonus. This makes the extra time we spent making two phone calls on what should have been a one-call close worthwhile. All we have to do now is make sure we turn this referral into a bonafide prospect.

LETTER 8.1. GETTING A CONTRACT RENEWED BY LETTER

This letter is intended for those "B" or "C" customers whom we don't have time to reach either personally or over the phone. It could also apply to those situations where we have a lot of small customers or when the renewal of the contract is almost a given and the notification letter is only a nice courtesy. Be careful, however, about *assuming* that anything is a "given" without doing some preparation and some homework. Too many salespeople have found that their customer base has shrunken by making these kinds of assumptions.

Dear (Customer):

Your new money-saving service agreement on your XT4 copy machine for next year is enclosed. You may be interested in some of the changes that have been made. Here are the highlights:

1. The annual service contract fee has been increased by only 6 percent. The total *value package* to you has been increased by several times that amount. Let me explain why I can make that statement:

2. The preventative maintenance program has been expanded so that we will be replacing the copy machine masters and replacing the toner on *every* call to ensure that your copies will always look sharp and fresh. *And*, you will get a discount of *50 percent* when we do this in connection with a service or preventative maintenance call.

3. The service recap enclosed shows that you would have paid $_____ for service calls over the past year if you did not have a money-saving service agreement. This is $_____ less than the total cost of the agreement.

Please review the terms of the agreement, let me know if you have any questions and send the signed contract back to me in the enclosed postpaid envelope.

—EXTRA BONUS—

If you get the signed agreement back to me before the September 30th expiration date (it's now around the end of July), we'll start you *immediately* on the expanded PM program.

P.S.: I'll be calling you in the next few weeks to set an appointment to talk about our new color copier which has enlarge, reduce, and document feed capabilities.

CONTRACT RENEWAL LETTER SUMMARY

Let's review some of the things we did in this letter:

1. We didn't pussyfoot around about the price increase. It's there and we can't deny it, so we defuse any negative reaction by bringing it up right away. Notice that we said "*only* 6 percent."

2. We then went immediately to the concept of the *value* of the contract to get the attention away from price as the only reason for the "agreement."

3. We followed up by providing a *benefit*. Actually, this "expansion" of the preventative maintenance program will cost us *nothing*. Our service people have been replacing masters and toners at no charge and this has been the proverbial bone of contention with the home office. Now, we've resolved the issue to the home office's satisfaction and made it look like a real customer benefit.

   (Actually, it *is* a *real* customer benefit since most of our customers "forget" to change masters and replenish toner because they don't like doing it. If they are absolved of this chore, they won't think twice about the fact that they are paying for it and will, instead, focus on the 50 percent discount. They will also be a lot happier with their copies.)

4. We did our homework and reminded our customer of all the service calls we've made in the past year. Further, we quantified this benefit in terms of dollars so the contract for next year, even with the price increase, still looks like a bargain.

5. We provided the necessary "action step" by asking for something specific to happen—send the contract back. *And*, we provided a benefit to the customer for doing this sooner than he has to, a benefit that will cost us nothing.

6. We saved the "P.S." for the introduction of our next effort to sell these customers another copier or to upgrade their present ones. (You remember that the "P.S." is the third most important part of a letter—after the name of the person to whom it is addressed and the name (and title) of the person who signs the letter.) We just may whet some appetites in an innocuous way and pave the way for our next call. (If it seems as if we are always "paving the way" in our calls, *it's true*. *Every* effort should always be a prelude to our next success.)

7. Finally, we kept the letter short and sweet. The fewer the questions that are raised about the price increase, the fewer we will have to answer. We will entertain objections if they come up, but we certainly aren't going to invite them. We act like the most natural thing in the world is to renew and that anything else would be unnatural.

IN CLOSING

This chapter should have served to take some of the fear and apprehension out of renewing contracts. We discussed and illustrated several issues:

1. Don't be afraid of the renewal process. Your customer signed last year's contract to obtain a benefit for *him*, not to do you a favor.

2. *Always* provide a new benefit, whether or not your home office has provided you with one. You could, for example, offer to check in every 2 months to provide training for any new employees. Just incidentally, this allows you to access the customer's need for additional machines or for an upgraded machine. It also provides the opportunity to perform the most-neglected sales function of all—ask for referrals.

3. *Do your homework.* That is, anticipate possible objections to the renewal and be prepared with answers whether or not you cover these in one phone call or one letter or several. The most effective way to do this is by providing facts and figures that you put together *at your customer's request.*

9

Using Customer Complaints as an Opportunity

INTRODUCTION

There are several themes that we've expressed many times throughout this book that are particularly appropriate for this chapter:

1. Every cloud has a silver lining.
2. Every "problem" contains the seeds of its own solution if we will only look *inside* the problem.
3. There are few adversities we will face that cannot be turned to our advantage.
4. "We are all faced with a number of great opportunities brilliantly disguised as insoluble problems."—paraphrased from John Gardner in *Self Renewal*.

We might also add one other suggestion so you will learn to *enjoy* what you are doing. That is, get enjoyment from the *process* or the *means* instead of just the *ends*: The rainbow is real—the pot is not. So, enjoy the rainbow—the process—because the "pot" never turns out to be what you thought it would be anyway.

Customer complaints are a way to *enjoy* the process, believe it or not. You can have 19 successful transactions with a customer and a problem with the twentieth. You will be measured, for better or worse on what happens on the twentieth. The most important thing a customer is looking to you for and the way you will be measured as an effective salesperson is how you are able to answer the question "What did you do for me when I had a problem?"

Problems *are* opportunities and the solving of them can be very gratifying as we'll see below. The important thing to remember, especially for customer service people, is that *customers are the REASON for our business, not an interruption of it.* Being very professional salespeople, we would much rather have a customer voice a complaint that we can handle than remain dissatisfied and stop doing business with us.

We'll assume during this chapter that *you* are your *own* customer service department. If you are fortunate enough to have an administrative assistant or even a customer service or sales service person or department, the same lessons will apply and you can teach them to your people.

SCRIPT 9.1. TURNING A POLICY COMPLAINT INTO A SALE

> OBJECTIVE: Well, we don't really know what our specific objective is because we don't know what kind of customer complaint call is going to come in. Let's just say that our overall objective is to turn all customer complaint calls into advantages and opportunities for us.

MS. PORTMAN (CUSTOMER): (not exactly in a clam frame of mind) Stu, are you guys out of your minds?
SALESPERSON: Well, sometimes I think we are. Can you tell me what your real question is, Sally?
MS. PORTMAN: What I have in mind is this nonsense about our having to pay a site location license fee to the manufacturers you represent for every single copy of the software package we want to use at different locations. We've copied the packages before and we'll continue to copy them.

> TIP: There's no point right now in reminding Ms. Portman that what she has been doing in the past and plans to continue to do is illegal. Let's figure out the dimensions of the problem so we know what it is that we're addressing.

SCRIPT 9.1A GETTING TO THE NUB OF THE COMPLAINT

SALESPERSON: Sally, how many locations are you talking about that will want to use this package?
MS. PORTMAN: Three now, maybe five in the next year.
SALESPERSON: And, what is your specific objection to the policy that, as you know, *all* software manufacturers are insisting upon?

> TIP: Before getting embroiled in a fruitless discussion, let's make sure that we know the exact nature of the problem we are dealing with by following our usual technique of asking questions. We got in the subtle suggestion that we and our manufacturers are not the only people who are enforcing this policy. Also, allowing Ms. Portman to talk about her perceived (or, perhaps, real) problem and blow off steam will make her a lot more reasonable and the discussion a lot more rational.

MS. PORTMAN: I *bought* this package for a lot of money and it seems to me that I should be able to do what I very well please with it.

> TIP: It would be tempting here to remind Ms. Portman of the statement that came on the package that made it clear (unfairly or not) that she *couldn't* do what she pleased with it and agreed to this provision by unwrapping the package. This would be a logical answer to an emotional complaint—not likely to be very productive. Let's draw Ms. Portman out a bit further.

SALESPERSON: Sally, how do you feel about copyright laws that exist for *written* publications?

MS. PORTMAN: What does that have to do with anything?

SCRIPT 9.1B. PUTTING THE COMPLAINT IN PERSPECTIVE

SALESPERSON: Just this: Whether we like it or not, the courts have decided that making copies of books or newsletters without permission is illegal.

> TIP: Now, we've brought *two* third parties into our argument—the analogy of printed publications and what publishers' policies are, and copyright laws that are already on the books.

MS. PORTMAN: What does that have to do with my using my software package the way I want to?

SALESPERSON: Well, the courts have also decided that software packages are like books—you can't reproduce them without the permission of the publisher.

MS. PORTMAN: Why in the h--- did they do that?

SALESPERSON: I guess they figured that producing a software package involved a lot of up-front expenses—at least as much as writing a book—and that the software producer should be able to get his money back. (Now we pause and wait for the next move.)

MS. PORTMAN: This is beginning to make sense.

SALESPERSON: (Silence. This is another of those times when the best thing we can do is keep our mouths shut. We'll give Ms. Portman a chance to think and we'll learn what direction she's going off in next.)

MS. PORTMAN: Stu, are you there?

SALESPERSON: Yes. I was just waiting for you to tell me what you would like me to do.

MS. PORTMAN: Well, I guess the policy does make some sense. But, I don't want to go to jail and I don't want to spend $695 for every location that could use this software package. What do I do now?

> TIP: Perfect. Our customer has convinced herself that the policy is a reasonable one without our having to get into any kind of argument. Now we can, in an avuncular way, help her out.

SCRIPT 9.1C. RESOLVING THE BASIC COMPLAINT ISSUE

SALESPERSON: Well, we can get you a site license deal for every other location in which you would like to use this program. It would cost you only $200 per location.

MS. PORTMAN: Besides not going to jail or subjecting my company to a lawsuit, what do I get for my 200 bucks?

SALESPERSON: Good question. Besides the fact that it makes your use of the program legal, the manufacturer has worked out a deal with us to *support* each location.

MS. PORTMAN: What does that mean?

SALESPERSON: It means that *each* location will get updates of the package as they become available and updates of the training manual.

MS. PORTMAN: This is beginning to sound worthwhile. What else will it do for me?

SALESPERSON: Isn't that enough?

MS. PORTMAN: I guess so. But you always seem to come up with something else that you call part of your *value package*. That's why I do business with you.

SALESPERSON: You're too sharp for me. Okay. Here's another benefit: Do you know that we've worked out a deal with the manufacturer where we train your people on the use of the package as a part of the price?

MS. PORTMAN: Yes. That's why we pay those exorbitant prices to you instead of buying from a mail-order house.

SCRIPT 9.1D. SELLING THE EXTRA VALUE OF OUR PRODUCT

SALESPERSON: Well, the "extra" in our *value package* in this case is that we provide the same kind of training for *each* of your locations that we provide for your main location when we first installed the package.

MS. PORTMAN: You'll really do all that for us?

SALESPERSON: Yes, *and*, this same feature applies to that database package we've been talking about. Why don't I work out all the details of the site licensing program and bring it to you? At the same time, we can talk about installing that database package you need.

A very successful automobile dealer uses a theme that goes something like, "Let us sell you a lemon—then you'll find out how good we really are." They look for *problems* that can be turned into *opportunities*. In our case, we not only dealt effectively with the problem raised and solidified our position as a *value package* supplier, but turned the complaint interview into an opportunity to discuss a different product we have been unsuccessful in selling to this customer so far. The techniques we used will also work as successfully over the phone.

SCRIPT 9.2. CREATING GOODWILL FROM A PRODUCT
APPLICATION COMPLAINT

Sometimes the customer really is wrong about the way he is trying to use a product or just hasn't read the instructions. This is still an opportunity for us to cement a relationship and pave the way to future sales.

OBJECTIVE: Handle a "the customer is wrong" complaint in a way to provide satisfaction, build goodwill, and benefit future sales.

SALESPERSON: Yes, may I help you?

MR. REA: I hope so. The last two people I talked with made me feel stupid.

TIP: Obviously the idea that "the customer is king" and that customers are the reason for our jobs, not an interruption of them, has not gotten across to everyone in our organization. We make a note to get out a formal procedure memo, or, depending on where we are in the organization, a "suggested" procedure for our manager to review.

SCRIPT 9.2A. LETTING THE CUSTOMER VENT (CATHARSIS)

SALESPERSON: Why don't you tell me exactly what the problem is and I'll see how I can help?

MR. REA: I bought one of your answering machines. The electrical cord plugs into the electrical outlet, but the telephone plug won't fit my telephone outlet.

TIP: At this point, we know exactly what the problem is, but let's take an extra minute to calm this customer down and make him feel better.

SALESPERSON: Could you describe your telephone outlet to me? Does it have four holes?

MR. REA: Yes. Just like all the outlets in my house that handle all the phones.

SALESPERSON: Mr. Rea, do you have your instruction manual handy?

TIP: This is a subtle, polite reminder that the manual is the first place to go for help. By getting the manual in the customer's hands and having him use it, we may head off the next problem.

MR. REA: Yes, right here.

SCRIPT 9.2B. GETTING THE CUSTOMER TO RECOGNIZE THE PROBLEM

SALESPERSON: Okay. Would you turn to page nine. Do you see paragraph four and the illustration just below that where we suggest that, if you have a four-prong outlet, you will need an adaptor.

MR. REA: Uh-huh. I guess I missed that the first time through the manual. Why don't you people supply the adaptors with the machines?

SALESPERSON: Well, only about 10 percent of the phones in our area use that type of outlet, so we make the machine for the vast majority.

TIP: This is the ''reasonable explanation'' step. We certainly are not going to tell Mr. Rea that he has an old, outmoded system.

MR. REA: How do I get one of these things?

SCRIPT 9.2C. SOLVING THE PROBLEM CREATIVELY

SALESPERSON: Any telephone store and a lot of retail electronic stores would carry them. However, if you can wait a couple of days to install your machine, I'll be happy to send you one.

MR. REA: What's that going to cost me?

SALESPERSON: Nothing.

TIP: At this point, Mr. Rea would pay us two or three times the value of the adaptor just to get the problem solved. On the other hand, it would cost *us* more than the adaptor to process his check.

MR. REA: Nothing? What's the catch?

SALESPERSON: There's no catch. We want all our customers to be satisfied with everything they buy from us. If you'd like, you could tell your friends that we're good people to do business with.

This is the way a lot of customer complaints are—some silly, little thing that could result in a big problem or the return of the merchandise if not handled promptly and properly. They can also be opportunities to build goodwill that no amount of advertising could buy. The small cost of offering to send the adaptor free is worth it. Contrast this with the way we often get treated—sent all over town (or back to the factory) for something that isn't worth 10 minutes of our time.

SCRIPT 9.1. HANDLING A COMPLAINT WHERE WE GOOFED

No matter how hard we try or how customer-oriented we try to be, mistakes will be made. Sometimes it's because manufacturers don't pay enough attention to the fact that they can correct defects in the factory for less than $1 that could result in a $75 service call in the field. Sometimes it's an honest mistake.

We can't pretend that they don't exist—and the sooner we get the word out about what we are doing to correct the mistake, the smaller the problem will be.

> OBJECTIVE: Call our customer's attention to the fact that the instruction manual was inadvertently left out of one week's shipment of machines. Solve the small problem *now* before it becomes a bigger problem.

Dear (Customer):

IF YOU RECEIVED A SHIPMENT OF OUR MACHINES DURING AUGUST, PLEASE READ THIS LETTER IMMEDIATELY.

During the week ended August 15th of this year, the instruction manuals were left out of the cartons of our Model 642 machines.

We've researched our records to determine the shipments to you during this period and are sending enough instruction manuals to cover the machines you received without manuals.

We're sorry about the inconvenience, but wanted to get the manuals to you right away rather than wait for you or your customers to discover the problem. If you have already sold these machines, we would be happy to send a manual with an apology letter to your customers.

You know that this kind of error is not typical of the kind of product or service we usually provide, so we would be pleased to work with you to resolve any problems that arise.

P.S.: We've had some requests in the past year to provide adaptors for those few customers who have the old-type telephone outlets. We're enclosing with the instruction manuals a *free* adaptor for each machine you bought during this period.

SUMMARY—THE "WE GOOFED" LETTER

Let's review what we accomplished with our handling of the situation and this letter, compared to the way situations like this are sometimes handled:

1. We didn't want this to look like just another sales letter, so we printed it on cherry stock and put a big headline at the top of the letter. Our customers and our salespeople know that this bright red paper means "urgent bulletin."

2. We rushed out the letter as soon as we found out what happened so we could defuse the situation by having our customers find out about the mistake from *us* instead of being embarrassed by finding out from their customers or their salespeople.

3. Instead of offering to send manuals to customers who requested them and transferring the burden of our mistake to our customers, we did some homework and found out who got the machines and will automatically send the right people the manuals. This has the extra advantage of confining the knowledge of the mistake to a small customer base.

4. We took the further step of offering to send manuals and apology letters to our customers' customers if they wish. We may not get many takers on this offer, but we get points for making it. If we get a lot of takers, our market research department has a nice addition to their end-user lists.

5. We reminded our customers that this is atypical of our company and offered to help in other ways to remedy the situation—another point-getting move.

6. Our P.S. threw in another low-cost customer benefit that might make some customers even happy we made the mistake we did.

LETTER 9.2. TURNING SHIPPING DELAYS TO OUR ADVANTAGE

Few factories or distributors are able to work out a completely effective JIT (Just in Time) inventory system where the in-stock inventory exactly matches customers' incoming orders. For most companies, there will always be peaks and valleys and products that sell a lot better than forecasted, no matter how efficient the production system. There will be production delays and problems in getting raw material from our vendors. As we did in the previous letter, we're going to 'fess up to these problems before they become an irritant to our customers and try to turn a problem into an advantage:

Dear (Customer):

SUBJECT: BOY, CAN YOU SELL MACHINES!!!

When we introduced our 642 answering machine this spring, we thought we had a winner. Our forecasts looked so optimistic that we had to practically bribe our production manager into producing so many.

Well, your orders and our sales have exceeded even our most optimistic forecasts. As you know, this has stretched our lead time for shipments from the normal one week to four weeks.

Of course, we're gearing up for a new, higher production level. In the meantime, however, we'd like to suggest an interim solution—a blanket purchase order program. Let me explain how that would work:

1. You anticipate your needs for the next 6 months and send us a blanket purchase order spelling out your requested shipping dates.

2. We'll handle these shipments as first priority on the basis of earliest *purchase order date* first. In other words, *your* November shipment called for by an August 15th purchase order will take precedence over an order received in September from someone else.

3. We can't promise upward adjustments in your requested shipments, but will consider downward adjustments if you've been overly optimistic. We expect to have a waiting list of customers who would be happy to pick up the machines.

We feel that this is the best solution to protect those of you who have invested in training and promotional programs and ensure a fairly steady and reasonably secure supply of product.

Your district manager will be working with you in the next few days on the details of the program. In the meantime, your questions, comments, and suggestions, as always, are welcome.

P.S.: We've taken your suggestion and are now using a larger switch lever for the playback control. This feature is incorporated in the machines that have been shipped during the past month.

Let's review what we accomplished in the way we handled the situation and with this letter:

SUMMARY—THE SHIPPING DELAYS LETTER

1. We admitted the problem and turned it into a positive. Everyone wants to be associated with a winner and we gave our customers credit for the win.

2. We made it clear that we were aware of the problems the delays might cause our customers and promised a long-term solution in the form of higher production.

3. We worked out an innovative solution that will be most responsive to those customers who can and will anticipate their orders because of the programs *they* have effected. It's the *fairest* answer to the problem we could come up with. Having purchase orders in hand doesn't do our forecasting ability or our clout with production any harm either.

4. We promised field follow-through to ensure that the program will be well-implemented. Naturally, a sales bulletin was issued spelling out all the details and a blanket purchase order coordinator appointed to handle details.

5. The entire tone of the letter was upbeat and suggestive of a winning company, a winning product, and, if you consider the alternative, a happy problem to have.

6. Our postscript provided yet another benefit and improvement and got us points for being customer-responsive. Too many companies are afflicted with the NIH (Not Invented Here) syndrome. That is, if the engineering department didn't think of an idea, it can't be very good. *Smart* companies *listen* to the marketplace and implement customers' ideas. *Customers' ideas*, even if mediocre, will work better than the seller's brilliant ideas because the customers will want to make them work.

This letter, admittedly, was written as though it came from the regional or home office. While this may be the best source, a modified version of the same program and letter can be implemented or suggested by field salespeople. It might even be the route to your next promotion, proving how smart you are in reading this book.

Unfortunately, shipping delays or other problems are not always the result of happy circumstances. Let's look at a letter covering an unhappy situation:

LETTER 9.3. SHOWING HOW WE CARE ABOUT PRODUCT QUALITY

"Zero defects" is a desirable quality assurance objective. As we mentioned previously, a $75 service call can sometimes be prevented by a $1 correction in the factory. Quality problems *do* occur, however, and have to be dealt with in the same forthright manner.

> OBJECTIVE: Admit our quality problem, provide a solution that will be in our customers' interest, and turn the problem into as positive a situation as we can under the circumstances.

Dear (Customer):

DID YOU EVER HAVE ONE OF THOSE DAYS WHEN NOTHING SEEMS TO GO RIGHT?

Well, we had a week like that recently with our Model 642 machines. We took your suggestion and incorporated a larger switch lever for the playback control on the machines. Naturally, we tested this thoroughly in our plant and it seemed to be working fine.

Unfortunately, we tested it in our Minnesota factory. It seems that, in hotter climates, the lever expands and binds against the housing. We've corrected the problem and have tested the machines under all kinds of weather conditions, but you may have a problem with machines with serial numbers from 360246 through 361471.

If you have any of these machines, you might want to replace the switch lever (a 30-second operation). Your district manager has a supply of the new levers which he will give you free of charge with an instruction sheet on how to make the change.

We're in the process right now of tracking down those of you who received these machines. Unfortunately, this is a manual job that will take some time. In the meantime, let your district manager know if you have these machines and want to replace the levers.

We're sorry about the inconvenience this may cause and we'll do whatever else we can to correct the temporary and limited situation. Your comments and suggestions on ways we can do this are welcome.

P.S.: In correcting the problem, we realized that a grooved lever would make the machine even easier to use, so we've also made this change.

Let's review what we did to make the best out of an unfortunate situation:

SUMMARY—PRODUCT QUALITY PROBLEM LETTER

1. We admitted the problem rather than hoping it would go away or not be noticed by more than a few people.
2. In the headline, we asked customers to identify with our problem. *Everyone* has some days when he or she seems to be running in black-and-white while the world is in technicolor. It may not always be completely appropriate to ask for sympathy, but it sometimes works very well.
3. We subtly invited customers to share some of the responsibility for the problem. After all, a larger switch lever was *their* idea wasn't it?

4. We told our customers in a straightforward manner the whole story of how the problem arose, indicating that it has been corrected.

5. We offered free replacement levers. This doesn't completely make up for the inconvenience, but shows that we want to help resolve the problem.

6. We said "We're sorry . . ." So many letters on recalls or explaining problems and defects omit this simple step. Instead, the tendency seems to be to take a defensive "What do you expect from us?" approach. In business as well as in personal life, the three most important words are often not "I love you," but "I was wrong."

As was the case with Letter 9.2, this letter could be implemented on a local field level, particularly if the problem is a local one or affecting only a few territories. Local implementation has the additional advantage of including a personal promise by the local salesperson to work with customers on the problem.

With computers, word-processing programs, and desktop publishing equipment, the letter could even be personalized with an "I'll be out to see you September 19th to help you resolve any questions" message. The downward spiral in the cost of such aids and the necessity to communicate by means other than personal calls suggests that you get this equipment if you don't have it already.

SCRIPT 9.3. TURNING A PERSONNEL COMPLAINT INTO A POSITIVE—NUMBER ONE

We, of course, are always friendly, courteous, and kind to our customers. But our customers often deal with other people in our company and the experience is not always positive. It *is*, however, our responsibility to deal with these situations since we are the main contact with the customer and have the most to gain. Let's look at how this kind of complaint can be handled.

> OBJECTIVE: Deal with a situation where our service person (it could be a product service or customer service person) has gotten our customer ticked off. Turn it into a positive. Because of our good relationship with the receptionist, we got tipped off to the problem before going in to see Mrs. Putnam.

MRS. PUTNAM: Well, if it isn't the representative of the company that doesn't like our business.

SALESPERSON: (pause, while seemingly taken aback) Mary, I want to assure you that we not only *like* but very much *appreciate* your business. (With sincerity and humility) May I ask what happened to give you the idea that we didn't?

> TIP: We're not going to get anywhere by being defensive or even letting on that we know about the situation and providing an immediate answer. Even if it were obvious that we did know, getting the story from Mrs. Putnam will cool her down besides ensuring that we have the whole and accurate (from Mrs. Putnam's view) story.

SCRIPT 9.3A. GETTING THE WHOLE STORY

MRS. PUTNAM: Your serviceman told me that our people had been abusing the machines.

SALESPERSON: Is it possible that they have been?

TIP: We know that this isn't the real issue, so asking the question doesn't hurt and will help later in isolating the *real* problem.

MRS. PUTNAM: Sure it's possible. We get a lot of turnover and some of our people can't turn on a typewriter without breaking the switch. That's not the point, however.
SALESPERSON: (Pause. Let's see what direction Mrs. Putnam will take.)
MRS. PUTNAM: (Glare.)

TIP: Well, pausing and silence doesn't *always* work. Let's go on with our questions.

SALESPERSON: (humble and sincere) May I ask then what the point is?
MRS. PUTNAM: It was the *way* he said it—like we were all a bunch of idiots who got up every morning thinking only of terrible things we could do to the machines.
SALESPERSON: Mary, you've known Tom for over a year. Is this typical of the way he usually acts?

TIP: We already know the answer to this, but let's keep asking questions until Mrs. Putnam begins to get close to an answer.

MRS. PUTNAM: (beginning to cool down) Well no. He's always been a little cool, but usually professional and efficient. I don't understand his attitude now.

TIP: The problem is no less severe, but it's now put in perspective. We've also reminded Mrs. Putnam of our usual standards. Now let's increase the perspective by relating *this* problem to one with which Mrs. Putnam is familiar.

SCRIPT 9.3B. PUTTING THE COMPLAINT IN PERSPECTIVE

SALESPERSON: How has your administrative assistant, Mandy, been lately. You recall that you were pretty upset with her a few months ago?
MRS. PUTNAM: I don't know what this has to do with what we're talking about. Mandy was going through a divorce. Once that got resolved, Mandy was fine.
SALESPERSON: (Pause.)
MRS. PUTNAM: Oh, I see. Is that what is happening to Tom? Why didn't you say so?
SALESPERSON: Well, I'm not sure that's exactly what is happening and I really feel uncomfortable discussing someone else's personal business.

TIP: We want to keep this conversation businesslike, don't want to spread gossip and don't want to get into Tom's personal affairs, but we've succeeded in placing some doubt in Mrs. Putnam's mind so she has to take a fresh look at the situation.

MRS. PUTNAM: Well, if that *is* the case, I can see why Tom might be a little irritable. Boy, now I feel badly about how hard I was on the poor guy. I really laid into him in front of the whole office.
SALESPERSON: I don't think you should feel badly. You couldn't know what is going on inside Tom's head. *And*, we expect our service people to always act professionally and courteously.
MRS. PUTNAM: What do we do now?

TIP: We put Mrs. Putnam *on* the hook, or let her put herself there. Now it's appropriate to take her *off* the hook so she doesn't feel guilty. People don't like associating with or doing business with people whom they feel guilty toward.

SCRIPT 9.3C. SMOOTHING OVER THE SITUATION EFFECTIVELY

SALESPERSON: Why don't we drop it, if you don't mind, with my apologies for what happened? I'll talk with Tom, not about this situation, but in general and see what I can do to help him and the company's relationship with our customers. I won't mention your name, but he just may get the point.

MRS. PUTNAM: Gee, I'm really sorry I bawled you out like that just now. It wasn't *your* fault and now I can understand where Tom is coming from.

> TIP: Now would be a good time to drop the subject, quitting while we're ahead. We can only lose by pursuing this any further.

SALESPERSON: No problem. Would this be a good time to talk about that document feeder we discussed a couple of weeks ago?

Another adversity turned to our advantage. We didn't get defensive and we didn't defend Tom or his actions. We asked questions that allowed Mrs. Putnam to come to her own conclusions so she has to "own" them. We were deliciously subtle about the causes which *might* have caused the actions and quit before the subject got beaten to death. How can Mrs. Putnam refuse to listen to us now about the document feeder?

SCRIPT 9.4. TURNING A PERSONNEL COMPLAINT INTO A POSITIVE—NUMBER TWO

Sometimes our "out" in explaining an employee's or colleague's actions is not so easy. Let's deal with another complaint that requires somewhat different handling to get it resolved. In this case, we weren't tipped off about the problem in advance.

> OBJECTIVE: Deal with our customer's complaint about the way he gets treated by our customer service people whether he is calling about a problem or to place an order. Turn it into some kind of advantage if we can.

SALESPERSON: Good morning, Mr. Seastrand. How can I help you?

MR. SEASTRAND: You can put that bunch of clowns in your customer service department on the next space shuttle or a junket to Siberia.

SCRIPT 9.4A. COOLING OFF THE CUSTOMER BY LETTING HIM TALK

SALESPERSON: You know, I sometimes used to feel that way too—until I got to the factory and found out what kind of pressure those people are under, especially in the morning. But, you obviously want to discuss a specific problem and I want to hear about it. Why don't you tell me?

> TIP: We dropped the hint about the pressure and made the subtle point that we, too, felt the same way *until* we got all the facts. Then we returned to Mr. Seastrand's agenda.

MR. SEASTRAND: This morning was the last straw. I called about an order and was put on hold for over 3 minutes. Then I was told that I had the wrong order number and would have to look up the right one. This, when I had my order sitting right in front of me. Finally the guy admitted that *he* had punched in the wrong number and said that I would have to call back this afternoon because the order was still being processed. Why couldn't *he* call *me*? If I didn't need the stuff for a customer I'd have suggested a place where he could put the order.

> TIP: Unfortunately, this is not atypical of the way our customer service department sometimes operates, especially in the morning rush when they are trying to get orders to the factory floor and answer customer calls at the same time. Equally unfortunate is the fact that the customer service department reports to the warehouse manager who reports to the production vice-president instead of to the marketing organization, so our manager has been able to do little to correct the situation.

SCRIPT 9.4B. RESOLVING THE SITUATION BY ASKING FOR HELP

SALESPERSON: Well, I don't blame you for being upset. Let me ask you a question. You know that customer service doesn't report to me or even to my manager. You've also seen how a lot of other factories operate. What suggestions would you make?

> TIP: In a subtle way, we've taken ourselves off the hook for *direct* responsibility for the problems, but we still have *indirect* responsibility since it is our company and we are the representative.

MR. SEASTRAND: I have enough trouble running my own business without being a consultant for yours.
SALESPERSON: I can appreciate that. I'm really asking for a favor and some specific help on how we can improve our service to you. You've told me before that most of your other factories do a better job than we do and I'd like to be able to pass some specific suggestions on to my manager.

> TIP: Tossing the ball back to Mr. Seastrand, however unfair that may be, takes the main focus away from the complaint and puts it on a solution. This should have the additional benefit of stimulating Mr. Seastrand to work with us for the moment on a "same team" basis instead of as an adversary.

MR. SEASTRAND: Well, one of the biggest problems is that I'm always talking to different people. Some of my suppliers assign specific inside salespeople, with specific backup people, to my account. That way, the people get familiar with me and I with them.

SCRIPT 9.4C. TURNING THE SITUATION INTO A POSITIVE

SALESPERSON: That sounds like a good idea. Look, I can't promise immediate improvement, but I'll call my manager *and* write a letter with that suggestion.

> TIP: Besides doing this, we'll try to get our manager to call or write Mr. Seastrand so he at least knows that the home office understands the problem, appreciates the suggestion, and will try to do something about it.

MR. SEASTRAND: How much do I get paid for this?
SALESPERSON: Larry, I appreciate the suggestion *and* your patience. I'll work out something for you.

> TIP: Mr. Seastrand really hasn't been patient and we can't blame him. Giving him the name, however, may encourage him to play the game. People have a way of living up to what you tell them you expect from them—negatively or positively.

MR. SEASTRAND: Don't send me any more keychains.
SALESPERSON: I'm sure we can do better than that. In the meantime, may I make a suggestion? Our customer service people are really rushed in the morning trying to get orders to the factory so they go out as soon as possible. I know that we should be ready to do business with you on *your* timetable, but you would get better service if you called in the afternoon to check on orders or ask any other questions.
MR. SEASTRAND: I suppose we could do that. I'm pretty busy in the mornings too.
SALESPERSON: Larry I'm really sorry about the problems you've had. I know my manager is trying to work with production to get them resolved. In the meantime, please let *me* know if you feel there is anything I can do to help.

This was a tough situation. We know the problem. Our manager knows the problem. The best we can do is listen, get our customer and us on the same team, keep putting pressure on our manager, and vociferously make our requests for change at the next sales meeting.

We can also call the customer service representative in question, listen to *his* problems, and ask what kind of message he thought he was communicating to our customer, despite the problems the representative has.

We might also suggest to our manager that he invite the production and/or warehouse manager to our next sales meeting to hear firsthand what the problems are. One-on-one meetings in the home office may be effective, but they are no substitute for hearing 10 or 20 salespeople voice the same complaints in a captive situation.

IN CLOSING

We covered only a few of the kinds of complaints we get every week if not every day, but the pattern will be the same for all complaints:

1. Listen, listen, listen.
2. Ask questions to make sure you have the full story and to give the customer time to blow off steam and cool down a bit.
3. Get behind the initial complaint to find out what is *really* upsetting the customer. The initial complaint may be the *real* complaint, but try to dig out as much information as possible. In the process the customer gets to tell his story which provides a kind of catharsis and cools him down further.
4. Don't be afraid to apologize or say "I'm sorry" when an error occurs. At the same time, don't get defensive about company policies. Explain the logical reasons for them as best you can no matter how illogical the customer may seem to be.

5. Remember that, as the company representative, you have to defend company policies and actions even when they appear indefensible. In this case, getting suggestions and offering to pass them along show that you understand the problem without your joining in criticism of your company.

6. Tell the customer that you understand the problem and appreciate his patience, whether he is being patient or not. Give them the name and they'll often play the game.

7. LISTEN, LISTEN, LISTEN.

10

Boosting Business Through Appreciation and Referrals

INTRODUCTION

One of the best ways to keep customers happy and get more business from them is to express appreciation in a more formal way than saying "thanks" for an order. One of the best ways to get more customers and hence more business is to get referrals from satisfied customers. The two can be related as we'll see later in this chapter.

In expressing appreciation, most companies will send out "Seasons Greetings" cards imprinted with the name of the company and either run through the address labeling machine or handwritten by some poor secretary who wishes she had time to get her own cards addressed and may even do this at the same time. This is hardly a warm, sincere greeting or expression of appreciation and gets buried in the seasonal avalanche of mail. If your company supplies these cards, you might as well use them, but add a personal note. If you don't send cards you could be conspicuous by your absence, like not showing up at a trade show that won't do you much good.

Christmas or Hanukkah gifts add an additional touch, particularly if they are tastefully chosen, but sometimes get buried in the pile as well. One year, instead of sending Christmas or Hanukkah gifts to my key customers, I waited until the beginning of the next year and enclosed a personal note thanking them for their business during the previous year. It went over well. It made it clear what the gift was for and stood out because it was the only gift received during January. Whatever your seasonal appreciation policies and practices are, try to make them tasteful and personal. Let's look at some other ways we can express our appreciation.

SCRIPT 10.1. EXPRESSING APPRECIATION FOR PAST YEARS' BUSINESS

One idea that will make your expression of appreciation stand out, whether it includes a gift or not, is to send it out on the anniversary of the first order you received from a customer. This marks a special occasion that you both share and reminds the customer how long you have been doing business together. The mailings will also be staggered throughout the year so you won't have a 30-day push to get the job done.

OBJECTIVE: Express our appreciation to our customer for the business he's given us over the number of years we've been doing business together, cement the relationship in an even more binding way, and pave the way to getting referrals from this customer. (The appointment has been set up ahead of time with no purpose spelled out for it.)

SALESPERSON: Good morning, Mr. Stillman. You're looking well today.

TIP: Mr. Stillman is very proud that, at 72 years of age, he still plays tennis and looks at least ten years younger. Not mentioning this would get the interview off to a bad start.

MR. STILLMAN: Thank you. Not bad for 72, eh? Ran 2 miles this morning.
SALESPERSON: That's great. I sometimes have trouble *walking* 2 miles.
MR. STILLMAN: You young fellows just don't take care of yourselves. Stu, this isn't your regular time to be here and I know that our purchasing people placed a big stock order with you last week. What's up?

SCRIPT 10.1A. SETTING UP THE APPRECIATION GESTURE

SALESPERSON: Well, I was doing my regular monthly analysis of accounts, tracking trends, and all that and realized that this week marks the twenty-fifth anniversary of doing business together.

TIP: Of course we didn't just happen to come across that piece of information. We have a tickler file of all customer anniversaries that we consult at least monthly to use this way of showing our appreciation to our customers for their business.

MR. STILLMAN: Has it only been that long?
SALESPERSON: In our business, 25 *weeks* is sometimes a long time. But it's been 25 *years*.
MR. STILLMAN: You came in just to tell me that? You could have called on the phone.

SCRIPT 10.1B. PRESENTING AN APPRECIATION AWARD

SALESPERSON: Actually, I want to do more than just *tell* you this. (Reaching into briefcase) I'd like to present you with our 25-Year Distinguished Customer Award.

TIP: You (or your company) has made arrangements with a trophy supplier to have a batch of 5-, 10-, and 25-year plaques made up. A phone call or simple order gets them custom-engraved.

MR. STILLMAN: That's really nice. It looks like that metal is real silver.

TIP: Silver, of course, is the "traditional" gift for a twenty-fifth anniversary. Our local greeting card shop gave us a complete list of traditional gift materials—paper for first, gold for fiftieth, etc.

SALESPERSON: It is. And, knowing about how you're always complaining about not having your mineral water handy enough, I'd also like to present you with this silver carafe that will keep your mineral water cold and handy all day.

MR. STILLMAN: Well, thank you Stu. (Looking at carafe) And, engraved too. You think of everything. That is really thoughtful.

TIP: It didn't cost us much more to have the carafe engraved with the occasion and, of course, our company name. Besides making the gift more significant and memorable, it's an advertisement and constant reminder of the occasion and of us and our company.

SCRIPT 10.1C. MAKING THE GESTURE EVEN MORE MEMORABLE

SALESPERSON: I have one more surprise. I called the local paper earlier this week and they agreed that its about time you were recognized in some way. I have a photographer outside who would like to take a picture of me presenting you with these awards and expressions of our appreciation.

TIP: This is an often-overlooked but relatively simple-to-arrange, extra touch. It's one thing for a nice transaction to take place between the two of you or even a group, but far more significant if it appears in the local paper or trade press. In this instance we can turn a simple award presentation into something Mr. Stillman will remember for years.

MR. STILLMAN: I'm going to get my picture taken?

SALESPERSON: Yes. *And*, the editor wants to do a feature story on the history of your company in this town and your career. When I talked with her, she was very receptive to the idea.

The extra little (or not so little) touches we can add to this kind of recognition and "thank you" can do more to cement relations with customers than weeks of slick sales calls and marketing efforts. This was an elaborate effort—and while we won't go to quite this extent for *all* our customers, some of the points illustrated above will apply to any customer. Let's pick up after the photo-taking exercise has been completed.

SCRIPT 10.2. GETTING REFERRALS THAT MEAN FUTURE SALES

This is the easiest and most effective way to broaden our customer base. It allows us to be *invited* in to see the prospect at the request, or at least at the suggestion, of a satisfied customer.

OBJECTIVE: Use our relationship with a satisfied customer, particularly when we have done something above and beyond the call of duty, to obtain recommendations and the names of qualified prospects.

MR. STILLMAN: Stu, that was fantastic. I haven't been so excited since I won the senior *senior* tennis tournament at the club.
SALESPERSON: It was my pleasure, Mr. Stillman, and nothing compared to the business *and* help I've gotten from you over the years.

TIP: Referring to the "help" puts Mr. Stillman in the role of *mentor* and further cements the relationship. A mentor doesn't easily stop doing business with his disciple.

MR. STILLMAN: Still, I feel that there is something I would like to do for you to repay that nice gesture. Tell me *something* I can do.
SALESPERSON: It's really not necessary, but if it would really make you feel better, there is one thing you could do that would be very helpful to me.

TIP: It may be a bit gauche to parlay this nice occasion into a referral-getting effort, but Mr. Stillman seems sincere about wanting to do something for us. If he didn't insist, we would not bring up the subject right now, but would call back a week later for the same purpose.

MR. STILLMAN: Just name it—as long as it won't cost me a lot of money.
SALESPERSON: It won't cost you a dime. You probably know a lot of people who could use our products and services. What I would appreciate is the names of just three of your business friends or acquaintances whom I can call and say that you recommended that I get in touch with them.

TIP: We emphasized *business* friends because we don't want to put Mr. Stillman on the spot with his personal friends.

MR. STILLMAN: Why sure. I'll not only give you three names, but I'll call them personally and ask them to hear what you have to say.

This happened to be an especially fortuitous time to ask for referrals, but there doesn't have to be a special time to do this and we don't have to wait 25 years. We will do this with other customers as soon as we have demonstrated our ability to provide a satisfactory product or service—the sooner the better.

One other note: we have a good relationship with Mr. Stillman, but he won't be around forever. We have to be sure that we have cultivated a good relationship with the person who is likely to be Mr. Stillman's successor.

SCRIPT 10.3. TURNING REFERRALS INTO PROSPECTS

All the referrals in the world aren't going to do us any good if they are not followed up upon promptly and effectively. As a general rule, 20 percent of our time should be spent on developing new prospects, and referrals follow-up is the most effective use of this time. Here's how we'll do this:

OBJECTIVE: Turn the referrals we've gotten into prospect appointments. If we don't get an immediate appointment, leave the door open for a follow-up call and the placement of the prospect on our prospect mailing list.

SALESPERSON: Good morning, Mr. Storms. Jim Stillman suggested I give you a call. (Pause.)

TIP: We pause to get the prospect's reaction to Mr. Stillman's name. If he says "Jim who?" we know we have a little work to do.

MR. STORMS: Oh, yes. Jim said you would be calling and spoke highly of you. What can I do for you?

SALESPERSON: We've done a lot of work for Jim in installing his computer system and training his people on how to use the software packages we also installed. He found our work very helpful and thought I might be of some help to you.

MR. STORMS: Well, I wish I had talked with you 6 months ago. We've just finished putting in a computer system in the past month.

SCRIPT 10.3A. GATHERING USEFUL INFORMATION

SALESPERSON: I'm glad you're smart enough to realize what a system can do for you. May I ask you a question? How is it working out for you?

MR. STORMS: Not too badly. I understand that there are always bugs to get out of the system and that it may take us another year before we're getting the maximum advantage out of it.

SALESPERSON: Really? I think if you talked to Jim Stillman, he would tell you that he was surprised at how few "bugs" there were in *our* system and that the system was up and running in less than a month.

TIP: This is a good time to pause and get Mr. Storms' reaction. He could get defensive about any perceived criticism. For all we know, the computer installer could be his son-in-law.

MR. STORMS: Really? That certainly hasn't been our experience—far from it.

TIP: Okay, now we know from the words and tone of voice that Mr. Storms is unhappy. We can proceed a bit more aggressively.

SALESPERSON: May I ask who your supplier is?

MR. STORMS: Well, Diane, our office manager has a son who is a computer whiz. He made most of the arrangements for hardware and software.

TIP: Now we know just how far we can go. We won't be knocking a legitimate competitor and just may be able to be useful to Mr. Storms.

SCRIPT 10.3B. SETTING UP AN APPOINTMENT CLOSE

SALESPERSON: I see. As I'm sure you know, Mr. Storms, it's very difficult for any one person to keep up with everything that is happening in the computer field whether we're talking hardware or software. That's why we have a staff of 50 people who are each in their own way constantly reviewing new products.

TIP: Pause and see if he will take the bait.

MR. STORMS: I guess you have a point, but we're stuck with the system we have now.
SALESPERSON: I'm sure the system you have is a good one. You just might have some problems with the installation and training of your people. (Pause.)
MR. STORMS: Okay, so what do I do now?

SCRIPT 10.3C. CLOSING THE APPOINTMENT

SALESPERSON: Let me suggest this: Why don't we get together for 15 minutes. If after that time you don't think we have anything to talk about, we'll say "It's been nice" and I'll leave. If you do feel we can be helpful, I'll meet with some of your people, find out where you are with your computer, and come back with a proposal on how we could be helpful.
MR. STORMS: I don't want to spend a lot more money replacing or even redesigning a system that I've already spent plenty on.
SALESPERSON: I'm sure that won't be necessary. Our company has been able to be helpful in a lot of similar situations and we haven't replaced a system yet. It usually involves small changes and some additional training from one of our specialists. We could spend that 15 minutes next Tuesday morning or next Wednesday afternoon. Which would be better for you?

If we had run into a stone wall about doing anything with the system or had found that Mr. Storms was completely satisfied, we would have thanked him and suggested that we get back in a month or so to see if there might be some need we could fulfill. Mr. Storms would go on our mailing list *after* a personal letter thanking him for talking with us. We want to be careful about being too pushy with a friend of Mr. Stillman's.

LETTER 10.1. EXPRESSING APPRECIATION FOR BUSINESS TO PAVE THE WAY FOR MORE

The approach described in SCRIPT 10.1 is not something that we will be doing every day. As good as the idea is, it needs to be reserved for special occasions or we would spend all our time doing it. With a large customer base, a letter could do the job:

OBJECTIVE: Cement our relationship with customers by expressing our appreciation in a special, other than "Seasons Greetings," way.

Dear (Customer):

HAPPY FIRST ANNIVERSARY!!!

You didn't know that you have an anniversary? Actually, it's *our* anniversary—we've been doing business together for one year.

I wanted to tell you that I've appreciated your business during the past year and especially the help you've given me in getting started in a new territory.

You've helped me learn how to determine what your real needs are and how my company and product can fulfill them. This has made me a better salesperson and, I believe, allowed me to be more helpful to you.

I especially appreciate . . . (Briefly mention some specific, significant event to personalize the letter.)

I'm looking forward to working with you in the future to develop an even more effective and mutually rewarding relationship.

IN CLOSING

As salespeople, we're pressed daily to get orders, handle customer problems, and respond to home office requests. It's easy to forget to express appreciation in a formal way and even easier to neglect referrals as a source of new prospects. As effective salespeople, we want to be searching constantly for ways to work smarter instead of harder. Saying "thanks" and getting referrals is a good way to work smarter. Combining the two efforts, if done in a tasteful way, can be even smarter.

APPENDIX

Quick Scripts for Any and Every Occasion

"I DON'T NEED ANY . . ."

In this appendix we'll include some brief scripts addressing specific sales objections or situations. The objective in most cases will be to keep the conversation open in order to get more information from the prospect that will enable us to hone in on the specific objection and address it more effectively. Sometimes this can be done in a friendly way and at times it may be appropriate to shock the prospect. "Shocking" is a last resort to be used when you feel you can only lose an order or request for an appointment once.

> TIP: Don't be too quick with responses. This could indicate that you're using a canned pitch and haven't really thought about the prospect's question or objection. Also, during your response, don't hesitate to use the kind of pauses suggested earlier.

11.1   Do you need more profits? As we discussed, our product will pay for itself in 6 months.

11.2   Would you like better cash flow? Our service can speed up your accounts receivables collection by 30 percent.

11.3   That's what a lot of our satisfied customers in companies like yours said at first. Now, they wouldn't be without the product.

11.4   May I ask what you are basing that assumption on?

11.5   As you know, *need* is only one reason for buying. I think we can show you how beneficial this product would be for you.

11.6   Do you own a VCR, a stereo, or have a radio in your car? (Pause.) You probably didn't *need* any of these, but I think you would agree that they make your life more pleasant.

11.7   Maybe you don't . . . *today*. However, I think it would make sense for me to show you what our product can do so you'll know when you *do* have a need.

11.8   I used to feel that way too—until I found out what our product can really do.

11.9   Think of how many things you've bought that you really didn't *need*. Would you like to do without them today?

11.10   You know, I've never heard that from anyone who has seen our literature or a demonstration.

11.11   Have you checked with your people on this?

11.12   Maybe you don't. (Pause.) Could you suggest someone in your organization who would?

11.13   That's interesting. (Pause.) The inquiry card we received from your company indicated that you did. Can we check this out further?

11.14   I don't understand. (Wait.)

11.15   Could you explain that to me?

11.16   Have you ever seen a product like ours in operation in a company like yours?

11.17   Do you know the ABC company? Would you say that they are pretty astute people? Well, I have a recommendation letter from them that I'd like to show you.

11.18   Have you *ever* used a service like ours?

11.19   Did you know that we've installed over 100 systems in companies like yours?

11.20   That's interesting. Could you tell me why your company is different from most of the others in the same industry you are in?

11.21   It sounds like you may have had a bad experience with a similar product. Would you mind telling me about that?

11.22   If you haven't had a bad experience and have never used our product, can you really be sure that it wouldn't work well for you?

11.23   A great deal has happened to make products more reliable in the last three years. Wouldn't it make sense to take a look at *today's* offering?

11.24   Well, as you know, that company is no longer in business and you've just pointed out why. I'd like to show you why *we* are still in business.

11.25   I know you are the kind of person who enjoys learning new techniques. (Pause.) Why don't we set a date for you to see a demonstration?

11.26   Really? (Pause and wait for the prospect to reveal his *real* objection.)

11.27   That's exactly why we should get together soon. Waiting until you *need* our service could cost your company a lot of money.

11.28   Suppose I told you that the cost was a dime? Would you be interested then? So, there is at least a *want* if not a *need* at some price. Let's get together and see what the price is.

11.29   Is cost the issue? I think you'll be amazed at how affordable our system is today.

11.30   Did you know that there have been recent tax law (other law) changes that require this kind of service for most companies?

11.31   Suppose we were to place a demonstration model with you for two weeks? At the end of that time, if you still feel that there is no need, we'll yank the machine and thank you for your consideration.

11.32   Isn't your company in the same kind of business we are? (Pause.) That is, we both investigate a company's needs and make sure our products meet those needs. We are both in business because we are able to do that effectively.

11.33   Our experience is that most companies who install our equipment realize a 25 to 30 percent return on the investment. Do you really want to give that up?

11.34   Isn't it important to you to be able to improve your office staff's productivity?

11.35   A friend of mine told me that you are erecting a new building. Sometimes circumstances change when facilities change. Wouldn't it be sensible to make sure you have checked out all the options available?

11.36   Mr. Prospect, what is the *real* reason you're reluctant to discuss this further?

"I'M HAPPY WITH MY PRESENT SUPPLIER"

Prospects resist requests for appointments and orders for a number of reasons, the most important of which is fear of some kind. Fear of changing suppliers is one of the most prevalent. The prospect has developed a relationship with his current supplier and it's only natural that he would prefer to remain with the known, however imperfect, than take a chance on an unknown.

This objection, more than any other one, has to be dealt with sensitively and with understanding. You can't put down the current supplier because this would question the prospect's judgment in choosing the supplier in the first place. Nor are slick one-liners a good answer. Here, more than in any other circumstance, the questioning and listening technique is called for.

12.1   Of course, or you wouldn't be doing business with them. But, wouldn't an alternative supplier make sense to you?

12.2   Most people are, but circumstances change. How many suppliers whom you were doing business with 5 years ago do you still use?

12.3   Mr. Prospect, could you tell me what you feel your present supplier does best?

       Yes, they are good at that, but everyone can't do *everything* best. Could you tell me what you feel they do least best?

12.4   Mr. Prospect, do you know how many previously large and well-known companies in this industry have gone out of business in the past two to three years? Wouldn't you agree that it would make sense to have an alternate lined up?

12.5   I understand, but why not give us a chance on a small order and see what *we* can do for you?

12.6   There must be *one* area in which we could outperform your present supplier.

       Why don't we get together and discuss how our total service offering (product line) could meet some of your needs?

12.7   I'm not sure what that means? Is anyone ever *completely* happy with anything?

12.8   Gee, I don't know how to address that. (In a friendly, nonthreatening tone) Perhaps you're living on a different planet.

       I don't know *anyone* on Planet Earth who is *completely* satisfied with anything. Do you?

12.9   May I ask how long you've been doing business with your present supplier?

       Yes, I can understand your reluctance to switch *if* we were talking about your giving us *all* of the business you are now doing.

       What I'm suggesting is that you check us out and see if we deserve a small portion of that business.

       Would next Wednesday morning be convenient for a 10-minute presentation of what we can do?

12.10 I'm sure you are. What I'd like to discuss with you is our new product line that no one else in the industry is able to offer you.

12.11 I'm sure you would agree that *no one* can possibly do *everything* best.

Wouldn't it make sense for you for us to get together to discuss our complete *value package* and see if there are any gaps we might fill?

12.12 May I ask who your present supplier is?

They are a fine company, and I can't give you a single reason for your switching all your business form them to us. (Pause.)

Well, perhaps there is *one* reason to switch some of the business—I think you would find our new Flashcoat line superior to anything now available in the industry.

We have a 15-minute presentation on this line that purchasing agents in companies like yours have found very interesting.

Would you be available next Tuesday for a demonstration of what I mean?

12.13 Mr. Prospect, do you get a medical checkup on a regular basis?

Wouldn't you agree that a checkup on the product lines you are using is also important?

You really don't expect to find anything wrong in a medical checkup, but you do it anyway.

Why not a checkup on what we can provide compared to what your supplier is doing?

12.14 Of course you are. But, did you know that our warranty period is twice as long as anyone else's? Is the warranty period important to you?

12.15 I really respect that kind of loyalty.

Would you also agree that you have a loyalty to protect and enhance your company's profits and to pursue *every* opportunity that might do that?

12.16 Would you say that your company management is completely happy with their total profits?

Of course, no one ever is. What I'm suggesting is a way that we might be able to make your management even happier.

12.17 I respect that. But, just as an ''insurance policy'' I'd like to do a point-by-point comparison of our product line with that of your current supplier.

You'd find that useful, wouldn't you?

12.18 I can understand that. But, everyone's product line has changed so much that a current review of offerings might make a lot of sense.

12.19 Mr. Prospect, may I tell you a brief story?

I had a friend who had lived in Rhode Island all his life. He grew up there and went to school there. He was convinced that Rhode Island was the best and *only* place to live.

Then he was transferred to San Diego for a two-year stint and was dismayed. At first, he didn't even sell his house in Rhode Island.

To make the story short, he refused the transfer back to New England when it came up and is now very happy in San Diego—all because he had the opportunity to make the comparison.

Wouldn't such a comparison of product lines make sense to you?

12.20 (When the objection seems weak) Yes, I understand that. May I give you three more reasons why it would make sense for you to review our line?

12.21 I'm glad you told me that. Now, I know how hard I have to work to get a piece of your business.

12.22 (Before the objection comes up) You're probably happy with your present supplier and I certainly wouldn't suggest that you immediately start doing business exclusively with us.

  However, wouldn't you agree that a review of other offerings from time-to-time makes a lot of sense?

12.23 (Before the objection comes up) I'm sure you're doing business with someone with a comparable product line.

  What I would like is a chance to discuss your needs with you and see if there are some ways in which some parts of our line might fit better.

12.24 (Before the objection comes up) I'm sure you're happy with your present supplier.

  I understand, however, that you are the kind of person who is always interested in learning something new that might be useful.

  I can be there either Tuesday or Wednesday and promise to keep my presentation to 20 minutes.

12.25 (Before the objection comes up) I'm sure you already have a supplier for this line.

  However, the whole ball game changed on August 1st when we introduced our 528 model.

  I'm sure you'll want to know what this can mean to you. Would Thursday or Friday be better for you?

12.26 You know, that's what just about every one of my present customers told me the first time I called.

  What would you say is the reason I have a large customer base now?

12.27 Do you know Dave Stuart at Harkins & Wendell?

  That was the first thing he told me when I called. I have Dave's permission to tell you that we are now getting a large portion of his business.

  Why do you think Dave is doing business with us?

12.28 Most people I talk with are.

  However, we've shown our customers what it means to be absolutely *delighted* with a supplier.

12.29 Sherie Morra at ABC Moving and Storage was too.

  Then she tested our product against what she was using and decided to use us.

  I understand that you know Sherie and how sharp she is. Doesn't this indicate that doing a similar test would be a good idea for you?

12.30 I can understand that. Did you see the writeup in *BH Magazine* last month that rated us number one in the industry for post-sale service?

12.31 I respect that. Did you know that our warehouse is 1,000 miles closer to you than theirs?

  Is saving a day or two on shipments important to you?

12.32 Most people are. Did you know that our warehouse is equipped to provide 24-hour turnaround?

  Why don't you give us a try the next time you need something in a big hurry?

12.33　Yes, and that made a lot of sense before we announced our new advertising program. Is a 5 percent cooperative advertising allowance important to you?

12.34　They're a fine company and you should be congratulated for your good judgment.

　　　There is *one* area, however, where we really excel. I'd like to discuss your needs with you and see if excellence in this area makes sense to you.

12.35　Mr. Prospect, our company has the highest number of service people per sales dollar of any company in our industry. Is that important to you?

12.36　(After much discussion—last resort) In that case, I don't see why you would be at all interested in our line. (Pause.)

　　　You must be an exception to the other companies I've talked with. It would be helpful to me if I knew just why you are different.

12.37　(After much discussion—last resort) Mr. Prospect, what is the *real* reason you are reluctant to even compare my line to what you are now using?

"I DON'T WANT TO SEE YOU (SET UP AN APPOINTMENT WITH YOU)"

The most common reason given for a prospect's not wanting to see you is that he's "too busy." This probably ranks ahead of "I'm happy with my present supplier" as a put-off. There are certainly prospects who are (or at least feel that they are) really busy. Be grateful. If they weren't busy, it could be because their business is off so they are poorer prospects.

However, we all have 168 hours in a week and make choices about what we are going to do with that time based on what is important to us. The critical thing to do is to find the *real* reason for the refusal of an appointment. The first reason given is rarely the real one. As we have suggested in previous chapters, this means active questioning and careful listening.

13.1 Perhaps I haven't explained clearly enough what the benefits to you and your company are.

I think the first 5 minutes of our meeting would clarify that to your satisfaction. Do you have 5 minutes Thursday afternoon?

13.2 Did I make it clear that the only obligation I'm asking you to assume is to participate in a 7-minute presentation that companies like yours have found interesting and useful?

13.3 Mr. Prospect, what do you *now* do in terms of sales training for your people?

Well then, wouldn't it make sense to at least *look* at a professional program?

A wise man once told me, "If you think training is expensive, consider the cost of the alternative." Can you really afford this cost?

13.4 Mr. Prospect, I'm really surprised. You have a reputation as being inquisitive, open-minded, and receptive to new ideas.

Is there something I've said that may in any way have offended you?

13.5 Did I tell you that we've been able to cut 30 percent from cleaning costs in companies like yours? I did?

Oh. (Pause) Are you telling me that you are not interested in saving 30 percent?

13.6 Mr. Prospect, I know that nine out of ten people calling on you promise to save you money. If I send you copies of some of the letters we've gotten from companies like yours where we've made this promise come true, would you see me then?

13.7 Mr. Prospect, what is your understanding of exactly what it is that I'm asking you to do?

That's right—no cost, no obligation, and no pressure, but a lot of *value* to you. Now, doesn't that sound like a good deal?

13.8 (Prospect is Italian) Mr. Prospect, I know you eat lunch even if you *are* too busy to go out.

Suppose I pick up two of Mama Luigi's fabulous meatball sandwiches Tuesday and we'll spend 20 to 30 minutes attacking them and talking?

13.9 I understand that your company will be marketing your own proprietary computer software package.

Wouldn't you like to explore the new opportunities you now have to use our product line?

13.10   If you weren't busy, you probably wouldn't be a very good prospect for our product line.

We usually sell only to busy, flourishing companies. Why don't we get together next Thursday and I'll show you why 20 minutes with me will be the best time you've spent all week?

13.11   Mr. Prospect, what do you feel your time is worth in terms of dollars per hour?

If I could show you a way to more than triple that as a return on your investment, wouldn't you agree that a 15-minute time investment would be well worth your while?

13.12   Mr. Prospect, you probably feel that your time is worth a great deal and rightly so.

Well, I feel that my time is worth a lot, too.

You're making a 20-minute investment in seeing me, but *I'm* making a *2-hour* investment in going out to see you.

Do you really think I would use my time this unwisely unless I had something to say that would be useful to you?

13.13   You know, it's really difficult to describe our product over the phone.

This makes it tough to give you a really good reason to see me, but that's also why it's so important to both of us.

How about if I stick my head in the door for 2 minutes with the product in my hand?

If you don't want me to stay after you see it, I'll thank you for the 120 seconds and leave.

13.14   You know Kris Wendell at ACE Plumbing & Heating don't you?

Well, Kris (who is now a very good customer) just bawled me out last week for not being persistent enough so she could have started using our system even sooner.

I don't want to face a chewing-out from *you* down the road, so why don't we get this first appointment completed this week?

13.15   What I hear you saying is that you aren't interested in cutting your health insurance costs by 20 to 30 percent.

Can that really be true?

13.16   Mr. Prospect, I'm sitting here with a signed purchase order from a company in your industry.

You would recognize the name if I were able to share it with you.

Their reaction was exactly the same as yours when I first called.

Now, I think you're at least as smart as they are.

How about 10 minutes on Wednesday to prove me either right or wrong?

13.17   Mr. Prospect, companies in your industry average an 18 percent return on investment.

I've sent you copies of letters from companies like yours documenting a 20 to 30 percent return through the use of our system.

Is your company really doing so much better than the industry average that you can afford to pass up this kind of return?

13.18   I'm glad you're so busy.

Mr. Prospect, *time-saving* is what I'm talking about. A 15-minute time investment with me today can show you how to save about 2 hours a month from now on.

13.19 Yes, I *could* send you our catalog.

Then, *you* would have to spend a lot of time matching up our products with your needs.

What I'm offering to do is to save you that time by learning about your needs and then picking out the products that will meet them.

13.20 I guess you haven't had a chance to see the coverage we've gotten in the trade publications on our new product line.

You see, we've had people calling *us* as a result of this, but *you* are my best prospect because the line is so right for your company.

Why don't I bring along some of the coverage we've gotten with the important points highlighted and we can go over them together?

13.21 I can understand your being busy.

Who else in your organization would be interested in learning how to increase word-processing productivity by 50 percent?

13.22 Mr. Prospect, *someone* in your organization can make effective use of our product (service).

Can you tell me who that would be?

13.23 Mr. Prospect, I've had at least 50 percent of my present customers tell me that on the first call. Perhaps we could save two more calls by setting up an appointment now.

13.24 I can understand your being busy.

But, as you know, we have 168 hours in a week to spend in any way we choose.

We set our priorities to get done what we want to. I'm suggesting that a 20-minute appointment to discuss the system I described briefly is of the highest priority to your company.

13.25 I know you're very busy from 8:00 to 5:00.

Would a breakfast meeting or an after-five meeting work best for you?

13.26 Are you going to be at the regional trade show later this month?

Good, let's plan on a cup of coffee together, say around 10:30 on Friday. You should be ready for a break about then.

13.27 You mentioned the regional trade show.

I'm going to send you an invitation to our hospitality suite which is just off the show floor. Would you jot down a tentative time for us to get together on the RSVP card?

13.28 Ms. Prospect, you know my manager, Mr. Boss, is one of the most respected people in this field.

He thinks that your company should be a prime prospect for this new product. How can I go back to him and tell him I can't even get an appointment with you?

13.29 Mr. Prospect, we expect a bandwagon reaction to this new program once it gets around.

However, I think that *your* company is positioned to make the best use of it, so I'd like you to have the first opportunity to see it.

Do you really want me to give away this opportunity to someone else?

13.30 Mr. Prospect, have you ever tried a product like this before?

(No) Then, could you tell me how you *know* that it wouldn't be right for you?

(Yes) Then you know the *general* advantages of this type of product. I'd like to show you *specifically* why and how ours is better.

13.31 Do you gamble, Mr. Prospect?

(No) Then, why take a chance on missing out on what could be a great opportunity for you?

(Yes) Okay. When I come in to see you, I'll lay $10 on you desk and you match it. If you agree that it was worth your while to see me, I pick up the two ten's. If you don't, you pick them up.

13.32 Mr. Prospect, I'm having trouble understanding this. Usually, companies like yours are anxious to get the kind of information I'd like to discuss with you. Could you tell me why you feel that the 20 minutes I asked for would not be in your interest?

13.33 (Almost last resort) You know, I really have trouble believing that.

What could be more important than saving 30 percent on the roofing for your new building?

13.34 (Almost the last resort) There must be at least one set of circumstances under which you would really want to see me.

Could you describe that situation to me?

13.35 (Last Resort) Mr. Prospect, what are you afraid of in refusing to spend 15 minutes with me?

13.36 (Last Resort) Is the reason you don't want to see me because I'm a woman (man)?

13.37 (Last Resort) Mr. Prospect, this is the third time I've called with a request for an appointment to discuss a service I *know* you'll be interested in. Are you testing me for perseverance?

"YOUR PRICE IS TOO HIGH"

"Your price is too high" could be expressed in any number of ways but this objection usually means that the prospect is not sold on the *value* of the product or service. If people bought automobiles strictly on the basis of price, we would all be driving black stick-shifts without radios or air conditioners. Much of the time, the prospect is dragging out this old cliché just to regain control of the sales interview. Let him have control by asking questions that will serve *your* purpose, show that you respect his opinion, and make it seem like the prospect really is in control. And remember, *you get control by giving it up*.

People *do* like to buy and they like to buy *value*. They just don't like making decisions. They have to be convinced of the value of the product or service in terms of *their needs*. They need to be reassured that *your* product or service is, indeed, the best bargain, given your total *value package*. As before, this means careful questioning and empathetic listening to discover how the prospect perceives value and how your product or service can provide it.

14.1   That might be true.
         May I ask what you are basing that assumption on?

14.2   You know, of course, that *quality* always costs. Is quality important to you?
         Let's review how the extra quality features in this product will meet your needs.

14.3   I can understand why you might say that.
         That's what most of our present customers said the first time they saw the product.
         When they found out how much easier it was to use than anything else on the market, they changed their minds and are now very happy with the price.
         Can we go over that list of features again?

14.4   You know, that's just what nine out of ten people say when they first see the product.
         Why, then, would you say that we have a large customer base and are growing at the rate of 25 percent per year?

14.5   I'm not sure I know what you mean.
         What is *your* idea of a fair price?
         May I ask what you are basing that on?

14.6   I don't understand.
         Is there some other product you have in mind that you are comparing this to?

14.7   Let me ask you a question.
         Is it better to save $5,000 on a $1,000 investment or to save $1,000 on a $500 investment?
         Let's review the cost-savings features we're talking about with the installation of this system.

14.8   That's probably true. You see, we try to be 10 percent *better*, not 5 percent *cheaper*.

14.9   May I ask what you are comparing our product to?
         Does *their* price give you some idea of the value that *they* put on *their* product?

14.10   May I ask what *intangibles* you've considered along with the product itself?

    Why don't we take a look at the convenience of service, our staff of backup people, the extra features this product has, our large customer base, and the length of time we've been in business?

14.11   Have you considered the cost to your company of *not* installing this system?

    As I recall, we determined together that your present machining costs are way too high.

    Let's take another look at the cost-effectiveness study we worked on together.

14.12   What features of this product would you be willing to give up to get the price down to where you think it should be?

14.13   Mr. Prospect, in the early days of television, the TV set was probably perceived as a very expensive radio with just one added feature. You know, of course, what that feature was.

    Do you think that one added feature was worth several hundred dollars extra in price?

    Let's look at what *our* extra features are worth.

14.14   What price do you need on this component in order for you to make money on the final product?

    Okay, now let's look at what *we* need in order to be able to give you this price. (Payment up front, firm blanket purchase order commitment, bulk packaging, limited returns, etc.)

14.15   Have you considered the cost of *not* having a quality training program?

    Let me tell you a couple of horror stories with which I'm familiar.

14.16   Do you place a value on your and your people's time? I think you agreed that your people could be up to speed on *our* system two weeks sooner than with the less expensive system.

    Let's figure out what this means in terms of labor cost savings, to say nothing about convenience, because your operations will be interrupted for a shorter period of time.

14.17   How much does a cup of coffee cost in the coffee shop downstairs?

    How many cups do you drink in a day?

    Well, the daily cost of purchasing our machine is *less* than that.

    For less than the cost of your coffee, do you think you can afford to be *without* this equipment?

14.18   How long do you think this equipment will last?

    Well, dividing the cost by the years of use, means that you will pay less than a dollar a day.

    Do you know of anywhere else where you can buy this kind of insurance for so little?

14.19   Mr. Prospect, I know that this fire-resistive file costs many times what a conventional file does. However, how will your boss feel if your department's records are destroyed by a fire and you didn't at least *ask* for a fire-resistive file?

14.20   Mr. Prospect, I agree that this fire-resistive file is expensive.

    But, where are you putting the records you would need tomorrow if you have a fire tonight?

14.21   Mr. Prospect, would you like a *free* payroll service? Well, that's exactly what you get with this software package that will handle your cost and general ledger accounting for less than a dollar a day.

14.22   Mr. Prospect, would you like this *free* daily records organizer? Why?
       Well, that's exactly what this system will do for your entire company.
       Does this put the price in better perspective?

14.23   Don't you carry *quality* merchandise in your other sales departments?

14.24   Perhaps you *can't* afford this.
       Why don't we make sure by getting together and reviewing *exactly* what we are proposing?

14.25   Mr. Prospect, isn't that like saying I can't *afford* to get my car serviced?
       Don't you *save* money in the long run by doing this? Aren't we talking about the same thing with the maintenance program we've proposed?

14.26   Mr. Prospect, doesn't it cost you money to have your car serviced regularly?
       Would you stop doing this to save money?
       Doesn't it *save* you money in the long run?

14.27   I can understand your concern about saving money for your company. After all, that's your job.
       So far, we've concentrated on *cost* or *price*.
       But, are we really talking about *price* or are you more interested in *value*?
       Let's review the *value* features of our product.

14.28   Mr. Prospect, I've prepared a point-by-point comparison of our product with the less expensive product you're considering.
       As we go down the list, would you put a value on the features you would be giving up if you were to purchase the less expensive product?
       Well, using your estimates, it seems that you would be giving up $300 of value to save $100 in cost.

14.29   Mr. Prospect, is the product your company makes the cheapest in the industry?
       Oh. Then how do you stay in business?
       What I hear you saying is that you provide *value* to your customers as part of a total *value package*.
       That's exactly what I'm talking about with *our* product, so we really share the same philosophy about satisfying customers and why they buy.

14.30   Mr. Prospect, are your *really* sure that we are talking about the same product?
       Let's look at this feature comparison sheet.
       I think you'll find that our product is unique.

14.31   Mr. Prospect, I notice that you drive a Lincoln.
       Is it worth more than a Ford? Why?
       Isn't that what we are talking about in looking at the price of our product?

14.32   I'm really surprised that you would say that.
       We're under constant pressure from our manufacturing and engineering people to *raise* prices.
       Do you think that *they* might know something about the product that *we* don't?

14.33   Mr. Prospect, we are the fastest-growing (largest, oldest) company in our industry.
       Do you think we could be there if a *lot* of people didn't think that our product offered *value* even at a higher price?

14.34 **Mr.** Prospect, the price differential between our machine and our competitor's is $200.
I'm going to give that $200 to you *double*.

You see, $400 is the value our customers put on the *service* you get with *our* machine.

14.35 Mr. Prospect, what do you think it costs you to have your copy machine out of service for a day or two? And how many days was it out of service last year? Isn't that more than the difference in the cost of our machine?

You see, with our machine, you get a guarantee of *4-hour* service or we add a month to the length of your service contract.

14.36 (Last resort) Mr. Prospect, *price* is never the only reason for not buying.
What is your *real* reason?

"OUR PURCHASES ARE ON HOLD RIGHT NOW
(WE ARE NOT OPEN TO BUY)"

This is one of the most difficult areas to tackle. It may, in fact, be next to impossible for your prospect or even a regular customer to place an order. However, the situation is no reason to abandon or ignore the prospect or customer. If he is truly unable to place orders, your competitors may slacken off in their attempts to sell. This creates an ideal time to create long-term goodwill. You may even get an order in the short term. Some companies announce freezes to make their buyers think through and fight for the really legitimate expenditures, so without undue pushing, you might assume that the situation doesn't exist until just before you hit a brick wall.

15.1   I understand, but the freeze won't last forever.

I still think it would be a good idea for you to hear my presentation so you're ready to act when the freeze is lifted.

15.2   I understand. You're probably on hold because inventories are too high or cash flow is poor.

Wouldn't your company like to know how to improve cash flow, especially right now?

15.3   Mr. Prospect, you and I have worked on this proposal for a long period and have invested a lot of time in it.

We both know that it will be good for your company. What if I get my boss to call your boss without getting either of us in hot water?

We might just get an exception made, but I didn't want to do this without clearing it with you first.

15.4   Mr. Prospect, we have put a lot of work into this proposal and we both want it.

Since my boss knows your boss, why don't I have him call and see if *they* can break this logjam?

15.5   Is your company looking for a way out of the situation that caused the freeze?

Good. I think our system can do just that.

Why don't we get together and let me show you how we can help be a part of the solution rather than adding to the problem?

15.6   You know that this situation is only temporary.

Let's sit down now and work out a stocking plan as though you were open to buy.

When the situation ends, we'll be able to just throw a switch to make things happen.

15.7   Boy, this sounds like the ideal time for us to talk since our system is designed to help companies like yours not get into situations like this.

15.8   Yes, the same thing is true throughout the industry. But, we're still selling our system despite the current conditions.

Wouldn't you like to know what we've done for companies like yours to make this happen?

15.9 Do you remember that account you recommended to me, Building Fasteners, Inc.?

Well, they are in the same situation you are and I have their purchasing agent's permission to tell you about the plan we worked out to enable them to still buy our line.

15.10 I understand that cash flow is the main problem. Would you like to hear about the deferred payment plan our company has put together?

15.11 What exactly does that mean? (Probe for a clue to your approach, especially if it's a new prospect and you suspect that it may be a convenient put-off.)

15.12 Has this ever happened before?

Did you stop buying *everything* then?

15.13 In a way that's good news.

You recall that your reasons for not installing the system previously had to do with being too busy and not wanting to interrupt your people.

It sounds like this would be a good time.

15.14 Most companies do this from time to time to improve short- or long-term profits.

I'm pretty sure I can show you how our product will help you accomplish that goal.

Who else should be at our meeting?

15.15 Do you know the real reason for being on hold?

I see. Well, I think I can show you how our system can help solve those problems in both the short run and the long run.

Would Tuesday or Wednesday be better for you?

15.16 You know, I had two retailers who reacted differently the last time there was the fear of a slow holiday season.

One was conservative. He cut back across the board and stayed cut back.

The other was careful. He ordered more often in smaller amounts, increased his store's promotional efforts, and kept a plan on hand for when business turned back up.

Only one of these retailers is still in business.

Can you guess which one?

15.17 Surely this doesn't apply to a product (service) that will *save* you money.

15.18 Mr. Prospect, perhaps I haven't made it clear that our product will *help* the situation that caused the freeze in the first place.

15.19 Mr. Prospect, if the chair in your vice-president's office broke and couldn't be repaired, would you buy him a new one?

I see. Then the freeze isn't absolute is it?

15.20 Let's see. You are closed to buy in toys, but open to buy in sporting goods.

Well, sporting goods stores buy and sell our product. I see no reason why this product couldn't be considered a sporting goods item. Do you?

15.21 I see no problem with your capital equipment budget being closed.

Since we both know that you need this equipment, I'll get in touch with a leasing company and bring in the deal for you next week.

15.22 You can't spend more than a $1,000 on a capital equipment item?

No problem. There are really two components to this item—one costs $800 and the other $600.

15.23   Since your capital equipment budget is closed, let's put in a piece of used equipment on a month-to-month rental basis.

At the end of 3 or 6 months, we'll take back the used equipment and apply your rental payments to the price of a new machine.

15.24   Since it's the sales department that wants these dictating machines, why don't we have the individual salespeople buy them and charge them off to their own budgets?

15.25   Mr. Prospect, do you still want this system?

Good. Why don't we put our heads together and see if we can come up with a way for you to get it despite your current situation?

15.26   There has to be a person or group responsible for implementing and monitoring the freeze.

Why don't you set up a meeting for us with him or them and let's see what we can do.

15.27   Let's go ahead with our proposal anyway.

I'll put it together with some input from you.

Then we can both present it to your management.

If they get upset because of the freeze, you can tell them that it's my fault.

15.28   You know, sometimes companies put freezes on just to make people *justify* expenditures.

Since we both know that this system is cost-effective, we should be able to get approval despite the freeze.

Why don't you set up an appointment with the committee for both of us?

15.29   Mr. Prospect, the last time our company offered a deal like this, television hadn't been invented. In fact, F.D.R. was in the White House.

What do we have to do to get an exception made to the general "hold" policy?

15.30   Your budget will reopen in two months, but we both know you need the equipment now.

Give me your check dated January 2nd and we'll install the equipment next week.

15.31   Isn't there *something* we can do to let you take advantage of this special deal?

By the time you're off "hold," this deal will be as dead as Don Quixote.

15.32   If you saw a real profit opportunity, surely your company would make an exception. (Pause.)

15.33   Suppose some of your present equipment out in the factory broke down.

You'd find a way to get it fixed or replaced so you wouldn't lose production, wouldn't you?

Installing our product is just as important and would have the same effect.

15.34   We've installed our system in other companies whose capital budgets were frozen.

Why do you suppose they made an exception?

15.35   (When there is no hope of reopening—only alienating your prospect.)

Okay. I'll call you in a month or so.

Be sure to let me know if I can do anything to help in the meantime.

15.36   (When there is no hope of reopening—only alienating your prospect.)

I understand.

I'll see you next year.

Is there anything we can do to help you through this freeze period?